The MIRACLES of the QUR'AN

القرآن الكريم

Shaykh Muhammad Mitwalli ash-Sha'rawi

مكتبة دار التقوى
DAR AL TAQWA LTD

بسم الله الرحمن الرحيم

ISBN No. 978-1-870582-01-8

Translated by: Dr. M. Alserougii.

Edited by: Abd Al-Latif Salazar, Muḥammad Isa Waley and Mrs Huda Khattab.

Printed and Bound by:

IMAK OFSET, Istanbul
Tel: +90 212 656 49 97
www.imakofset.com.tr
info@imakofset.com.tr

Contents

Part III:

PART I

Chapter 1

What is a Miracle?

The Qur'ān is Allah's speech revealed to His chosen Prophet Muḥammad as a challenge to man and jinn.* This challenge was not extended to the angels, as Allah did not grant them free will. They are committed to obey His commands willingly and submissively. The Qur'ān is, therefore, a challenge to those who have freedom of choice, as well as the mental capacity to distinguish between right and wrong.

A miracle is a divine act which defies and transcends universal norms and laws, which Allah grants to His messengers and apostles in order to convince people of the truth of their message. With this heavenly support mundane laws and natural phenomena are caused to yield in such an overwhelming way that all attempts at rational explanation are defeated.

Knowing that His messengers would inevitably be challenged to perform such miracles, Allah bestowed upon them this power. Thus was Abraham able to withstand burning by the fire; Jesus restored sight to the blind and raised the dead; and Moses parted the Red Sea. The miracle of Muḥammad (SAW) was the Qur'ān itself.

The difference between the miracles of Allah and other supernatural [events] artifices is in the challenge these miracles presented to the strengths of the people to whom a particular messenger has sent.

A true miracle defies all natural laws established by Allah, which could not be violated or suspended, except by His Will.

---

* Note: Jinn are the beings composed of smokeless fire which inhabit the intermediary realms between earthly and angelic spheres.

The exact object of each Messenger's miracle was a challenge to the particular traits of each of the groups of people to whom they were sent.

A miracle would be futile if it did not achieve its desired effect on its witnesses. For it to have full impact, it should relate to an area of knowledge in which its intended audience are well versed. For example, if the people for whom a Messenger has been sent excel in medicine, sorcery or philology, the miracle should also concern these fields.

Only in this way can a miracle fulfil its purpose. This rule has been observed in all the divine miracles performed by the Messengers and Prophets of Allah.

Divine miracles are not limited to challenges they present to the people before whom they occur, but are also designed to provide them with the capacity to perceive them as signs of His power over all things in the Universe.

This was illustrated by the miracles in which Allah protected Abraham from the burning fire, and caused Moses the infant to be rescued from drowning in the Nile. In both these miracles, the laws of nature were suspended, through the will of Allah and their physical properties neutralised.

Abraham's miracle was designed to challenge the idolators who by burning him alive sought revenge against him after he had insulted their idols. This punishment, besides being a challenge to Abraham's God, and a demonstration of the power of their idols was meant to serve as a warning to anyone tempted to defy the idols.

One may ask, why would Allah leave His servant Abraham to go through this horrifying experience? Why did He not inspire him to flee his tormentors? Had Allah helped Abraham to escape this the idolators would have had reason to continue believing in the superiority of their idols, over the power of Allah. At the same time, they would have persisted in believing that Abraham was incapable of escaping their idols' wrath. Abraham's ordeal by fire was necessary for this miracle to take place in order to demonstrate to the idolators the falsity of their idols. Any heavenly assistance to Abraham before actually being forced into the fire would have deprived the miracle of its full impact. The idolators would have then been able to attribute their idols' inability to destroy Abraham, to such an intervention. But Allah wanted the whole act to be carried out in order that the full impact of the miracle be comprehended. Thus, when Abraham was hurled into the fire Allah caused its nature to burn to be suspended, enabling Abraham to stand within the flames unharmed as a challenge to the idolators.

The purpose behind this miracle was not to save Abraham from his fate *per se*. If this had been Allah's wish, He would not have enabled the idolators to capture him. He actually wanted them to watch Abraham standing in the burning fire unscathed, in defiance of their idols. This proved that the idols were incapable of inflicting harm on the apostle who had insulted them. Only in this way could the idolators be convinced of the falsehood of their idols and of the truth of Abraham's God. Of this miracle Allah says: [in the Qur'ān:]

> "We said: O fire, be coolness and peace for Abraham." (al-Anbiyā' 21:69)

There is a great similarity between Abraham's miracle and that of the rescue of Moses from the Nile. In this miracle, Moses' mother was inspired by Allah to abandon him on the river so that he would be spared certain death by the Pharaoh. To abandon a helpless infant to a turbulent river prey to all its hazards was the last thing a mother could possibly conceive of doing.

Under normal circumstances it would have been wiser to hide the child or to flee with him out of Egypt. Instead, Moses' mother was inspired to choose this option despite the obvious hazards.

Within her decision however, was a purpose. For Allah wanted the young infant to be surrounded by these dangers in order to demonstrate His providence and His power. By obstructing the natural course of such an action, believers and non-believers alike were shown that in the grip of danger and death safety and life could be found if Allah so willed.

The prostration of the Magicians

Each messenger brought to his people a miracle commensurate with the kind of knowledge they most excelled in. Thus, because the people to whom Moses was sent excelled in magic, the form of the miracle which he challenged them with was of a magical nature. The magicians who observed Moses performing his miracle were among the first to believe in him and in Allah. Being in a better position than others to judge that the miracle was the supernatural work of a divine power and not the result of a magical skill, they were overwhelmed by what they witnessed. In recognition of the true faith that Moses was commanded to convey to them they fell on their knees in prostration. The Qur'ān says:

> "And the magicians fell down prostrate, crying: We believe in the Lord of the Worlds, the Lord of Moses and Aaron." (al-A'rāf 7:120-2)

Being better acquainted with the art of magic, the magicians could distinguish between what was artifice and what was a divine miracle. And so they were the first to declare their faith in the God of Aaron and Moses. Overwhelmed by the new revelation, the magicians forgot the Pharaoh's promise of gold and silver, as well as the torture that awaited them for their failure to defeat Moses. Pharaoh's might and oppression paled before the power of this true God and His faith. This was the greatness of the divine miracle and its holding power on people's minds and souls. Through such miracles, the vehement antagonists were instantaneously converted into faithful believers, ready to relinquish all mundane wealth and power.

Similarly, the challenging miracles of Jesus focussed on medical phenomena because his people were well advanced in medicine. He restored sight to the blind, cured lepers, revived the dead and demonstrated powers beyond human knowledge.

Because the Arabs at the time of Muḥammad were masters in philology and unsurpassed in elocution and the miracle therefore came in the form to challenge their understanding from the vantage of their linguistic skills.

The Qur'ān with its literary inimitability was all the more astonishing because Muḥammad himself was illiterate when the Qur'ān was revealed to him. When the Arabs failed to match the language of the Qur'ān, they accused Muḥammad of sorcery and even of being insane.

The miraculous features of the Qur'ān are not confined to its linguistic inimitability. Indeed, it is filled with miraculous signs that will remain a challenge to mankind for eternity. One of the miraculous features of the Qur'ān lies in the ever-expanding nature of the meanings contained in its verses and their inexhaustible capacity to accommodate even the most recent scientific discoveries.

A miracle can transcend the laws of nature or defy the characteristics of natural phenomena without posing a specific challenge to man. In this kind of miracle, Allah does not seek to challenge mankind, but to show His domination over the universe and man's incapacity to understand such occurrences in terms of cause and effects. Consequently, a true believer should always be prepared to attribute those happenings which he cannot find an accountable cause to the will of Allah.

The Omnipotence of Allah

The miracle of the virgin conception of Mary, as depicted in the Qur'ān, is a clear example of Allah's absolute power and His domination over the happenings of the universe. The immense significance of this miracle is that it involved a physiological phenomenon taking place which could not have occurred under the normal working of the laws of nature.

By discarding the natural process whereby male and female unite to produce an offspring Allah demonstrated His absolute power and domination. This was to convince mankind that creation need not necessarily follow the rules of cause and effect or be subjected to it. For Allah has the capacity to ordain a thing to be and produce effects without prerequisite engendering causes.

Here, Allah is involved with four different processes of creation to demonstrate that the reproduction and perpetuation of the human species can be fulfilled without the necessity of physical contact between male and female or their participation, if He so ordains.

These four processes are namely: the creation of Adam from dust; the creation of Eve from Adam (or female from male); the creation of mankind through the union of male and female and lastly the birth of Jesus from a female without being touched by a male. Thus has Allah accomplished the four kinds of creation of the human race.

The three creative processes in which the male/female role has been eliminated are divine miracles accomplished by Allah alone in isolation of cause and effect.

Although birth and reproduction have been ordained to occur in accordance with the principle of cause and effect, or union between male and female, the fruitfulness of any such union rests with Allah's will and providence. About this divine will, the Qur'ān says:

> "Unto Allah belongs the sovereignty of the heavens and the earth. He creates what He will. He bestows female (offspring) upon whom He will, and bestows male (offspring) upon whom He will. Or He mingles them, males and females, and He makes barren whom He will . . ." (al-Shūrā 42: 49-50)

The issue emphasised here is not the presence or absence of causes, but rather the deciding and governing will of Allah Who has the power to make causes and effects fruitful or to impede them from achieving their natural end or purpose.

Allah tells believers not to succumb to despair or confusion if they fail to account for causes or effects, because ultimately it is He alone that determines all causes and their effects as He wills, regardless of laws or norms. With this knowledge at hand, the believer is better prepared to confront the upheavals of daily life with greater confidence in Allah's providence and omniscience. This faith rekindles his heart and soul with renewed hope. The thought of unaccountable happenings occurring is no longer disturbing or frightening. Once this faith takes root in the believer's heart, the true believer firmly holds the conviction that Allah is capable of ordaining happenings and events in isolation of their due causes.

This unwarranted despair is referred to in the Sūrah of the Family of Imran (Āl 'Imrān), wherein Allah says:

> "(Remember) when the wife of 'Imrān said: My Lord! I have vowed unto You that which is in my womb as a consecrated (offering). Accept it from me. Lo! (You, only You) are the Hearer, the Knower. And when she was delivered she said, My Lord! Lo! I am delivered of a female. . . " (Āl 'Imrān 3:35-6)

The sentence "I am delivered of a female", spoken by 'Imrān's wife, indicating her disappointment that the child born was not a male, illustrates the kind of despair which we are cautioned not to let infiltrate our faith in Allah and His wisdom.

'Imrān's wife had pledged to offer her unborn child to the service of Allah and had, therefore, felt certain that He would give her a son who, in her reckoning, would be better able to serve Him. This was an unfounded belief to which God replies:

> "(Allah knew best of what she was delivered). The male is not as the female." (Āl 'Imrān 3:36)

In this verse, Allah again cautions us not to judge His decrees and plans in terms of our imperfect knowledge and logic. In all divine acts is a purpose that might not be obvious at the time of their actual manifestation. This verse also corrects the misconception that males are superior to females in the service of Allah or in fulfilling His purpose. Hence came the reminder that 'The male is not as the female.' In other words, the daughter 'Imrān's wife had given birth to was much more worthy than any son she could have wished for. Allah alone knew what the great significance of the birth of this female child to mankind would be.

Following the death of Mary's father, Zachariah was appointed her guardian, which entailed providing for her. But whenever he visited her in the sanctuary where she worshipped, he noticed that she was never short of food. When he asked her where it came from, she replied:

> "It is from Allah. Allah gives without stint to whom He will." (Āl 'Imrān 3:37)

So, even at this early age, Mary understood that Allah is not bound by any law or rule and that He gives as He wills, to whom He wills.

In preparing Mary for her predestined role, Allah planned that she should be offered by her mother to His service in the temple, and that her guardian Zachariah should be one of His Apostles. Her spiritual education began by being instilled with faith in Allah's power to make things happen independent of their natural or established causes. She was given evidence of this when He provided her with food that was unlike any found on earth and with fruit out of season. When Zachariah beheld this divine miracle he praised Allah and begged Him for a boy.

A second miracle to take place was the annunciation to Zachariah that his request had been granted and that his wife would give birth to a boy. Listening to this divine intimation Zachariah remembered his old age and the infertility of his wife and asked:

> "My Lord! How can I have a son when my wife is barren and I have reached infirm old age?" (Maryam 19:8)

Through His angel Allah replied: "So (it will be). Your Lord says: It is easy for Me, even as I created you before, when you were naught." (Maryam 19:9)

This prophecy was intended to consolidate Mary's faith in Allah and in the miracle which she herself was destined to perform acting as a mental and spiritual conditioning. Despite these divine signs however, she continued to doubt the possibility of such a conception, asking Gabriel, who had come to announce to her Allah's will:

> "How can I have a son when no mortal has touched me, neither have I been unchaste?" (Maryam 19:20)

To reinforce her faith and reassure her of His almighty power, Allah said to her through Gabriel:

> "So (it will be). Your Lord says: It is easy for Me. And (it will be) that We may make of him a revelation for mankind and a mercy from Us." (Maryam 19:21)

What Allah was saying to Mary was "Do you wonder at what is happening to you after all that you have seen of My limitless power?".

Another Āyah (3:49) tells us that Jesus was given the power to "heal him who was born blind, and the leper, and . . . raise the dead by Allah's leave". In other words, the true healer was Allah Himself. He was, likewise, the One who gave life and took it. The verses leave no doubt but that in all these miracles the true doer was Allah Himself even though they were performed by His Messenger.

On the other hand, we have the second class of miracles which Jesus could perform spontaneously, using the divine powers already vested in him. Unlike the former class, Allah revealed to him the secrets of these (latter) miracles and gave him access to His knowledge regarding them. Thus, although he was given the power to revive the dead, neither he or any other Prophet was given the secret of life and death.

Despite the portents and miracles that demonstrated the power of the Absolute and the support it gave Jesus from the moment he was born until his death, the Israelites rejected his message and refused to believe in his God. They seemed to alienate themselves further from Allah and began to plot against him and cast doubt about his message, exactly as they had previously done to Moses. Even when they seemed to have rid themselves of the attraction of the material world, their faith did not last long and they always regressed to their old ways and the worship of matter, as is stated in the following verse:

> "But when Jesus became conscious of their disbelief, he cried: Who will be helpers in the cause of Allah? The disciples said: We will be Allah's helpers. We believe in Allah, and bear witness that we have surrendered (unto Him) [or: are Muslims]" (Āl 'Imrān 3:52)

Thus Jesus began to look for true believers and supporters when he discovered that all the miracles and evidence he brought the Israelites could not weaken their deeply-rooted corruption and love for the material world. In seeking disciples to carry on his message after his ascension, Jesus was showing his despair that the Israelites would never see the light of truth, that they would ever cease to fight his religion. He put all his hope in spreading his message to mankind in his disciples and the few supporters who truly believed in his God, and began to teach them the content and purpose of his divine message. He explained to them the commands and injunctions contained in his message and made them pledge to spread it throughout the whole world, and correct the false allegations and misinterpretation which he knew the Jews would propagate to destroy the new religion.

Indeed the message of Jesus was an embodiment of the limitless power of Allah's will, which was manifested throughout Jesus' life. It showed itself most vividly when Allah revealed to 'Imrān's wife that He alone knew best why she should give birth to a girl. The same divine power showed itself in providing Mary with food unlike any other. It was also shown when Allah blessed the aged Zachariah's barren wife with a child. Finally the immaculate conception and birth of Jesus, his ability to speak and defend his mother when he was but a few days old gave further evidence of the Almighty will of Allah.

Unchallenging Miracles

The miracle of the birth of Jesus was not one to challenge the mistaken beliefs of a particular people. Rather, its purpose was to stand as a testimony to Allah's infinite might. Another miracle, the purpose of which was not to challenge but to show Allah's incomparable power and control over the laws of nature, was His parting of the Red Sea for Moses. The followers of Moses had been trapped between the soldiers of Pharaoh and the sea and were facing certain destruction. But at this moment, when all natural indications pointed to their inevitable doom, Moses still maintained his faith in Allah's power to intervene. Praying for divine intervention, he then faced his followers and urged them not to despair or lose faith in Allah's providence saying:

> "Nay, verily! For lo! my Lord is with me. He will guide me." (al-Shu'arā' 26:62)

With this appeal, Moses actually surrendered the whole affair to Allah's supreme will. This was at a moment when human efforts to avoid annihilation was useless. Answering his appeal, Allah inspired him to strike the water with his staff:

> "Smite the sea with your staff. And it parted . . ." (al-Shu'arā' 26:63)

This miracle defies all the known laws of physics which govern liquids. The sea's parting by Moses' smiting of its surface cannot be explained in terms of physics. The only possible explanation for this miracle is in terms of the absolute power of the Almighty, Who can simply "*say unto a thing 'Be', and it is*".

In contemplating these miraculous events which are, indeed, acts of Allah, one often finds that the natural pattern that had been interrupted to allow the miracle, returns to normality. Thus the fire that was commanded to be as coolness and as peace to Abraham regained its heat following the miracle's accomplishment. Likewise did the parted sea return to normal after Moses and his followers had safely crossed it.

The miracle of the Qur'ān, being Allah's speech, draws its everlasting validity and vitality from the eternal attributes of Allah Himself.

A second remarkable feature of Allah's miracles with which He supported His messengers, or used as portents of His supremacy over creation, is that His agents were always from among the weakest and most humble of His creatures on earth. Having selected them, He then provided them with the power to perform miracles which baffled and bewildered the minds of those who witnessed them.

Because these tangible miracles were performed only once, their impact was greatest on eye-witnesses. For those who had not seen them, they were matters of hearsay which had they not been affirmed in the Qur'ān would have possibly been dismissed.

It is sometimes said that scientific advancements might allow man to duplicate such supernatural phenomena as miracles. This assumption is indicative of man's conceit and sceptical nature. Divine miracles will continue to challenge mankind until the Day of Resurrection. No other mortal being could ever smite the sea with a rod and cause it to part, as Moses did.

While arrogant people may contend that modern medicine is capable of curing leprosy and restoring sight to the blind, nevertheless none could achieve these cures by simply touching the one inflicted as Jesus did. Still others may argue that nowadays one can fly to Makkah and back more than once in a day. But Muḥammad on his Night Journey was not transported to Jerusalem in a plane, and no one apart from him has been able to levitate unaided by mechanical means. Despite man's tremendous advancements in space exploration, no one has yet been able to depict the first heaven, let alone that found beyond.

This power was exhibited in the miracle performed by the small birds during the attack on the Ka'bah by Abraha's army with its elephant. The enormity of this miracle was so confusing and perplexing to the intellect that it engendered some doubt in the minds of some later believers who read about it in the Qur'ān. Some scientists found it too difficult to understand and tried to account for the destruction of the elephant and Abraha's army by hypothesising that the birds might have been carriers of infectious diseases that caused the death of the marauding army.

All this is but mere conjecture, because as we have said earlier, there were eye-witnesses on the day of the incursion, and they would certainly have ridiculed Muḥammad (SAW) if the revelation he imparted to them had been false.

Allah bestowed the same divine power upon Moses, enabling him to part the sea. It was likewise bestowed upon Jesus enabling him to cure the leper and the blind and revive the dead.

He gave Abraham the power to revivify when He commanded him to cut a bird in pieces, put each piece on a separate hill top, then call the bird back. When it heard his call it came to him. We must, however, understand that all that Abraham did was to call the bird and that it was Allah Who permitted the miracle to happen.

What does all this imply? The analogy is true as far as all human interaction is concerned. We should not wonder when we witness an oppressor being overcome by a weak or helpless person, or when the defiant are broken down by natural causes. It is a reminder to all of us that Allah never slumbers and that His divine justice, though it may come late, never fails to be implemented.

Chapter 2

The Difference between The Miracle of the Qur'ān and Other Miracles

The miracle of the Qur'ān sent to the Prophet Muḥammad differs from those of other Messengers and Prophets in many respects. In the Qur'ān there are many miraculous aspects which demand a considerable degree of contemplation before their secrets are unlocked. When this happens it becomes apparent that within the Qur'ān are layers of meaning which throw new light on the superficial significance of its verses. This miraculous feature may be in one single letter which alone may denote immeasurable meanings. For each successive generation, the Qur'ān offers new and relevant meanings, proportionate to the development of knowledge and the growth of that generation's intellectual aptitude. In other words, they are applicable to the constantly changing perceptions of the human race, expanding in meaning as man's exploration of the universe and his search for knowledge about his life and existence increases. From this we see that the Qur'ān was not intended solely for one people or nation, but came for the benefit and guidance of all, as a complete and comprehensive religion, providing knowledge for all generations. If these teachings were limited to one century or generation the divine everlasting objective of the Qur'ān would have long since diminished. But the Qur'ān is constantly regenerating new meaning, providing a continual source of guidance. Thus today we are able to perceive from some revelations subsequent meanings to those of our predecessors.

To clarify this feature of the Qur'ān, it is essential that we distinguish the precepts of worship, on the one hand, and on the other the laws that govern this universe and its phenomena.

By precepts of worship we mean the discipline which Allah decreed and defined for the human race to follow and observe. Specific commands such as 'do this and not that', 'this is lawful and that is not', are not liable to alteration or misinterpretation. They should be practised and followed exactly as they have been elucidated by the Prophet Muḥammad at the advent of Islam and the revelations of the Qur'ān. Likewise, there should be no disputing the five daily prayers (*Ṣalāt*), *Shahādah* (the witnessing of Allah's unity), *Zakāh* (alms), *Ḥalāl* and *Ḥarām* (what is prohibited and what is permissible), the laws governing marriage and divorce and so forth. Everything Allah legislated for humanity has been clarified and elucidated by His Prophet and is uncontestable. No one can argue that the daily prayers ought to be four and not five, no matter what justification is used. This is absolutely forbidden. These laws are commands to be observed and on which man's deliverance or damnation depends. There can be no speculation.

When the Qur'ān was first revealed to Muḥammad, the human race lacked the basic knowledge necessary for understanding and perceiving the complex facts it contained. Because of this paucity of knowledge, many phenomena such as the sphericality of the earth and its movements in the solar system, or the notion of relativity embryology, were simply touched upon in the Qur'ān, leaving their profound exploration and identification to the inquisitive minds of future generations.

The miracle of the Qur'ān is that it yields its knowledge to each mind within its capacity and degree of intellect. It gives to the mind that which satisfies it. Thus we find the illiterate quite content to listen to the Qur'ān being read or recited. The literate obtain a great deal of contentment and satisfaction from reading it or listening to its meaningful elucidation. The highly-educated find its miraculous features challenging and stimulating to their mind and thought. This is because within the Qur'ān the basis for all knowledge a man may attain by Allah's will, at any period of time, can be found. When such knowledge is attained and the relevant verses for enlightenment sited, one is overwhelmed by their consistency and authenticity. For example, in the Qur'ān we find the following descriptions:

a. ". . . Rabb al-Mashriq wa'l-Maghrib . . ."
"Lord of sunrise and sunset, or east and west."
(al-Shu'arā' 26:28, al-Muzammil 73:9)

b. "Rabb al-Mashriqayn wa Rabb al-Maghribayn."
"Lord of the two easts and Lord of the two wests."
(al-Raḥmān 55:17)

c. "Rabb al-Mashāriq wa'l-Maghārib."
"Lord of sunrises and sunsets, or of easts and wests."
(al-Ma'ārij 70:40)

In the first instance we find that the words al-Mashriq (east) and al-Maghrib (west) refer to the direction of sunrise and sunset. There was no contradiction between the meaning of the quotation and the mind at the beginning of Islam. In the second quotation "al-Mashriqayn (the two easts) and al-Maghribayn" (the two wests) were understood to indicate both direction and position. This is the same as saying "This is the east, or this is the west", and pointing with one's hand in either direction to determine where the sun rises or sets. It was meant by "Rabb al-Mashāriq wa'l-Maghārib" that each country on earth had its own sunset and sunrise, or east and west and that Allah was Lord over all. These were the plausible explanations available or possible at the beginning of Islam.

Examining these descriptions in the light of today's scientific evidence, we discover another meaning totally compatible with that evidence. The quotation "Lord of east and west" is now conceived as a generality. But Allah has combined the word "east" with the word "west" because there is no east without west, nor sunrise without sunset. The spherical shape of the earth pre-determines this phenomenon, so that when the sun is setting in one place it is also rising in another. Hence came the divine usage of the phrase "Lord of east and west" and not another. For in those days, mankind believed that sunrise and sunset were two unrelated phenomena, as they could be seen by the naked eye to face each other on opposite sides of the globe.

The extended meaning is likewise discernible in the second phrase "Lord of the two easts and Lord of the two wests". It is now known that the earth rotates on its axis from west to east, taking 24 hours (or one day) to make one complete rotation. This causes day and night. Because the earth is spherical the sun can shine on only one half its surface at one time. As it spins in space, places receiving light from the sun (or half of its total surface) move into a zone of darkness and those in darkness (the opposite half) gradually move into daylight. Thus, it can be said that each half of the earth has its own sunrise and sunset, or east and west, and that there are, therefore, two easts and two wests.

We find the more elaborate and progressive meaning of the third description "Lord of easts and wests" is also consistent with advancements in astronomy. We now know that there is no such thing as one static east (or sunrise) or one static west (or sunset) for any one country, but that there are many, due to the unsensed daily progression of the seasons and the corresponding shift in the angle of sunset and sunrise.

We also know that during a single rotation every place on earth has its particular sunrise and sunset, in an ever-changing pattern, as the earth moves along its orbital path around the sun. In other words, the sun never rises or sets at the same angle as that of the previous rising or setting, even though the direction remains unchanged.

During the holy month of Ramadan, the times of prayer for Muslims continually vary according to the earth's revolution round the sun. It is this movement that causes the variation in time, and it is this variation in time and in the angle of sunrise and sunset which led to the conclusions about the earth's sphericity and its movement. If it were flat as was once believed there would have been only one unchanging position for the sun's setting and rising, with no seasons.

The term "Lord of east and west" must not be thought contradictory to the two descriptions mentioned. Even scientific progress which has unfolded many of the secrets of the universe and its phenomena, does not find discrepancy between their meaning but confirms their veracity.

When we contemplate the relativity of time and the divine organization of the universe we are able to grasp the fundamental purpose and wisdom underlying the immaculate harmony and uniformity which ensure that around the world prayer is continuously taking place.

It is evident that the meanings of the above mentioned were planned by Allah, The Source of all knowledge, to expand with human knowledge and scientific exploration. While offering appropriate meaning at the onset of Islam, they yield a more elaborate meaning today, and it is likely that future generations may discover an even deeper meaning in them.

Therefore we see that one miraculous feature of the Qur'ān is its ability to offer knowledge to each generation according to its capacity without contradicting existing facts, in harmony with the realities of the universe, yielding new and more profound meaning to successive generations.

For each of Allah's Messengers there was an exclusive miracle and that of the Prophet Muḥammad was the Qur'ān itself. With the very nature of the Qur'ān standing as a miraculous proof of the Prophet's divine mission, Allah ensured that both the code of injunctions and its eternal message would be forever safeguarded from human falsification.

In the past Allah entrusted the task of safeguarding and preserving the authenticity of holy scriptures to His worshippers. However, in the course of time they allowed copies of the text in which the written record of the Messenger was preserved to become corrupted allowing for inaccuracies to appear. Some of what had been delivered to them was forgotten, and the meaning of what they did still remember distorted.

To protect the Qur'ān's integrity, Allah made it clear in His divine verse:

"Lo! We, even We, reveal the Reminder and lo! We verily are its Guardian" (Surah al-Ḥijr 15:9) that He had undertaken the task of its preservation. Moreover, as the Qur'ān itself is a miracle, it was essential that its textual authenticity be preserved, as corruption of the text would diminish the miracle.

One can discern from the reverence in which Muslims hold the Qur'ān another of the divine safeguards that guarantee its authenticity. Despite the lack of spiritual concern that generally characterises present day living, there has, nevertheless, been a resolute effort to preserve and propagate the text of the Qur'ān. Throughout the Islamic world it is common for a Muslim to possess one or more copies of the text. It is carried in cars, while at home one or more copies can be found. It is even fashionable for ladies to attach gold or silver lockets, containing miniature versions of the text, to their necklaces. This same zeal that affects both Arab and non-Arabic speakers alike, can even be found extending to the non-Muslims. From enthusiastic Germans inscribing the whole of the Qur'ān upon a single sheet of paper, to Japanese printing and producing exquisitely designed versions an astonishing attitude can be detected. When they are asked about their motives for such work, they are unable to justify the reasons other than confirming the impression that they were propelled in their endeavours by an innate and irresistible spiritual force which they themselves could not fathom.

This determination and zest by mankind to honour, preserve and propagate the Qur'ān has no other explanation than it being an act of Allah and the fulfilment of the promise made by Him. It is not a human endeavour *per se*.

Oddly enough, many of those who keep a copy of the Qur'ān in their cars, homes, pockets or on their library shelf are not always so eager to implement its divine injunctions, and frequently fail to give any convincing justification for this paradoxical behaviour. It appears, therefore, that despite our reluctance to carry out and adhere to the norms of behaviour prescribed in the Qur'ān, our jealousy and care to preserve it has not diminished.

In the past, Allah's Messengers were sent to different societies and communities to remedy their ills and guide them to salvation. As each of these communities had its own particular afflictions, messengers were sent with the predetermined task of remedying those ills alone. In some instances, more than one messenger was sent. Sometimes these communities were widely scattered and knew nothing of the other's existence. Each messenger's task was, therefore, designed to treat the ills of a particular community or society. These afflictions were not always the same. Some communities were pagans and worshipped man-made idols, while others wallowed in sinful living or festered in corruption and dishonesty. As transport and communications have developed, the whole of mankind has become one large community. As a result of this development, people of all nations have come closer to each other and as they have so have their ills and afflictions, so that one nation's suffering eventually affects the others.

This situation necessitated a remedy that was universal, while being powerful enough to eradicate those ills such as greed, lust, and other social and spritual diseases that have continually plagued mankind.

As a result, Allah sent the Qur'ān as a means of deliverance for the whole of mankind. It came as a cure to all human ills, including those which had not been anticipated when the Qur'ān was revealed, as well as those which have since emerged. Only Allah knew that they would arise in the course of time, thus giving mankind unquestionable evidence of the divine miraculous nature of the Qur'ān.

Another miracle unique to the Qur'ān is in the way it has pinpointed the foundation of all learning. The Qur'ān tells us that Allah taught Adam the first names: "And He taught Adam all the names (al-Baqarah 2:31)". This verse indicates that access to teaching and knowledge for all people begins with the act of naming.

Speech is the foundation of civilization and culture, as well as of all knowledge that comes from Allah to mankind. In the Qur'ān Allah tells us that it was He who taught Adam all the names, thus giving us the universal rule for the acquisition of knowledge and the first step in language teaching. The first thing that a child is taught is how to pronounce words such as 'Mummy' and 'Daddy'. Once a child has learnt how to pronounce names, he progresses to more complex expressions. Both the educated and the illiterate are endowed with the divine gift of speech, which is the medium of all understanding among people as was first established by Allah when He taught Adam the names.

The Qur'ān as a precept and discipline for life

Another remarkable feature of the Qur'ān is that it explores and prescribes some remedies for all mundane and spiritual problems afflicting mankind. As a 'remedy' its fundamental objective is to cure any widespread corruption or deviation from pre-established moral values and ethical norms. The Qur'ān deals with all these shortcomings and prescribes remedies for them. Far from falling short of dealing with contemporary issues confronting mankind, it is as relevant today as when it was first revealed.

However by failing to perceive the wider and more profound meanings of the Qur'ān, man sometimes misses the remedy. There is no fundamental issue concerning man's existence in this universe that is not inherently dealt with. The Qur'ān is fundamentally a discipline of worship and guidance in establishing a right way of life. Thus, when the Qur'an tells us to explore the earth for evidence of Allah's greatness, or to study the universe for knowledge and enlightenment, or to toil and produce, or build and populate the earth, it is, in fact, delineating rules which should govern man's movement within Allah's universe.

In our endeavour to achieve our goals, we must be armed with unwavering faith in Allah's grace and infinite justice, as well as with the firm conviction that we are divinely guided subjects whose principal concern should be the fulfilment of Allah's plan for mankind as expressed in the Qur'ān. For Allah does not assist or reward those who ignore His decrees or stray from His path. By failing to follow Allah's directions one should not hope to share their fruitful ends.

By straying, nations lose mobility and become decadent

when they diverge from Allah's way, failing to implement His injunctions.

It is unreasonable to give lip service to the directives Allah has prescribed in His message and expect His blessings and rewards. It follows that there is no action without reward, and no reward without action. This is the core and kernel of Allah's precepts and discipline. It is this equilibrium which constitutes harmony and beauty in life and existence as a whole. Indeed, this balance would become meaningless if the industrious and the idle, the studious and the lethargic, the productive and the negligent were equally rewarded, irrespective of their effort or yield. If this became the rule, beauty and harmony would eventually disappear and be replaced by grossness and the lack of drive, motivation, ambition, ingenuity, creativity and the desire to excel. There would be no addition to one's cultural heritage.

Chapter 3

The Miracle of the Language of the Qur'ān

The Qur'ān, being the speech of Allah, cannot be rivalled, transcending as it does all human diction and linguistic ability. At the time of its revelation, the Arabs, who were considered to be expert in the skills and arts of the Arabic language, were astounded by its clarity and unsurpassed beauty. They became exasperated by their inability to match its diction or exquisitely expressed meaning. A number of scholars, after failing to compose anything to challenge its eloquence and rhetoric, claimed that some mysterious supernatural power had caused their efforts to abort, compelling them to give up. This claim, apart from its face-saving aspect, implicitly recognised the divine origin of the diction of the Qur'ān and the heavenly power it embodied. These features should, however, be contemplated and viewed in relation to the Messenger to whom the Qur'ān was revealed.

It is natural, as well as logical, to assume that because the Qur'ān is Allah's speech, it should therefore, be most clear, eloquent, meaningful, intelligible, unsurpassable and miraculous. But although the Qur'ān, like any other diction, strictly observes the rules of eloquence and rhetoric, defined by Arab philologists as the appropriateness of speech to the needs of a situation, it actually goes far beyond the restricted scope of human speech. The Qur'ān addresses itself appropriately to an infinite number of situations while applying itself to the most profound of human needs, using the same words and expressions – an accomplishment entirely beyond the reach and power of human rhetoric and elocution.

No fruitful discourse can truly be achieved or serve its purpose without some knowledge of the workings of the listener's mind. Furthermore, the style and manner of speech varies according to the degree of education and the status of the person spoken to. We do not address a president in the same language as when speaking to an uneducated person. The words with which we try to pacify an aggrieved person are not the same that we use to rebuke a stubborn offender. Our style and language usage are modified to the needs of the situation and the mental and emotional state of the listener.

In contrast, the language of the Qur'ān uses the same expressions and the same words when speaking to the educated and the illiterate, the offended and the offender, the agressive and the peace-loving. It conveys to each the meaning that is appropriate to his situation and satisfactory to his needs and state of mind. Thus, it soothes the angry, fills the heart of the desperate with hope, reminds the oppressor of Allah's divine justice, and the lustful of the vanity of this transient world and the infinite rewards of the next. It speaks to them using the same words regardless of their education, socio-economic status, or psychological state or tendency; and answering all their varied needs. Throughout the world one can find people of all walks of life passively listening to its words and verses being elucidated or recited, which seem to reach their inner souls unhindered by barriers of any kind.

This unparalleled ability of the Qur'ān to address a multitude of people of different origins and cultures, penetrating their innermost selves and bringing to them comfort and peace, is one of its most outstanding and miraculous features.

It is not easy for someone to describe exactly how he is moved by the Qur'ān, which shows the extent of its depth and its diffusion throughout one's mind and soul. Its influence on the self is so overwhelming that it is impossible to single out any distinct feeling or reaction. The only explanation for this is that the Qur'ān actually reaches beyond our conscious awareness. If one could consciously become aware to what extent this happens, perhaps we could discover why one is so responsive to the language of the Qur'ān.

Despite constant research on and analysis of the language of the Qur'ān by both scholars and philologists to find the underlying element which gives the Qur'ān its unsurpassed meaning, it continues to elude them. This is because man's unconscious faculties seem to respond to Allah alone, regardless of any external factors, be they social, cultural, or psychological.

Because of the Qur'ān's impact on such deep levels of consciousness, Muḥammad's adversaries dreaded people listening to it, particularly the non-believers. Its influence on those who listened to it was so powerful that Walīd ibn Mughīrah, a staunch opponent of Muḥammad, after listening to its recitation said: "It indeed overflows with sweet clarity; it is fruitful at its lowest and prodigious at its highest, and towers over all human diction."

This same soothing and overwhelming power of the Qur'ān was experienced by 'Umar ibn al-Khaṭṭāb before embracing Islam. Having learned that his father-in-law and sister had denounced their old religions and declared their allegience to Muḥammad and the new faith, 'Umar rushed to their house filled with rage. However, arriving to hear the Qur'ān being recited, his anger soon vanished and shortly afterwards he himself became a Muslim.

The spontaneous emotional change in 'Umar happened because the words of the Qur'ān stirred deep within, bringing him calm. In the same way, the verses which cause the hearts of believers everywhere to throb with elation are equally able to produce the same effect in the heart of someone who has yet to believe in Allah.

There are within man inborn talents and faculties known only to Allah. He alone can reach them and cause them to respond to His words without the soul detecting their true nature.

This divine ability of the Qur'ān to remain appropriate to an infinite number of situations confounded Arabs and non-believing scholars alike. They tried to justify their failure to comprehend this miracle by accusing Muḥammad of sorcery. They claimed he had cast a spell on those tempted to listen to him, admitting that no human could produce diction appropriate to so many situations or could influence people's thoughts unhampered by their different aptitudes.

If Muḥammad was a sorcerer and could cast a spell on those who listened to him recite the Qur'ān, how as it that some listeners were influenced by the spell but not others? If the Qur'ān was indeed Muḥammad's own composition, why weren't Arab scholars and linguists able to rival the Qur'ān? Advantaged by their knowledge in diverse literary fields and the arts of diction, such scholars were in a superior position to Muḥammad who was known to be illiterate. What prevented them from exposing him if he was an impostor as they claimed? The answer is that the Qur'ān is Allah's speech, and no man can compete with Him. To those opponents Allah says:

> "It is not poet's speech – little is it that ye believe! Nor diviner's speech – little is it that ye remember!" (al-Ḥāqqah 69:41-2)

Even the answer is not without challenge, for poetry is governed by metre and other literary devices. The assumption that the language of the Qur'ān was metrical verse in which the rules of poetry are observed was utterly false. The Arabs, more than any other people, knew this because of their superior skill in poetry. Their hypocrisy and denial of Allah were affirmed by Allah's saying to them, "Little is it that ye believe!"

Similarly, the allegation that the Qur'ān was the language of a soothsayer is equally unfounded. Apart from the fact that a soothsayer, like anyone else, is prone to forgetfulness as the years go by, he may need to modify his speech to the needs of each new situation. Hence came Allah's remark "Little is it that ye remember!" Furthermore, a soothsayer's words burdened with conventions of speech which, no matter how elaborate, cannot apply to more than one situation by using the same words and referring to one thought.

Another miraculous feature of the Qur'ān is its superb use

of both metrical composition and prose, in such exquisite harmony that the shift from one style to the other is barely perceptible. This intermingling of metrical and non-metrical composition is present throughout the whole of the Qur'ān, as the following verses exemplify:

> "Lo those who ward off (evil) are among gardens and watersprings. (And it is said unto them: Enter them in peace, secure. And we remove whatever rancour may be in their breasts. As brethren, face to face, (they rest) on couches raised. Toil cometh not unto them there, nor will they be expelled from thence . . . Announce (O Muḥammad) unto My slaves that verily I am the Forgiving, the Merciful, and that My doom is the dolorous doom. And tell them of Abraham's guests. (How) when they came unto him, and said: Peace. He said: Lo! we are afraid of you." (al-Ḥijr 15:45-52)

When reading the original Arabic of the above verse the reader moves from metric composition to prose without experiencing the slightest change of style or mode.

The same mingling of metrical and non-metrical composition can be observed in the following verse from the Surāh of Yūsuf (12). In this chapter, the wife of the ruler al-'Azīz commands Joseph to come out and face the women whom she has assembled,

> "Come out unto them! and when they saw him they exalted him and cut their hands exclaiming: Allah blameless! This is not a human being. This is no other than some gracious angel. She said: This is he on whose account ye blamed me. I asked of him an evil act, but he proved continent, but if he do not my behest he verily shall be imprisoned, and verily shall be of those brought low." (Yūsuf 12:31-32)

Although the original version of the phrase translated as: 'This is he on whose account ye blamed me' is indeed metrical diction in which the rules and technique of Arabic poetry are observed, it is almost impossible for the listener to detect the shift from one form to the other, nor does this exquisite mingling impinge on the fluidity of expression or impair its meaning.

The Qur'ān is truly unique in its composition. It is neither prose nor verse, deriving its unique and inimitable eloquence and meaningfulness from the divine attributes and powers of its Maker. It is these same divine attributes which have set the Qur'ān above emulation and given it its transcendental powers.

When the non-believers failed to detract from the Qur'ān's credibility or give sound justification for their antagonism to it, Allah's speech and message to mankind, they focussed their attack on Muḥammad instead. They contended that if Allah truly sought someone to serve Him as His Messenger to mankind He would have favoured one of their highly esteemed dignitaries. They argued that Muḥammad's illiteracy and humble status within the community, as well as his humility, made him ineligible for such a divine task. This rancorous and conniving strategy is revealed in the Sūrah al-Zukhruf (43) where Allah says:

> "And now that the Truth has come unto them they say: This is mere magic, and lo! we are disbelievers therein. And they say: If only this Qur'ān had been revealed to some great man of the two towns."
> (al-Zukhruf 43:30-31).

These verses show how jealous, resentful, and confused the idolators were. Although they described the Qur'ān as mere magic, they nevertheless wished that it had been revealed to one of their unbelieving dignitaries, knowing that such a favour would have given them a pretext to herald the view that Allah had no feud with their idols. It would then have been easy for them to distort the message to suit their own ends, to tighten their grip on the minds of their followers and to ensure their submissiveness while expanding their wealth and power. To accept the message and abide by its imperatives and the discipline of Allah however, is to forfeit all this authority and corruption. This hidden trait is revealed in the Sūrah al-Qaṣaṣ:

> "And they say: If we were to follow the Guidance with thee we should be torn out of our land."
> (al-Qaṣaṣ 28:57)

The Meaning of the Muqaṭṭa'āt Letters

By their resentment of Muḥammad and in their defiance of Allah, the idolators consciously unveiled their hidden belief in the truth of the message and its miraculous nature. The very choice of Muḥammad (SAW) as the recipient of Allah's Message was itself miraculous. Still another miracle of the Qur'ān can be found in the mysterious usage of the so-called Muqaṭṭa'āt letters that occur in certain chapters.

The choice of Muḥammad (SAW) as the Messenger of Allah was miraculous because he could neither read or write. He had no knowledge of the skills of literature, yet he preached to mankind in a language that was unique in terms of its clarity, intelligibility and its inimitability. All these factors were clear indications to the Qur'ān's divine origin. An illiterate can utter words and reproduce sentences, but to construct new ones is something which no illiterate has been known to do. Many of the passages revealed to Muḥammad began with the letters of the Arabic alphabet, such as *alif, lām, mīm* as a further challenge to the sceptics. Despite his illiteracy, Muḥammad was able to pronounce those letters in which he had no education and which he had never previously heard spoken. If the Qur'ān were of Muḥammad's (SAW) own making, the pronunciation of the letters of the alphabet, which he had not learnt, would have been beyond his ability, for only a person who had learnt how to read and write could identify these letters and utter them correctly.

The skill of the maker

Another miraculous feature of the language of the Qur'ān lies in its power to use the same letters of the Arabic language in a unique way to produce new meanings unparalleled by man no matter how skilled one might be in the diverse arts of language. In fact this inimitability and incomparability can have only one explanation: that its originator is no mortal being.

To compare the skills of two artisans they must be given samples of the same raw material and then their performance assessed on the same task. If they are tailors, they must be provided with the same fabric. The raw material of language is its letters and words. The production is itself the norm against which the skills of the producers are assessed. The miraculousness of the language of the Qur'ān does not lie only in the fact that it is Allah's speech, but also by the fact that although made up of the same letters and words, it has not been rivalled.

The Arabs are noted for their rhetorical ability, eloquence and meaningful expression. They considered meaningfulness, clarity, harmony of sound, and intelligibility to be essential to any eloquent speech. They summed up all these features by stipulating that the best and most meaningful speech is that which is appropriate to the needs of a particular situation. According to this definition, it is obvious that knowledge of human needs is limited as no human speech, no matter how eloquent can be applied to the needs of more than one situation.

The language of the Qur'ān unlike human diction reaches beyond all human knowledge, applying itself to myriad situations and transcends all barriers. This is the divine and unfathomable power of the Qur'ān which makes it so easily accessible to the illiterate and educated alike. Although revealed the letters of the Arabic language, no one has been able to match it or equal its beauty and rhetoric. This is because the Qur'ān has come to mankind both as a challenge and as a proof of the identity of its Maker, and it will remain so until the Last Day.

Chapter 4

The Rhetoric and Eloquence of the Qur'ān

The language of the Qur'ān is unsurpassed in its accuracy of meaning and expression. Each letter and word has its place while the language is free from fault. These unique features are found manifested in the use of one single letter or a preposition, as is demonstrated in the following verse:

> "Say (unto the disbelievers):
> Travel in the land . . ." (al-An'ām 6:11)

Here, the reader may wonder why Allah has used the preposition *fī* ('in') instead of *'alā* ('on') as correct Arabic usage dictates. However, this structure may be justified if we assumed that the proposition *fī* ('in') entailed adverbiality, and considered the word *al-arḍ* ('earth') to be an adverb of the word 'walk', and the meaning permitted it. But in the Qur'ān there is no allowance for likelihood. Each expression is measured to fit strictly the meaning it conveys leaving no shadow of doubt as to its interpretation. Each letter or word has one definite meaning and purpose which unfolds itself readily to the inquisitive mind.

With the advance of science into the nature and function of our universe, we have come to learn that the earth is not limited to its terrestrial and aquatic components. It also comprises a gaseous envelope which cleaves to it and gives it life, and without which life on earth would have been impossible. People living on earth make use of the properties of this gaseous extension or atmosphere for their benefit and progress in exactly the same way as they make use of the rocky crust and the liquid surfaces, or land and sea. Thus, when we travel in an aeroplane at about thirty thousand feet above the surface of the earth we are still moving within the boundaries of the earth. We pass beyond this boundary when we cross the limit of the atmosphere and plunge into space.

This scientific fact was a mystery to man when the Qur'ān was first revealed. Only Allah possessed this knowledge. Now we know that we are living and moving amidst two layers of matter: the solid matter of the earth and the gaseous matter which is air. No one today is ignorant of the fact that the three states of matter are solids, liquids and gases, but this primary knowledge was not available to man fourteen centuries ago, and neither Muḥammad nor anyone else could have known this.

A further example of the accuracy of usage and clarity of meaning, where no redundancy or synonymity exists, can be seen in the following verses:

> ". . . And persevere whatever may befall you. Lo! that is of the steadfast heart of things." (Luqmān 31:17)
> "And verily whoso is patient and forgiveth – lo! that, verily is (of) the steadfast heart of things."
> (al-Shūrā 42:43)

In the second verse the preposition "of" (*lamin*) may pass unnoticed or be taken as an emphatic synonym. But this is not so, because every letter or word in the language of the Qur'ān is selected with the utmost care to convey one intrinsic meaning and definite purpose. There is no such thing as synonymity in the Qur'ān. Each letter and word has its own fixed meaning which no other word can express as accurately, irrespective of their seeming similarity.

If we consider thoughtfully the meticulous selectivity of the words in the above verses and their underlying meaning, we soon come to realize that there are two kinds of patience. In the first kind there is no direct adversary or person responsible for hardship or misfortune; for example a brick falling from a building under construction onto the head of an unsuspecting pedestrian, or the collapse of a newly-built house over peacefully sleeping tenants. In all incidents and mishaps of this nature no individual bears the responsibility for the victim's misfortune. It is therefore easy for the unfortunate man to restrain his anger and accept his misfortune as an act of Allah. This kind of patience does not require a great deal of energy and can be easily achieved.

But patience which is "verily of the steadfast heart of things" is that which involves an antagonist against whom a victim has the freedom to retaliate and avenge himself, but prefers to suppress his anger and vengeful tendencies and forgive him. This kind of patience is deemed by Allah to be worthier than the first, because in this kind the aggrieved is dominated by his instinctive anger and feelings of injustice, and has to exercise a great deal of self-restraint. He is restrained by his fear of Allah, and refrains from responding to evil with evil. In the above verses, Allah defines the merits of the two types of patience and their corresponding heavenly rewards. He also describes the human responses of retaliation that ought to be observed in each case by the faithful. Thus, in the first case they are commanded to accept what befalls them with humility and resignation to His will. In the second they are commanded to be forgiving and to maintain their faith in Allah's justice.

The preposition 'of' has obviously been used to accentuate the distinction between the kind of patience in which forgiveness is not a necessity, and that in which forgiveness represents a test of endurance of injustice and of the believer's trust in Allah's providence and will. This shows how a single letter or preposition can bear such depth of meaning and discriminating power in the language of the Qur'ān.

Addressing the inner self

The miraculous features of the language of the Qur'ān are not limited to the accuracy of its words and letters or to their suitability of meaning. They are also exhibited in its unequalled ability to reach the deeply-hidden desires and tendencies of human nature, thus illustrating the all-encompassing and perfect knowledge of its true Maker. When Allah commanded the Muslims not to allow the idolators to come near the Ka'bah, He said to them:

> ". . . The idolators only are unclean. So let them not come near the Inviolable Place of Worship after this their year . . ." (al-Tawbah 9:28)

Allah knew that this commandment would stir the economic aspect of the Muslim community, arouse their apprehension and give them reason to question its fairness. For these idolators who came from different parts of the Arabian peninsula represented an important source of revenue for the Muslim traders of Makkah. To exclude them would surely reduce trading activity creating a state of hardship and poverty among the Muslim community. But because Allah was aware of the impact His commandment would have on their minds and thoughts, He did not issue it as an indisputable imperative of religious righteousness. Instead He addressed their economic tendencies, and in doing so, He was able to dispel their apprehension. He reminds them in the same verse that He alone determines all mankind's sustenance and says:

> ". . . If ye fear poverty (from the loss of their merchandise) Allah shall enrich you from His bounty if He will. Lo! Allah is Knower, Wise."
> (al-Tawbah 9:28)

Allah cautions them not to let their fear of losing trade divert them from obeying His commands, telling them that He is capable of rewarding them in diverse ways.

The above verse has a significant bearing on our daily business activities, for although the Qur'ān has set the rules for these activities, we nevertheless always live in fear of possible hardship and poverty. This fear seems to make us oblivious of the assurance provided in the above verse: that

Allah alone is the Provider of all sustenance on earth irrespective of the means, and that no man will gain more, or less, than his predetermined share of Allah's bounty.

Allah, throughout the Qur'ān, always addresses human attributes and tendencies, accurately answering any uncertainty that His injunctions may arouse in the minds of His worshippers. But this accuracy may, sometimes, require some modification in the use of one word in order to convey a new, broader and more apt meaning. This unsurpassed dexterity of language is a dominant feature of the language of the Qur'ān, as can be observed in the following verse in which Abraham says,

> "Lo! They are (all) an enemy unto me, save the Lord of the worlds, Who created me, and He does guide me." (al-Shu'arā' 26:77-78)

Here a question could be raised as to why Abraham said "Who created me," and not "He is the One Who created me", which would emphasise the notion of creation.

The answer is that creation does not require confirmation or assurance, for no one except Allah has the power to create a human being, and, therefore, no confirmation of this power is necessary or needed. But as far as guidance is concerned, there are many people who pretend to possess this power or talent. Some have constructed disciplines along the lines of religion, while others have distorted them. Both have declared that their purpose was to guide mankind. Thus anyone could set out his own views and pretend that they are the worthiest disciplines of guidance for humanity to follow.

It was therefore necessary to stress that guidance is in the hands of Allah and is bestowed upon mankind according to His will and design. The situation required that the pronoun *huwa* ('He') be introduced in the phrase *fa huwa yahdīni* ('and He does guide me'), in order to stress this fact and remind worshippers that guidance is a blessing that only Allah can bestow. The verse goes on to confirm this precept,

> "And Who feeds me and waters me, and when I sicken, then He heals me, and Who causes me to die and then gives me life (again)". (al-Shu'arā' 26:79-81).

The pronoun huwa ('He') was introduced in the above verse because the actions needed confirmation that Allah was behind these blessings. It is only by His will that we are able to attain them. Both sustenance and cure from sickness are made possible by His will and providence.

In contrast, the pronoun 'He' was omitted in the last sentence because no one could pretend to possess the power of giving life or taking it away. The exclusiveness of this attribute to Allah needed no justification or confirmation. Thus, Allah adds one word or omits another according to the needs of the situation, so that the precise and desired meaning be accurately and adequately expressed.

If Allah had added the pronoun 'He' to the above verse, or omitted it altogether, it would have passed unnoticed, and the controversy that the Qur'ān was man-made would have continued unabated.

The accuracy of meaning and expression may sometimes require the restructuring of words; changing them from transitive to intransitive verbs and vice versa. The verb *saqā* ('to water') for instance, is sometimes used in four forms. This multiple and varied usage can be observed in the following verse:

> ". . . Their Lord will slake their thirst with a pure drink." (al-Insān 76:21)

In another passage, we notice that the verb *saqā* ('to water, to give a drink, or quench thirst') is used to denote an entirely different meaning:

> "If they (the idolators) tread the right path, We shall give them to drink of water in abundance."
> (al-Jinn 72:16)

Although the two words stem from the same root, the

omission or addition of a letter gives the modified word an entirely new and different meaning. The addition or the omission is not used for the sake of expediency or to avoid repetition of the same word. Actually each word has a definite meaning that cannot be substituted by any other word. Thus, the expression in the second verse "We shall give them to drink" means that although Allah has provided water in abundance for man, he has to look for its source, whether it is a well, a spring or river. In contrast the expression 'Their Lord will slake their thirst' entails no effort on the part of man, for in Paradise water will automatically come to the lips of the thirsty whenever they wish. There is no toil or effort for the dwellers of Paradise. All their wishes are answered instantaneously in response to their thoughts.

This differentiation in the use of words and their correspondent meanings is well demonstrated throughout the whole of the Qur'ān, as can be remarked in the following verses:

> ". . . What! Even though their fathers had no knowledge whatsoever, and no guidance?" (al-Mā'idah 5:104)

> ". . . What! Even though their fathers were wholly unintelligent and had no guidance?" (al-Baqarah 2:170)

Whereas to the casual reader the two words *lā ya'lamūn* (no knowledge) and *lā ya'qilūn* (unintelligent) may seem to refer to the same thing, a thorough examination of their full context will reveal their entirely different and true meaning:

> "And when it is said unto them: Follow that which Allah has revealed, they say: We follow that wherein we found our fathers. What! Even though their fathers were wholly unintelligent and had no guidance? The likeness of those who disbelieve (in relation to the messenger) is as the likeness of one who calls unto that which hears naught except a shout and cry. Deaf, dumb, blind, therefore they have no sense." (al-Baqarah 2:170-1)

and,

> "When it is said unto them: Come unto that which Allah has revealed and unto the messenger, they say: Enough for us is that wherein we found our fathers. What! Even though their fathers had no knowledge whatsoever, and no guidance? O ye who believe! He who errs cannot injure you if you are rightly guided."
> (al-Mā'idah 5:104-5)

Orientalists contend that the two words are synonymous in meaning; that knowledge and intellect are one and the same thing; and that an intelligent person is capable of gaining knowledge and comprehending it.

This contention is far from accurate as far as the meaning of the two words, as expressed in the above passages, is concerned. In fact, each word has its distinctive and intrinsic meaning. When Allah used the word *lā ya'qilūn* ('unintelligent'), He meant that the idolators did not understand anything about this universe and its divine portents, because they did not use their minds properly, and that if they had used their intellect, without bias or prejudice, they would have ultimately seen the truth. Thus, in using the word *lā ya'qilūn* ('unintelligent') Allah deemed them to be lacking in both reason and wisdom in matters of worship, as well as failing to perceive the true meaning and indication of the various divine portents in the universe and how it operates.

In contrast, by using the words *lā ya'lamūn* ('have no knowledge'), Allah deemed the idolators to be lacking in both knowledge and intellect which means that in addition to their lack of reasoning and inability to perceive the true meaning of this universe and the power that governs it, they were ignorant of what others have learnt or acquired. For a man who lacks intellect does not reason or see the link between universal phenomena and their Creator and co-ordinator. But a man who has no knowledge does not use his mind, nor does he even try to acquire knowledge from others who have the insight to see Allah's might through His portents and His universe. The acquisition of meaning could be accomplished from someone else's recording of knowledge or the elucidation of the phenomena of the universe. This kind of learning happens all the time. For instance, when one reads a book written by a scientist or a scholar, he learns from what they have been able to record or discover, or from the product of their thinking. Thus he can learn about gravity or astronomy or any other field without actual research or experimentation.

The word 'unintelligent', therefore, referred to those persons who were reluctant to exert any worthwhile and purposeful mental or contemplative effort over Allah's portents and their meanings. They expressed this reluctance when they said,

> "Enough for us that wherein we found our fathers."
> To which Allah commented,
> "Even though their fathers were wholly unintelligent?"
> (al-Baqarah 2:171)

He describes those insensitive to His revelations as the deaf, dumb and blind. But the idolators deemed by Allah to have no knowledge are those who refused to think or learn from others and were content with the religion of their forefathers.

A further illustration of the accuracy of the Qur'ān in the selection and use of words to convey new meaning can be observed in the following verse:

> ". . . and that ye slay not your children because of penury – We provide for you and for them . . ." (al-An'ām 6:151)

It is also demonstrated in the following verse from the passage of al-Isrā' which deals with the same issue:

> "Slay not your children, fearing a fall to poverty. We provide for them and for you . . ." (al-Isrā' 17:31)

On the surface there seems to be no difference in meaning between the sentences 'We provide for you and for them' and 'We provide for them and for you'. But a close examination of the two verses will soon reveal that the first refers to poverty which already exists, for a poor man's primary concern is how to provide for himself and his wife. He is in constant fear of the hardship he is bound to face if the size of his family increases. Hence came Allah's assurance "We provide for you and for them" (i.e. when they are born). He is telling him not to worry in advance about the difficulties of providing for his future children, because He alone determines the sustenance of all His creatures.

In the second verse the persons referred to are not poor, but although they are well provided for, they are still apprehensive that the birth of more children may create new difficulties, and eventually poverty. Here again Allah assures them that the birth of children will not take away any part of their parents' sustenance, and that each child's sustenance is being determined by Him at birth.

Some may ask, why did Allah not say, "We provide for all" instead of 'for you and them,' or 'for them and you'? The reason is that He wanted to make it clear that every creature on this earth has its own share of His bounty, which is divided among them according to His will and wisdom, and that no one can take even the smallest part of the other's share, nor does the birth of a new child diminish what had already been decided for his parents.

'You are the Mighty, the Wise'

The accuracy of meaning is impressively demonstrated in the following verse in which God speaks to Jesus:

> ". . . O Jesus, son of Mary! Didst thou say unto mankind: Take me and my mother for two gods beside Allah? He says: Be glorified! It was not mine to utter that to which I had no right. If I used to say it, then You knew it. You know what is in my mind and I know not what in Your mind. Lo ! You, only You, are the Knower of Things Hidden." (al-Mā'idah 5:117)

Then Jesus continues,

> "If You punish them, lo! they are Your slaves, and if You forgive them, (lo! they are Your slaves). Lo! You, only You are the Mighty, the Wise." (al-Mā'idah 5:118)

Jesus' saying "If You punish them . . . they are Your slaves" is a settled case, for we all are Allah's slaves, governed by His will. We must submit to His justice and providence and abide by His commandments and injunctions. But if we consider the situation to be one of forgiveness, why then has Jesus used the word 'Mighty' whereas the word 'Forgiving' would seem more appropriate? This remarkable and selective use of words and expressions illustrates the fundamentally surpassing power of the language of the Qur'ān. This same power is denoted in Jesus' plea 'If You forgive them', because it bears the actual meaning of forgiveness, for if Allah were not forgiving, how then could He forgive? In fact, ending the verse with the adjectives 'Mighty' and 'Wise', indicates that in addition to Allah's freedom and power to bestow forgiveness at will, no one has the right to question His acts. He is the 'Mighty' and the 'Wise' who gives no account of what He does. The word 'Wise' (al-Ḥakīm) has been introduced as a means of pleading for greater forgiveness and mercy for those who are misguided.

The tyrant, oppressor, sinner, transgressor . . . and evil, iniquity

Now let us explore the following two verses for further evidence of the Qur'ān's surpassing accuracy of expression:

> "And those who, when they do an evil thing or wrong themselves" (Āl 'Imrān 3:135)

and

> "Yet whoso does evil or wrongs his own soul" (al-Nisā 4:110)

Some may argue that both evil doing and sinful acts are tantamount to wronging the soul and both warrant punishment. They say that the conjunction 'or' is unnecessary, and see no difference between he who sins or does an evil thing, and he who wrongs his own soul. This is not so, and there is indeed a difference between the two, because he who sins is seeking quick pleasure and material satisfaction. His weak soul is overcome with the glittering attraction of worldly pleasures and gains. Among the misguided are those persons who are ready to forsake their religion and Allah's discipline for mundane vanity and rewards. Adultery, stealing, alcoholism and similar unlawful and unchaste habits are examples of evil deeds whose perpetrators have willingly sold their religion for transient worldly gains. But persons who wrong themselves do not necessarily gain anything from their wrong and unlawful acts. They do not satisfy any sensual or material desire, and yet will have to account for their unrighteous behaviour on the Day of Judgement. They have failed in this world and the next for having sold their religion and left their soul open to condemnation for the sake of hypocrisy and appeasement of others. Most notorious among these are the persons who commit perjury for no other reason than to please a corrupt and malicious man of power and authority, thus inflicting harm upon an innocent person, without securing any personal gain. In doing so they have done injustice to themselves and to the innocent victim. The same condemnation applies to persons who invent false accusations or distort true facts about someone else to deprive him of some reward or charity, or for the mere pleasure of causing misfortune and harm to others. Likewise these are those who pry into other people's lives then use their information for no other reason but to smear their reputation; or the senior official who gives an untrue report about one of his employees to hinder his promotion, for the benefit of another who does not deserve it.

Such people are unlikely to secure any material gain from such malicious acts. They all do injustice to themselves because they bear the burden of these sins when they are asked to account for them on the Day of Judgement. Herein lies the difference between them and the evildoers.

Darkness and light

In the Qur'ān the words "darkness" and "light" assume a much deeper meaning than in ordinary usage, as expressed in the following verse wherein Allah says:

> ". . . He brings them out of darkness unto light by His decree . . ." (al-Mā'idah 5:16)

When Allah speaks about light or darkness He never uses the plural form of the word 'light'.* One would say that the usage would be more appropriate if the plural of the word 'light' was also used in the above verse. (The word translated as darkness – al-Ẓulumāt – is plural). This would, perhaps, have been true if the reference were to the light of the day and the darkness of the night. But the verse is, in fact, referring to the darkness of the soul and the light of Allah's truth. Whereas the darkness of the soul can vary in intensity from one person to another, there is only one light and one truth. Therefore, not once in the whole of the Qur'ān has the plural form Anwār ('lights') been used. In contrast, the word 'darkness' has been repeatedly used in either its singular or plural form according to contexts. Every soul, or self, has its own particular lust, or darkness, and the darkness of one individual's soul cannot be identical to that of another. In many instances man becomes ensnared by his lust, and lusts cannot be numbered. This dark lust is the root from which stem all sorts of struggle among men. They kill, steal and are aggressive towards each other. The list of such acts is endless. They represent different kinds of darkness, and each kind harbours the lust of its owner. Each person is striving to satisfy a certain desire, regardless of his means, and each justifies his means in response to the dictates of his lust. Some may cloak their lust in such ideological doctrines as communism, capitalism, socialism and so forth. The main concern of each is to usurp that which is not lawfully his. They are clichés behind which is hidden the real lust which each man, or group, wish to feed and nourish, so

*In Arabic the words for 'darkness' and 'light' can be singular or plural.

that they can stand supreme, powerful and unrestrained by either ethics, moral values or any other authority or power.

Darkness, therefore, is not one, but is rather of many sorts. Light, in contrast, is one. It is the discipline which Allah has decreed for mankind, so that it can live in harmony with its own self and with Him.

Chapter 5

Is there Contradiction in the Qur'ān?

It has been alleged that some verses of the Qur'ān lack consistency of meaning owing to forgetfulness and an inadequate mastery of language on the part of Muḥammad (SAW). Furthermore this "logic" deduces that, since Allah is above error, the Qur'ān must, therefore, be Muḥammad's (SAW) own composition and not Allah's speech.

If those critics and sceptics spent as much time in an honest and unprejudiced study of the Qur'ān's language and its depth of meaning as in seeking defects or lapses of memory to justify their futile attempts of discrediting Allah's divine message to mankind they would have long ago discovered the futility of their endeavours.

The primary objective of these critics is to discredit Muḥammad (SAW) and the message he was ordained to deliver to mankind. They began by promoting the false notion that some verses in the Qur'ān lacked coherence and accuracy of meaning and were in many respects contradictory. They then postulated that the Qur'ān was Muḥammad's own composition, for 'Allah', they said, was above error.

Those critics were unable to perceive the true meaning of Qur'ānic verses which, though invariably vivid and clear to the believer's receptive eye and thought, remain imperceptible to the sceptic's mind.

This did not happen by accident, but by divine decree. For this provocative challenge and the misinterpretation of the Qur'ān by sceptics has been countered by a determined and vigorous analysis and elucidation of the Qur'ānic verses in question. These verses have been illuminated and clarified in a way that had not previously been fully explored or defined, resulting in further convincing evidence about the divine source of the message and the credibility of its bearer, Muḥammad (SAW). In other words, such an ungracious attack by sceptics has, contrary to their expectations, only enhanced the faith as regards both the message and the Messenger alike.

Amongst the verses that the critics have described as inconsistent and incoherent, are those concerning the creation of the Heavens and the Earth:

This is one of the principal issues, because it involves something which only Allah, the Creator of all things, knows. The sceptics have singled this out because it stands as the central pillar and core of the miracle of the Qur'ān. Any apparent misrepresentation would serve their case against the validity of the message and the credibility of the Messenger.

These sceptics contend that in a number of verses it is stated that the earth and the heavens have been created in six days, yet in the Sūrah Fuṣṣilat (41) the number of days is increased to eight. This is indeed true, for in the Sūrah of al-A'rāf Allah says,

> "Your Lord is Allah Who created the heavens and the earth in six days . . . " (al-A'rāf 7:54)

This is repeated in Sūrah Yūnus wherein God says,

> "Your Lord is Allah Who created the heavens and the earth in six days, then He established Himself upon the Throne." (Yūnus 10:3)

The same thing is affirmed in Sūrah Al-Furqān:

> ". . . Who created the heavens and the earth and all that is between them in six days . . . " (al-Furqān 25:59)

All these verses are in accord that the heavens and the earth were created in six days. There is no disagreement about that. But when we examine the passage in Fuṣṣilat (41) the story is told in a different context. Allah says:

> "Say (O Muḥammad, unto the idolators): Disbelieve you verily in Him Who created the earth in two days, and ascribe you unto Him equals? He (and none else) is the Lord of the Worlds. He placed therein firm hills rising above it and blessed it and measured therein its sustenance in four days, alike for (all) who ask. Then turned He to the heaven which was smoke, and said unto it and unto the earth: Come both of you, willingly or loth. They said: We come, obedient. Then he ordained them seven heavens in two days and inspired in each heaven its mandate . . ." (Fuṣṣilat 41:9-12).

Counting the number of days in the above verse the initial impression is that it took eight and not six as previously stated. Indeed, it took Allah two days to create the earth and the setting of mountains and the measuring of its sustenance took four days, and a further two days for the differentiation of the heavens. Looking carefully and thoughtfully beyond this apparent anomaly promptly dispells any confusion and superficial impression.

In fact the beginning of this last verse diverges distinctively from the other three verses. It is obvious that Allah is addressing those idolators who equate Him with their own man-made gods; He is telling us that those who exploit the information contained in this passage to raise doubt about its authenticity are equally interested in promulgating blasphemy and denying His Unity. When He says "Disbelieve you verily in Him who created the earth . . . ?" He is, in fact, telling us that in the course of time there will emerge unbelievers who will make use of this apparent contradiction.

This predictive power inherent in the foregoing verses puts the divine and transcendent origin of the Qur'ān beyond any worldly rhetoric. In the first three verses Allah is referring to the process of creation as a whole. But in the Sūrah 'Fuṣṣilat' He is speaking of the creation of the earth, which was accomplished in two stages. In the first stage, He created the globe in two days. In the second, He placed the mountains and blessed and measured its sustenance in two more days. The explanation is that the two days and the four days involve an overlapping process, the four days representing the total length of the time taken in creating the earth and placing the mountains.

This is the same as saying: "The train will arrive at station 'A' in two hours, and it will stop at station 'B' in four hours", meaning that the first stage will take two hours, but the entire distance (which includes the first stage) will take four hours; or when one says that laying the foundation of a house would take 4 months and that the completion of the entire house would take 12 months.

In fact in the three verses from the chapters al-A'raf, Yūnus and al-Furqān (25), Allah does not detail the various stages of the creation of the earth and the heavens, He refers to them as a part of a whole. But in Surah Fuṣṣilat He conveys a detailed description of the entire phenomenon which, He tells us, took four days. He then turns His attention to the heavens – an entirely new and independent stage of the creation, which lasted, according to the verse, only two days. But how long is one day with Allah?

This question is answered in Sūrah al-Ḥajj, where it is stated that "a Day with Allah is as a thousand years of what ye reckon." (al-Ḥajj 22:47)

From the above it is obvious that the alleged paradox may be attributed to a shallow and superficial interpretation of the verses in question, which, in fact, provide undeniable evidence of the Qur'ān's divine origin and miraculousness, anticipating the appearance of future disbelievers who would use this shift in meaning to cause confusion and perplexity.

Another point of contention concerns the Qur'ān's distinction between charitable deeds and kindliness. In Sūrah al-Mujādilah, Allah says:

> "You will not find folk who believe in Allah and the Last Day loving those who oppose Allah and His messenger, even though they be their fathers or their sons . . ." (al-Mujādilah 58:22)

In another verse from the surah of Luqmān (31) however Allah says:

> "But if they strive with you to make you ascribe unto Me as partner that of which thou hast no knowledge, then obey them not. Consort with them in the world kindly . . ." (Luqmān 31:15)

Here critics of the Qur'ān claim that the two verses are contradictory on the premise that in the former Allah forbids believers from being kind to those who oppose Him and His messenger, even if they are parents, and yet in the second, it is commanded to be kind to them.

Again the sceptics seem to have been content to scratch at the surface of the passage, and as a result have failed to grasp the deeper and more impressive meaning inherent in it. They have consciously, or unconsciously, confused the meaning of good deeds or benevolence with that of loving kindness. A good deed could involve, on the one hand, people whom one knows well, or complete strangers. A good deed may be motivated by momentary compassion. The beneficiary could be an individual in financial need, or a charitable society. These deeds are done for heavenly reward and nothing else.

Recipients of good deeds are not bound by obligation. Unlike good deeds, loving kindness is lodged in the heart and evolves from it. A good deed or an act of charity does not necessarily evolve from the heart, but kindness does. It lives in it and is stimulated by it. Loving kindness is a divine gift bestowed by Allah upon the hearts of those who have faith in Him and His commandments. Agnostic hearts are devoid of this divine gift. No one can have two kinds of heart and no heart can harbour agnosticism and devoutness simultaneously, or perform both tasks alternately or concurrently, as is stated by Allah in the Sūrah al-Aḥzāb, where He says,

> "Allah has not assigned unto any man two hearts within his body . . ." (al-Aḥzāb 33:4)

Allah has used the word '*loving*' (in 58:22) because of its connection with the heart. It is uncommon to find a believer being kind or loving to persons who inveigh against Allah and His messenger, even if he is closely related to them. This is the kind of love that flows from within the heart. In the second verse Allah, nevertheless, forbids offspring from being harsh to their parents or inflicting any pain on them, even if they try to force them away from Allah's faith. Allah commands children to be kind and charitable to their parents in recognition of all the care they have taken of them throughout different stages of their infancy and maturity, as well as because of their old age. He commands them not to hate or scorn their misguided parents, nor show them the same kind of love and kindliness as that which they would invariably and readily give to parents who shared with them the same faith in Allah and allegiance to his Prophet. Misguided parents are entitled only to the same charitable and civil conduct as that given to distant unrelated persons.

The command to be civil and respectful to unbelieving parents is, indeed, the ultimate lesson in behaviour and the dutiful relationship between child and parent. Children should observe these norms in order to gain Allah's unrestricted mercy which He does not withhold even from those who rebel against Him and His Prophet.

No one can assume that benevolent and charitable deeds are synonymous with kindliness and love, or that they are motivated by the same kind of feelings and emotions. Whereas the first are elicited by a sense of duty, the latter are convictions lodged in the heart which flow from it.

Two other verses deemed by some critics to be inaccurate and contradictory are the following:

> "And we have commended unto man kindness towards parents. His mother bears him with reluctance, and brings him forth with reluctance, and the bearing of him and the weaning of him is thirty months, till, when he attains full strength and reaches forty years he says: My Lord! Arouse me that I may give thanks for the favour wherewith you have favoured me and my parents . . ." (al-Aḥqāf 46:15)

Again in Sūrah Luqmān Allah says:

> "And We have enjoined upon man concerning his parents – His mother bears him in weakness upon weakness, and his weaning is in two years – Give thanks unto Me and unto your parents. Unto Me is the journeying." (Luqmān 31:14)

In both verses, Allah commends both parents, while placing more emphasis on the role and endurance of the mother. The opponents of Islam criticize these verses, assuming that they favour the mother and ignore the father, and that Allah is talking about a stage of childhood. They maintain that Allah begins the first verse by commending both parents, but then neglects the father while the verse enumerates the mother's role and merits and what she endures in her tasks of child bearing and child rearing. They also question the logic of addressing an unborn baby or a breast-fed child who can neither reason nor understand and conclude by asking whom the Qur'ān is actually addressing.

Here again we say that the critics have once more misinterpreted the verse and failed to deduce its underlying meaning. If Allah has favoured the mother with His commendation it is because she bears most of the burden of child bearing and rearing, both of which are either unregistered stages in the child's consciousness or hazily inscribed in an adult's memory. She devotes her entire life to caring for him until he reaches the age when he becomes dependent on his father for the satisfaction of his material needs.

The role of the father is firmly etched in the adult's conscious mind. One is aware of all that his father has done for him and is able to appreciate it and be grateful for it. In contrast he barely remembers anything of the mother's selfless role which began with bearing him and did not end until he was able to fend for himself. He has no recollection of the anxious and sleepless nights his mother endured patiently, every time he was sick or needed comforting. Hence the emphasis on the mother's role and the commendation that it should be constantly remembered and rewarded with equal care and kindness. Allah, indeed, commends both parents, but fearing that the scale might be tipped in favour of the father, whose role is more easily remembered and appreciated, He cautions the children against such bias or unbalance. Actually this same commendation was stressed by the Prophet Muḥammad (SAW) who was once asked to define who, after Allah and His Messenger, deserves most respect, to which he replied: "your mother, your mother, your mother, then your father".

Those who would seek to discredit the validity of the Qur'ān have also focused on those passages that deal with the Day of Judgement. One may cite the verse of Sūrah al-Naḥl which says:

> "The Commandment of Allah will come to pass, so seek not to hasten it . . ." (al-Naḥl 16:1)

This verse has been criticized on the assumption that it is grammatically incorrect. Sceptics argue that the phrase translated "will come to pass", the form of which in Arabic is a past tense, indicates a past action and that the phrase "seek not to hasten it" indicates a future action. In other words: if the commandment has been decided and the Last Day fixed why does Allah ask us not to hasten Him?

In responding to this criticism, it may be useful to begin by pointing out that when talking about Allah we should always be conscious of the fact that His capability is incomparable and is beyond our imagination. We should not compare our limited powers and means with His infinite might and foresight. We live in time, and our notion about it is strictly defined. But for Allah, time has no scope or limit. He is above time as understood and defined by man. Therefore, the verb "has come" derives its past tense in terms of Allah's unrestricted knowledge of time. So when He says 'has come' it should be understood that the decision has already been made and the Last Day has been registered with Allah's. It is a certainty. But Allah's knowledge of the things to come is conveyed to mankind at His will and when He ordains it to be, as stated in the following verse from Sūrah al-Naḥl.

> "And Our word unto a thing, when We intend it, is only that We say unto it: 'Be!' and it is". (al-Naḥl 16:40)

So in Allah's knowledge and design the Day of Judgement has already been set, but it will remain a mystery to mankind until the imperative 'Be' is uttered and the trumpet is blown. This is the reason Allah has told the faithful not to be hasty in seeking that Day before they are fully prepared to account thoroughly for their deeds. On the other hand, Allah is reminding the sceptics, who, through defiance and ignorance of the awesomeness of that Day, are urging its arrival. He conveys this reminder in the following verse:

> "And they find all that they did confronting them . . ." (al-Kahf 18:49)

Another controversial issue has stemmed from the misinterpretation of the following verse from the Sūrah al-Fīl (105) where Allah addresses Muḥammad and says:

> "Have you not seen how your Lord dealt with the owners of the Elephant?" (al-Fīl 105:1)

The critics claim that the phrase "Have you not seen?" is inappropriate, on the premise that Muḥammad was born in the same year of the incursion of Abraha referred to in this Sūrah and, therefore, could not have witnessed it. They add that the phrase would have been more accurate if such words as 'known' or 'learnt' were used instead of 'seen', and conclude their criticism with the assertion that language had betrayed Muḥammad. (SAW)

The obvious error regarding this critical interpretation of the verse in question is that the element of faith and conviction in all that Allah conveys to those who believe in Him has been overlooked. What He imparts to the faithful instantly takes the form of a perceptible vision. The Qur'ān is Allah's speech as it was delivered to Muḥammad who was not permitted to modify it or alter it. When Allah says to him 'Have you not seen?' it means that the seeing is a certainty and a constant vision for all believers. That is, because the seeing here involves a supernatural phenomenon that defies all natural norms. It is a miracle which Allah wants to impress on the minds of the faithful as if it had actually been seen.

The importance of the issue – which is fundamentally one of faith – was the underlying purpose for the use of the word "seen". Allah wants the faithful to visualize His might and power. The miracle Allah wants us to see is one in which He changed weakness into strength in a unique and formidable way which is beyond the reach and comprehension of man.

On this occasion, small birds (abābīl) carrying small pebbles of baked clay were able to defeat an army considered to be the mightiest army at the time – an incredible feat by human standards. But Allah willed it and, He enabled one of the weakest of all creatures to overcome and destroy one of the largest of all animals and the army that had mobilized it to destroy His House of Worship: the Ka'bah.

Some scientists have since tried to raise doubts about the miracle. They contend that the destruction of the elephant and the combatants was caused by infectious diseases. This cannot be true, because Muḥammad (SAW) was born in that year, and received the message forty years later, which indicates that many of those who had lived through this experience would still be alive when the verse was revealed to him. They would have been the first to deny it and to ridicule him if it had been false. But they refrained from any attempt to discredit its authenticity or refute it. They remained silent because they had seen the marauding birds as they attacked the invading army with their baked-clay stones. The silence of the elders of Makkah was undisputable evidence that the miracle had taken place exactly as it was revealed in the Qur'ān.

The truth of this or any other Sūrah, does not require justification, because Allah has the power and the capability to perform such supernatural feats and to say unto a thing, Be! and it is done. It follows, that in all issues demanding solid faith, Allah's speech mirrors the actual incident or feat and the image illustrated therein: the seeing is as true and as real as the words spoken.

Actually, Allah has emphasized 'seeing' (and not 'knowing' or 'learning') the miracle because its underlying significance and meaning touch many aspects of our interaction and relationships, as manifested in the constant strife between the helpless and the powerful oppressor; between the ruler and the ruled. It is aimed at instilling faith in the heart of the weak and the aggrieved while cautioning the tyrant. It is a reminder to all of us of Allah's omniscience. His divine justice is never far away and He is always on the side of the aggrieved and the helpless against the callous and the transgressor.

This is the kind of faith that every believer should be armed with. It lodges in the heart, and the true believer is overwhelmingly sensitive to it, as well as to Allah's might and His command of happenings relevant to all acts of right and wrong.

Yet another verse that has come to be criticized as a result of a misinterpretation is the following:

> "When the hypocrites come unto thee (O Muḥammad) they say: We bear witness that thou art indeed Allah's messenger. And Allah knows that thou art indeed His messenger, and Allah bears witness that the hypocrites indeed are speaking falsely." (al-Munāfiqūn 63:1)

Here the critics contend that the facts state in the verse are contradictory and lack coherence. They argue that if the hypocrites had witnessed that Muḥammad was indeed Allah's Messenger and that Allah also knew that he was; how could the hypocrites be condemned as liars, when their testimony was identical with that of Allah? They then define lying as the non-conformity of speech with the actual facts, and concluded that according to this definition, the admission by the hypocrites that Muḥammad was Allah's Messenger must be a false statement.

To respond to the above criticism it is necessary to detach the verb *bear witness* from the clause "that thou art indeed

Allah's messenger" before we can sort out the part of speech to which the lying is ascribed.

A true confession or testimony must evolve from the heart. If the conviction of the heart is absent, then the testimony is merely lip-service. God knew that the hypocrites' confession was false and devoid of any true faith or belief and that the hypocrites' objective was to beguile Muḥammad.

The verse is true in so far as Muḥammad is Allah's Messenger, but the lying is not ascribed to the clause "Muḥammad is Allah's Messenger." But the verb 'bear witness' is, and it is to this verb or act that the accusation of lying has been ascribed. This is the reason why Allah completed the first statement by saying:

> "And Allah knows that thou art indeed His messenger."

Here lies the fine distinction between the testimony or the verbal act, and the object of that testimony. The lying is restricted to the confession and not the object of the confession. Because the hypocrites' intention was to deceive, their confession was not genuine. But regardless of this deceptive confession Muḥammad (SAW) is truly Allah's messenger and Allah knows it.

Is there any evidence to indicate that Muḥammad's memory ever failed him as some would have us believe? Two verses might be cited to shed light on this question.

> "On that day neither man nor jinn will be questioned of his sin." (al-Raḥmān 55:38)

> "And stop them, for they must be questioned." (al-Ṣāffāt 37:24)

In the first verse there is a negation of questioning, but in the second the inescapability of questioning is affirmed. The critics used this discrepancy in their attack on Muḥammad (SAW), accusing him of a lapse of memory.

This misconception on the part of the critics is due to their failure to distinguish between the two purposes of any question, for a question is asked either to learn or to make the person questioned aware of the quality and quantity of his knowledge. When a pupil asks his teacher a question, his intention is to learn, but when the teacher asks his pupil a question he does not do this in order to learn, for his knowledge is greater than that of his pupil. He asks the question so that the pupil can assess the extent of his achievement or his limitations. He thus puts him in a situation where he cannot argue that he has studied well if the opposite is true. Exams are held not only for the purpose of assessing how effectively a teaching method is working but also to provide the learner with self-documented evidence assessing his own effort throughout the year. He is both the judge and the judged. He cannot argue or claim that he has been unfairly treated or assessed. His grade or mark is his witness.

In the verse "On that day neither man nor jinn will be questioned", questioning for learning or obtaining knowledge is discarded, for Allah already knows the sins every man and jinn has committed. He has no need to question in order to obtain knowledge. As for the second verse: "Stop them, for they must be questioned" it means that sinners are to be stopped to be informed of what sins they have committed, or in other words, to admit their sins.

The same meaning is emphasized in the Sūrah al-Ṣāffāt (37) wherein Allah refers to the hypocrites and says:

> "And (they) say: Ah, woe for us! This is the Day of Judgement. This is the Day of Separation, which you used to deny. (And it is said to the angels): Assemble those who did wrong, together with their wives and what they used to worship instead of Allah, and lead them to the path to hell; and stop them for they must be questioned." (al-Ṣāffāt 37:20-24)

The 'stopping' here is not for the purpose of questioning them about that which they have committed, but rather to confront them with it and make them bear witness to it.

In the same Sūrah, Allah asks:

> "What aileth you that you help not one another?" (al-Ṣāffāt 37:25)

Where are those gods whom you worshipped and set up as rivals to Me? Allah is not seeking an answer; He is simply reminding them of the fact that there is no other god but Him. The remark has its answer in their plight.

The following verses have also been declared by some critics to be inconsistent:

> ". . . Nor does any laden bear another's load . . ." (al-An'ām 6:164)

> "And no burdened soul can bear another's burden . . ." (al-Malā'ikah 35:18)

> "But they verily will bear their own loads and other loads beside their own . . . " (al-'Ankabūt 29:13)

The critics argue that these verses are contradictory and lack logical coherence, for whereas in the first two verses Allah has ordained that no one should bear more than his own burden of sins, He says in the third verse that sinners will bear other burdens besides their own.

Again, if those critics had searched more deeply beneath this seeming anomaly they would have reached the precise meaning of these verses. There is no obscurity or ambiguity in the first two verses. It is clear that no one will be allowed on the Day of Judgement to bear the burdens of others, as may happen in a worldly relationship. For example, a father may be willing to go to jail in place of his son in order to save him from such a punishment. This does not apply to spiritual offences on the Day of Judgement.

The third verse tells us otherwise, but a misunderstanding has arisen as a result of confusing the sinners referred to in the first two verses with the sinners in the third verse. The sinners mentioned in the first two verses are those misguided sinners who only disobeyed Allah's commands and His Prophet. They will be judged for their disobedience only.

But the sinners in the third verse are those who entice others to rebel against Allah and His commands. They are doomed and are to be judged for their own sins and some of the sins of those they have misled. This is emphasized in the Sūrah al-Naḥl wherein Allah says,

> "That they may bear their burdens undiminished on the Day of Resurrection, with somewhat of the burdens of those whom they mislead without knowledge. Ah! evil is that which they bear." (al-Naḥl 16:25)

In this chapter the allegation that some verses in the Qur'ān are inaccurate and lack coherence and consistency was discussed. This allegation has been exploited by some critics to construct a case against the origin and authenticity of the scripture and the credibility of Allah's Prophet, Muḥammad (SAW). In response we have been able to demonstrate some of the Qur'ān's miraculous and transcendent features, embedded in both its language and meanings, and how the two work to produce and convey perceptible ideas and facts.

Chapter 6

The Qur'ān and the Universe

There are many miraculous features in the language of the Qur'ān the significance of which demands a keen and sustained interest. The lack of thorough research beyond the apparent meaning of many of these controversial verses has been responsible for their misunderstanding by sceptics who presume that they lacked consistency. Allegations made by sceptics that the information recorded in the Qur'ān diverges from established scientific facts about the universe and its varied phenomena could be easily discarded on the premise that the Qur'ān is undeniably Allah's speech to mankind. And Allah, being the Creator of this universe, knows best how it functions. However it is useful to examine these allegations if only to show their superficiality and the malicious intention of those who make them.

It should be pointed out that the meanings of the verses of the Qur'ān are constantly regenerated from generation to generation. This continual increase of meaning is one of the Qur'ān's fundamental miraculous features, developing in proportion to the degree of knowledge revealed to mankind at Allah's will and timing. If this renewed contribution had been confined to one generation or one people it would have exhausted its message and purpose in a few years, and eventually the Qur'ān's miraculousness would have diminished. It would have reached the following generations devoid of divine power and spiritual conviction.

But this could never be the case. From the time it was revealed to Muḥammad (SAW) up until the present day, the Qur'ān's contribution to our knowledge about this universe has never faltered or ceased. On the contrary, it still provides further insight into the mysteries of the universe, in proportion to mankind's expanding knowledge and intellectual capacity. Today we draw upon broader meanings from the Qur'ān, far more significant in their implication than anything hitherto before perceived.

This ever-unfolding "newness" explains why Muḥammad's (SAW) elucidation of the message did not go further than the immediate commandments and injunctions relevant to man's situation in the universe and his relationship with Allah and His tenets of worship and their repercussions. He refrained from commenting upon the complexities of the universe and its functioning, in proportion to the scientific knowledge available at that time. He explained and taught what was necessary to promote and fulfil the objective of his divine message.

Since the initial revelation, the meanings within the Qur'ān have maintained relevance despite science's latest discoveries and theories, giving credibility to some and refuting others.

Regarding the Qur'ān and scientific theories, it might be useful to draw attention to the unsound and hazardous attempts by some overzealous students who make use of scientific theories to confirm the recorded facts found in the Qur'ān or to enhance its authenticity. No less dangerous than this attitude is the practice by some scientists and scholars who attempt to elucidate the Qur'ān in terms of these scientific discoveries or ascribe to some verses and facts the power of foretelling future events, only to be stunned later by discovering that they have been over-enthusiastic. Many have overlooked the indisputable fact that the credibility of the Qur'ān does not depend upon evidence from science or any other field of knowledge. The Qur'ān should not be regarded as a scientific text, but rather as Scripture with a system of discipline for leading a virtuous life, decreed by Allah for the benefit and welfare of mankind.

Allah, however, knew that in the course of time there would emerge sceptics who would proclaim the decline of the age of divine power and herald their allegiance to the power of science. To foil this impious misconception, Allah supported the Qur'ān with many scientific facts about the universe and its organisation which no one else but He knew at the time of the Qur'ān's revelation.

The following verse, whose meaning has remained hidden for centuries, has only recently begun to yield its wealth of scientific data. This happened when mankind became able to assimilate such complex knowledge.

> "We shall show them Our portents on the horizons and within themselves until it be manifest unto them that it is the Truth . . ." (Fuṣṣilat 41:53)

It is important to draw the reader's attention to the future tense of the verb 'show'. Actually the verse refers to the endless future; it addresses not only the present age or the one that follows, but rather the whole of mankind from now until eternity.

This regeneration of meaning and its inexhaustibility should not, however, be used as a justification to ascribe to the verses any meaning other than what they presently yield. We should approach the Qur'ān as a divine message that has come to provide us with knowledge about this world and organise our relationship with it and with its Creator. It has not come to reveal the fundamental laws of geometry, architecture, astronomy or any other science. In fact, Allah defines the Qur'ān's fundamental objective in the first verse of the Sūrah "the Cow", in which He says:

> "That is the Scripture whereof there is no doubt, a guidance to all those who ward off (evil)."
> (al-Baqarah 2:2)

Although the Qur'ān is primarily a scripture of guidance and worship, Allah has recorded in it factual knowledge capable of answering and clarifying any misconceptions that might arise in the course of time. Some revelations which touch upon scientific phenomena have not completely unfolded. All of them, however, are meant to discredit those heretics who hail the doctrine of science and decry the doctrine of faith and who, in their foolish and misguided conceit, have been oblivious of the fact that science, to which they vow allegiance, is of Allah's own making. It is He alone who unfolds the secrets of science to mankind when He wills. This knowledge which has been imparted to man should not be used to validate the Qur'ān.

The Qur'ān can prove or disprove the findings of science, but it is safer and wiser to refrain from correlating any scientific theory with the facts recorded in it until it has been proved and verified beyond any doubt. It is grievously wrong to hastily attribute something to Allah, only to discover, later, that it is untrue. All scientific hypotheses which disagree with the Qur'ān have been proved to be unfounded and lacking in empirical evidence.

It is often asked why the Qur'ān did not elucidate the scientific facts recorded in its verses to those who were alive at the time of its revelation, or to the generation who followed them. Indeed, the scientific knowledge and facts recorded in the Qur'ān involve universal phenomena which have a significant bearing on man's survival, regardless of how they function. Thus the energy of the sun, the earth's gravity and its rotation day and night, the development of the embryo and all similar phenomena are created to serve man and ensure his survival on earth. He need not be fully acquainted with the details of how they function in order to benefit from their useful properties.

There are millions who know nothing about the physiological processes of conception and pregnancy, yet this lack of knowledge does not stop them from having children. Similarly, there are millions who do not know that the sun is the main source of life on earth, and yet enjoy all the benefits derived from this distant star. Hence there was no urgent necessity, at that early stage, to explain these complex scientific phenomena or to those who lived at the time of the revelation of the Qur'ān and the generation who followed them. They were given as much as their intellect could assimilate, in proportion to the growth of that intellect.

There have been those who have contended that some of the facts recorded in the Qur'ān diverge widely from the empirically validated laws of science. This contention is both misleading and inaccurate. In fact, disagreement can arise only when the verses are either misinterpreted and their true meaning not understood, or when an unproved scientific hypothesis is exploited to inveigh against the Qur'ān. It is, therefore, safer and wiser to refrain from using science to justify Qur'anic facts because the Qur'ān, though higher than human knowledge, was not meant to be a reference to assess the validity of scientific discoveries.

> "And the earth have We spread out, and placed therein firm hills . . ." (al-Ḥijr 15:19)

The above verse is a good example of how misinterpretation has led sceptics to assume the existence of discrepancy between scientific evidence and the facts of the Qur'ān. They contended that the above verse meant that the earth was flat. This contention reveals their failure to understand its true meaning and its accuracy of expression. Actually the word 'spread out' is synonymous with 'extend'; an expression which we often use in our daily speech to describe our actual perception. Therefore, in this context there is no contradiction between what the Qur'ān portrays and what is visually observable.

When the sphericity of the earth was discovered, religious scholars in the Christian world called it blasphemy and condemned all advocates of this view on the premise that it conflicted with the teachings of the Bible. But fourteen centuries ago, Allah gave to mankind true evidence that the earth is a sphere. The simple fact is that wherever you stand on earth, whether it be in Africa, America or any other part of the globe, and look in front of yourself, you will always see the earth spread out before you, no matter how far you travel. This phenomenon has but one explanation: that the earth is a sphere. If it were square, triangular or any other flat shape it would be possible to reach its edge. Thus in one simple phrase the Qur'ān has revealed to mankind a scientific fact about the earth which was only discovered by scientists many centuries after its initial revelation to the human race.

The same fact has again been stressed in Sūrah 'Yā Sīn' wherein it is stated:

> "It is not for the sun to overtake the moon, nor does the night outstrip the day. They float each in an orbit." (Yā Sīn 36:40)

The above verse describes the organisation of our solar system and the harmony that governs its movement. It is scientifically known that the moon is bound to the earth's gravity, and that both go together in orbit round the sun in perfect balance.

The statement 'nor does the night outstrip (precede) the day' was revealed to rectify a false notion that prevailed among the early Arabs. It negates something which was not true, although it appeared to be so, and which therefore needed to be rectified. The Arabs used to say that night always preceded day. Their 'day' began with sunset and accordingly the month of Ramaḍān was confirmed after the sunset of the last day of Sha'bān. But if night preceded day, as the Arabs said, then day could never precede night. Here we are faced with two statements: the first is that night precedes day, and the second is that day can never precede night. Allah did not refer to the latter statement because it was a true fact; but He corrected the former which was indeed a misconception affirming that *"nor does the night outstrip the day"*.

With this answer, Allah affirms that day and night are always present, simultaneously, on both hemispheres. At the same time He has provided the evidence that the earth is a sphere, for the phenomenon of day and night accuring simultaneously could never happen otherwise.

Allah used the correction to tell us more about the earth. If the earth had been created flat the sun would have been facing the upper surface at the moment of creation, and consequently day would have occurred first; but if, on the other hand, the sun had been facing the lower surface, then night would have occurred first. But Allah states in the above verse that both day and night have been created at the same time. His saying that neither one preceded the other proves that the earth was created as a sphere, because this is the only shape which allows such a phenomenon to occur. Thus in a few words Allah has revealed to mankind a scientific fact which had remained a mystery for centuries until He deemed it suitable to make it available to science.

The rotation of the earth is another phenomenon which has been dealt with in the Qur'ān as an established universal fact. This is revealed in the following verse;

> "And you see the hills you deem solid flying with the flight of clouds: the doing of Allah Who perfects all things . . ." (al-Naml 27:88)

Mountains are considered to be a kind of stabilizing mass which eliminates the vibration and swaying of the earth. Their massiveness gives the beholder the impression that the earth is motionless and still.

To dispel such false notions and illuminate our perception, Allah tells us in the above verse that the mountains which may seem to us to be stationary and immobile are in fact moving in the same manner as the clouds sailing above them. But how? We all know that the wind is the force behind the movement of the clouds. But because the mountains are rooted in the earth they can move only if the earth on which they sit is moving. Nor are the mountains moving slowly; 'they are flying with the flight of clouds.'

Thus in a few words Allah provided science with the established fact that the earth is a sphere which rotates in space.

The word 'solid' in the above verse needs some explanation for it unfolds a second scientific fact concerning the sensation of motionlessness which one experiences when there is no other body in relation to which it would be possible to estimate the movement of one body. The verse explains our inability to sense the movement of the earth.

The fact that to the beholder, the mountains and the earth are all rotating together, and the absence of a stable background against which he could contrast their movement, make the sensation of immobility quite real. This sensation is felt most accutely when one is flying in an aeroplane. If the aeroplane is flying at a very high altitude beyond all atmospheric disturbances, with all windows sealed, and vibration nonexistent, it becomes difficult to sense the movement or speed of the 'plane. This is the sensation implied in the word 'solid'. Allah is actually giving us the reasons underlying our inability to sense or detect the movement of the earth and the mountains sitting on it simply by watching them; the fact that we are all rotating together, and the absence of a contrasting background that can be observed with the naked eye, make the mountains seem to be solid and still.

Allah, anticipating that the knowledge imparted in the above verse would be perplexing, asks us – in this verse – not to wonder at His accomplishments:

> ". . . The doing of Allah Who perfects all things . . ." (al-Naml 27:88)

Some may say that the description provided in the above verse is identical with the description of the Day of Resurrection. This is not true, because on that Day there will be no speculation or uncertainty about what is hapening or what is seen and sensed. On this, Allah says in Sūrah 'Qāf':

> "Now We have removed from you your covering, and piercing is your sight this day." (Qāf 50:22)

About the mountains on that Day, He says in the Surah 'Ṭā' Hā':

> "They will ask you of the mountains (on that day). Say: My Lord will break them into scattered dust."
> (Ṭā' Hā' 20:105)

The same destruction of the universe is again stressed in Sūrah Ibrāhīm:

> "On that day when the earth will be changed to other than the earth, and the heaven (also will be changed) . . ." (Ibrāhīm 14:48)

Certainly the above verses convey an entirely different perspective from the former. On the Day of Resurrection the mountains that may otherwise seem solid will be scattered into dust. The picture will be vividly clear, man will see both Hell and Paradise. He will see Allah. There will be no speculation as has been the case before.

The Qur'ān has touched upon many facts about life and human existence which science has only recently discovered. Some of these facts are extremely intricate and were little known to past generations. Neither Muḥammad nor anyone else could have attributed such facts to the work of Allah unless they were truly His, for had they proved to be inaccurate or false the credibility of the message, as well as that of the Messenger, would have been destroyed. It would be naive to suggest that Muḥammad (SAW) was unaware of this possibility, and one would have expected him to avoid such matters if he had had the slightest doubt about their source and truth. Why would he have broached such matters of which he had no knowledge and which until recently have remained part of the knowledge confined to Allah?

It is indeed remarkable to compare what Allah revealed to Muḥammad some fourteen hundred years ago concerning the embryo, with the most recent scientific discoveries in the field of embryology:

> "Verily We created man from a product of wet earth: then placed him as a drop (of seed) in a safe lodging; then fashioned We the drop a clot, then fashioned We the clot a little lump, then fashioned We the little lump bones, then clothed the bones with flesh, and then produced it as another creation. So blessed be Allah, the Best of Creators." (al-Mu'minūn 23:12-14)

Chapter 7

The Qur'ān and the Unveiling of the Unseen

When the Qur'ān was revealed to mankind, it challenged human powers and beliefs, as has been discussed in previous chapters. In its challenge, however, it unveiled mysteries of the universe, including the barriers of time, place and future. The barrier of place refers to those things which happen in an instant, and of which we have neither knowledge nor awareness because of their happening in one place while we are elsewhere. The barrier of past time refers to all things and events which took place in the distant past and remained, until their revelation, a secret to mankind. The barrier of the future refers to those future events which are beyond human prediction and control. In addition to these three barriers the Qur'ān has also penetrated the barrier of the human self and disclosed its deeply buried secrets.

The Qur'ān unveiled the barrier of past time by disclosing all that happened to ancient peoples and civilizations. It portrayed the history of previous Apostles and events which had remained a mystery until they were revealed to Muḥammad (SAW), thus enabling him to challenge and defeat those heretics bent on discrediting him and his message.

The unveiling of the barrier of the past is demonstrated in the following verses:

> "And you (Muḥammad) were not on the western side (of the Mount) when We expounded unto Moses the commandment . . ." (al-Qaṣaṣ 28:44)

> ". . . And you were not a dweller of Midian, reciting unto them Our revelation . . ." (al-Qaṣaṣ 28:45)

> ". . . You were not present with them when they threw their pens (to know) which of them should be the guardian of Mary . . ." (Āl 'Imrān 3:44)

> "and you were not beside the Mount when We did call; but (the knowledge of it is) a mercy from your Lord . . ." (al-Qaṣaṣ 28:46)

In the above verses, Allah not only disclosed to Muḥammad (SAW) what until then had been unknown history to man, but He also corrected what had been distorted of this history and of the previous Messages and His commandments.

Muḥammad (SAW) frequently challenged Christian priests and Jewish rabbis with these revelations, thus correcting what had been distorted and misquoted in both the Gospels and the Torah, at the same time confirming that which agreed with the true facts of the Qur'ān. He challenged them to disprove these true facts, including the miraculous conception of Mary and the birth of Jesus as portrayed by Allah:

> "Such was Jesus, son of Mary: this is a statement of the truth concerning which they doubt." (Maryam 19:34)

Allah removed the barrier of "Place" from Muḥammad (SAW) by revealing to him the deepest and most intricate functions and reactions of the inner self. However, before we delve deeper into these human faculties and endowments, it may be useful to draw the reader's attention again to the fact that the Qur'ān is Allah's speech and message to mankind and that reading it is synonymous with worship. Therefore it ought not to be modified, misinterpreted or misquoted. If such interference were later discovered it would destroy the Qur'ān's authenticity, as well as the credibility of the Messenger.

Now that the hazardous implications of such meddling with the Qur'ān have been pointed out, let us examine the following verses and the challenge they present:

> ". . . and (they) say within themselves: Why should Allah punish us for what we say? . . ." (al-Mujādilah 58:8)

The power of the challenge in the above verse lies in its touching upon the deepest recesses of the self and what goes on inside the human mind and heart. The idolators referred to could have belied Muḥammad (SAW) by simply asserting that they had never harboured such thoughts. Moreover, if such thoughts had not been cultivated in their minds, they would have been justified in discrediting Muḥammad (SAW) and the message he brought to them.

Thus in breaking through the barrier of place, the Qur'ān has penetrated the human inner life and self and brought to light the inner secrets and tendencies of those idolators, who were bent on discrediting the message. In this context Allah says:

> "Hast thou not observed those who were forbidden conspiracy and afterward returned to that which they had been forbidden, and (now) conspire together for crime and wrongdoing and disobedience toward the messenger? And when they come unto you they greet you with a greeting wherewith Allah greets you not, and say within themselves: Why should Allah punish us for what we say? Hell will suffice them; they will feel the heat thereof – a helpless journey's end!" (al-Mujādilah 58:8)

> ". . . Yet they will swear by Allah (saying): If we had been able we would surely have set out with you. They destroy their souls, and Allah knows that they verily are liars." (al-Tawbah 9:42)

> "They swear unto you, that you may accept them. Though you accept them, Allah verily accepts not wrongdoing folk." (al-Tawbah 9:96)

> "And if We would, We could show them unto you (Muḥammad) so that you should know them surely by their marks. And you shall know them by the burden of their talk . . ." (Muḥammad 47:30)

With these verses Allah has unmasked the conspiring idolators by unveiling their hidden malicious intentions. Certainly neither Muḥammad (SAW) nor any human could be endowed with such a miraculous power.

The same challenge may be noticed in the following verses from the Sūrah 'al-Tawbah' and elsewhere, wherein Allah cautions Muḥammad (SAW) not to trust those hypocrites who will come to him and swear by Allah that they are faithful to him and to Allah, while inwardly they believe otherwise and are intent on betraying him. In these verses Allah unfolds the thoughts that are hidden in the deepest recesses of the hypocrites' hearts:

> "and they swear a false oath knowingly."
> (al-Mujādilah 58:14)

In all the above verses Allah identifies the hypocrites with the heretics who have chosen consciously and deliberately to misquote and distort the meanings of the Qur'ān. Until then they had been successful in stilling their evil thoughts, and therefore they had the freedom to refrain from such hypocritical conduct. With this freedom of choice they had been placed in a situation where they seemed to have no alternative but to behave exactly as had been stated by Allah in the Qur'ān, without being able to retreat or abandon their predetermined role. Even more significant than this is Allah's uncovering of their innermost ambitions which they had never shared with anyone.

There are two kinds of secrets. The first kind are secrets which two persons confide to each other. The second kind involves secrets that one buries deep in one's inner soul and seldom reveals to anyone else. But in these verses Allah disclosed these hidden secrets to Muḥammad and the hypocrites alike, leaving the latter incapable of denying accusation.

It is important, to point out that the use of the future tense in the word 'swear' indicates that the act (of lying) had not yet taken place, but that it would happen later. Nevertheless, this prior revelation of the hypocrites' inner intent did not seem to influence them or dissuade them from lying, thus fulfilling what Allah had said they would do.

The Qur'ān also unveiled the future. This unveiling had to be in successive stages of which the initial stage involved events which were only necessary to convince both believers and misbelievers of its truth. The second stage involved events in the distant future whose revelation was necessary for the welfare and guidance of successive generations. Thus the challenge of the Qur'ān at the onset of its revelation focused on events that were destined to take place in the near future. As for the rest of mankind, the revelations involved universal phenomena.

It is important that we emphasize that the prefix "*sa*" (the Arabic letter 'sīn'), a synonym of the word 'shall', is used in the Qur'ān to indicate future events. Because the Qur'ān's authenticity is safeguarded by Allah and will remain intact and unchanged until the Last Day, it cannot be altered, modified or denied by those believers who worship Allah through it. Therefore, any attempt to link what has been foretold with any future events other than those clearly indicated, or to ascribe to its revelations an obscure meaning, is indeed a pernicious practice. The whole basis of faith may be shaken if it is discovered later that a particular interpretation was inaccurate. No one has the divine authority or foresight to predict what will happen within an hour or a day except Allah, let alone what will happen within years or centuries. Therefore, Muḥammad (SAW) himself could not have made such predictions unless he was certain beyond any doubt that the message was unequivocably true.

Because of the limitations of human capability to determine the course of events or to control time, Allah has not bestowed upon mankind the power to foresee the future. A person who decides to construct a building in a year's time, for example, cannot be entirely sure that his plans will be realized. Any number of factors such as the government deciding to repossess the land or a sudden shortage of labourers or of materials may upset his plans.

This power to control destiny is confined to Allah alone. Only He can say to a thing 'Be', and it is, whether this thing is decreed to happen in an instant or in a thousand years' time. This power of prediction has been demonstrated throughout the Qur'ān, for example in the following verse:

> "The hosts will all be routed and will turn and flee." (al-Qamar 54:45)

This verse was revealed to Muḥammad in Makkah when the Muslims were still a minority. They were so weak as a fighting group at that time that 'Umar ibn al-Khaṭṭāb expressed his despair of their ever being able to defend themselves against their enemy. But the Qur'ān had predicted that Muḥammad (SAW) and his few men would eventually be victorious and that their enemy would flee. More significant than this was the identifying of the enemy's leader, the description of his fatal injury and how he would die. Thus we are told:

> "We shall brand him on the nose." (al-Qalam 68:16)

This verse refes to al-Walīd ibn al-Mughīrah, one of Islam's arch-enemies who was killed in battle by a blow on the nose. Could Muḥammad (SAW) have predicted this event with such precision and detail? Certainly not.

The Challenge to Allah's enemies

Now let us consider the following verse from the Sūrah 'al-Masad' in which Allah gives a description of the fate of Muḥammad's uncle:

> "The power of Abū Lahab will perish, and he will perish. His wealth and gains will not exempt him. He will be plunged in flaming Fire, and his wife, the wood carrier, will have upon her neck a halter of palm-fibre." (al-Masad 111:15)

Here the Qur'ān speaks about Muḥammad's uncle, another notorious enemy of Islam. According to this Sūrah he would die an idolator and would meet his punishment in hell. He could have gone to Muḥammad (SAW) and announced his entry into Islam, then afterwards contested the validity of the prediction. All he had to do was to testify – even hypocritically – that Allah was One and that Muḥammad was His Messenger. But the Qur'ān predicted that only he and his wife would continue to reject Muḥammad (SAW) and Allah. It did not name or refer to the other idolators, who later declared their belief in Allah and His Messenger.

The miracle here is that the Qur'ān challenged an idolator (Abū Lahab) and defied him to change the course of his destined fate. It defied him in something wherein he had the freedom of action and decision. But Allah knew that Abū Lahab would persist and that he would not resort to hypocrisy and deceit as an attempt to save his soul.

The Qur'ān's Challenge to the Non-Arabs

The Qur'ān disclosed a great deal of knowledge regarding the universe to both the Arabs and the non-Arabs who lived at the time of its revelation to Muḥammad (SAW), as well as to their descendants. The examples are too numerous to be mentioned here. A few verses will show how the Qur'ān challenged the powers of non-Arabs.

At the onset of Islam there were two great empires struggling to extend their influence over the world. The Byzantines, although they resented Muḥammad's (SAW) message, did believe in Jesus, his religion and his God. The Persians however were idolators and heretics. The Byzantines were closer to the hearts of the Muslims, and the Persians were closer to the Arab idolators.

A war broke out between the two empires in which the Byzantium was defeated. The Arab idolators were delighted while the Muslims felt that the defeat was a setback to Allah's men and a victory for His enemies. Allah intervened and consoled the believers and strengthened their faith, when He revealed:

> "The Romans [or Byzantines] have been defeated in the nearer land, and they, after their defeat, will be victorious. Within ten years – Allah's is the command in the former case and in the latter – and in that day believers will rejoice in Allah's help to victory. He helps to victory whom He will. He is the Mighty, the Merciful." (al-Rūm 30:2-5)

The challenge continues:

> "It is a promise of Allah. Allah fails not His promise, but most of mankind know not." (al-Rūm 30:6)

Could Muḥammad have predicted the outcome of a battle that was to take place after ten years? Could any commander predict the course of any war, even if it were to occur within a day or two? Was Muḥammad (SAW) sure to live until this battle had occurred and been won?

Who else but Allah could have predicted the outcome of a battle between two nations so remote from and so alien to the Arabs? What would Muḥammad's (SAW) position have been if the battle had not taken place, or if it had happened and the Persians had emerged victorious? Would anyone have continued to have faith in him and his message? Certainly not.

If the Qur'ān was of Muḥammad's (SAW) own composition, as some heretics presumed, why should he entangle himself in such a hazardous and unpredictable issue? If it had been discovered to be untrue, it would certainly have destroyed his credibility and the message he conveyed. Why should he take upon himself such a challenge when no challenge existed, nor was he asked by anyone to touch upon the battle and its future outcome? Because the prediction was made by Allah, Whose knowledge encompasses both past and future, it was fulfilled exactly as it had been portrayed in the Qur'an.

We have previously said that the Qur'ān is not restricted to time and place, and that it will continue to enlighten mankind and be a challenge to man and his knowledge until the end of time. But in order to maintain this challenge, Allah has provided it with the miraculous power to offer something new to successive generations. It is obvious that many of the scientific facts imparted in the Qur'ān were too complex to be understood or believed by early contemporaries, and Muḥammad (SAW) had to bypass them in his explanations of the Qur'ān because of this very limitation, and to avoid being accused of insanity if he attempted to go deeper into such matters.

Indeed, the Qur'ān has touched upon the law of probability, Darwin's theory of evolution, the hypotheses on matter and soul and a great deal of what is being hypothesized in the field of science, and the attempts to sow doubts about Allah and the creation of our universe. All this scepticism has been anticipated and predicted in the Qur'ān. It has actually cautioned us about those who would emerge in the course of time and attempt to distort the truth about the creation of the universe and man.

If the information given in the Qur'ān about the embryo was inaccurate or false, then the Qur'ān would thus have provided the sceptics with the tool for its destruction. The Qur'ān has been decreed to be relevant until the Last Day. If science, after a thousand years or more, succeeded in disproving it, the whole issue of faith would be virtually destroyed. But because the speaker and the executor was Allah, it has survived all attacks and remained as challenging as on the day it was first revealed to Muḥammad (SAW). It will continue to give new evidence of its divine origin and nature as long as there is life in this universe. In earlier ages it challenged the idolators by unfolding their innermost thoughts. Today it still challenges all sorts of heresies and redirects the heretics' hostile efforts into a new direction favourable to the message of Islam, as is stated in the verse:

> ". . . but most of mankind know not. They know only some appearance of the life of the world, and are heedless of the Hereafter." (al-Rūm 30:6-7)

According to this verse man's knowledge is restricted to some apparent physical phenomena of this world and nothing else. That is because there are two kinds of knowledge. The first is readily available to man without restriction or limitation, and he is free to experiment and explore it. But he cannot have access to the second kind because it surpasses his mental capacity and perception. Here man has no alternative but to obey Allah's commands. It is a realm where man does not have the liberty to speculate. It is confined strictly to Allah and it is He alone who decrees how He is to be glorified. No mortal has the wisdom to question or debate these divine directives. In contrast, the former field of knowledge is wide open for mankind to explore and make use of what has been provided in it for his benefit. The diverse areas of this knowledge are clearly laid down in various verses of which the following is but one example:

> "Have you not seen that Allah causes water to fall from the sky, and We produce therewith fruit of diverse hues; and among the hills are streaks white and red, of diverse hues, and (others) raven black; and of men and beasts and cattle, in like manner, diverse hues?" . . .
> (al-Malā'ikah 35:27-28)

In the above verse Allah is referring to matter, as well as plants and animals. Then He adds:

> "The erudite among His bondsmen fear Allah alone . . ."
> (al-Malā'ikah 35:28)

Allah has singled out the erudite because the nature of their work, which focuses on exploring the various phenomena of our universe, and brings them closer to Him through their understanding of the divine power behind its creation and operation. Moreover, Allah has emphasized the diversity in one kind or species when He said, 'fruit of diverse hues'. In fact He wants us to pay attention to this phenomenon and its underlying causes and His limitless power over things, as is shown in the process of water and mineral absorption in plants. We know that dissolved minerals are absorbed in the roots of plants by the process of capillary action. At this point one has to ponder a little. Can these capillary tubes differentiate between dissolved minerals?

If we dissolve different minerals in a basin half-filled with water and then place vertically in it a number of capillary glass tubes, we will notice that the water level in the glass tubes is always higher than the water level in the basin. The water in each of the tubes contains equal samples of all the minerals dissolved in it. But in plants this process is performed in an entirely different way. If, for instance, we grow an orange tree next to a lemon tree, both will absorb their needed minerals from the same soil, and yet the oranges will always be sweet and the lemons sour. This is so because, although both trees absorb their minerals from the same soil, this absorption is selective. About this divine power Allah says in a passage in al-Ra'd:

> "And in the Earth are neighbouring tracts, vineyards and ploughed lands, and date-palms, like and unlike, which are watered with one water. And we have made some of them to excel others in fruit . . ." (al-Ra'd 13:4)

About material things He says,

> ". . . and among the hills are streaks white and red, of diverse hues, and (others) raven black."
> (al-Malā'ikah 35:27)

This is a definition of what is now known as geology and its diverse branches. After plants and non-living matter comes man, of whom God says,

> ". . . The erudite among His bondsmen fear Allah alone . . ." (al-Malā'ikah 35:28)

The word 'erudite' (*al-'ulamā'*) in this verse refers to those men who muse over Allah's creation. Truly an active and searching mind can explore a great deal of physical phenomena and can harness them for the welfare of mankind.

From the history of those inventions and discoveries which have been of great benefit to mankind, it is clear that they were accomplished by men who were immensely observant and sensitive to the most minute details of the phenomenon they explored. For without keen observation and experimentation no discovery could be accomplished.

Not infrequently we are tempted to bypass the laboratory or overlook the objective of the experiment and lean toward philosophizing about things of which we have no knowledge, or the knowledge of which is far beyond human reach. An example of this overreaching endeavour is when we hypothesize that matter is antecendent to the soul. In other words, man attempts to experiment with elements that defy experimentation and whose secrets are still confined to Allah, the Creator.

Of such persons we are told:

> "I made them not to witness the creation of the heavens and the earth, nor their own creation . . ."
> (al-Kahf 18:51)

Creation is an issue where human knowledge is impotent. We have neither witnessed the process itself, nor is it within our power to subject it to experimentation; all our knowledge about it has come directly from Allah, the Creator of all things. He has told us how man was made, and the way he was made is beyond all imagination. It is, therefore, vain to talk about matter and soul or which of the two came first. He who delves into such matters, the answers of which are still confined to Allah, does more harm than good to himself. We know about the elements of which the human body is made, but man has yet to know as objectively certain what constitutes the soul.

All sciences are based on experimentation with solid matter irrespective of theory or method. There is no such thing as American, French or Russian electricity, nor is there any such thing as English or German chemistry. There is but one electricity and one chemistry. The science of chemistry in any country is based on the same results of experimentation with matter in its three forms. The results are always the same irrespective of the identity of the experimenter, his feeling or the country he belongs to. This is why discord is non-existent with regard to scientific findings. But disagreement always occurs in matters where ambition and ideology are involved. Thus we find that ambition and greed, although similar in their purpose, are, nevertheless, contradictory. When these external factors intervene, the scientific facts and rules become confused and difficult to grasp.

Taking the issue of creation, we can see how the unbelievers helped unintentionally to prove the truth of the Qur'ān. Allah has given different names to the matter of which man was made. In some verses He called it dust, in others clay, or baked clay. There is no contradiction in the process of creation or the substances used. In fact if we examine the various substances named in the Qur'ān with reference to creation, we come to the conclusion that they indicate the various stages of creation itself, i.e. dust, mud, baked clay and clay like pottery. They represent the steps which ended with Allah's breathing of His spirit into the final product, whereof He says:

> "I made them not to witness the creation of the heavens and the earth, nor their own creation, nor choose I misleaders for (My) helper." (al-Kahf 18:51)

In this verse, Allah predicted a time when people would attempt to sow seeds of doubt in the minds and hearts of men regarding creation and He cautions us against them. The fact that such men have emerged and been able to propagate these misconceptions, of which Darwin's theory of evolution, the theory of probability and chance, and the theory of matter and soul are but a few examples, have indirectly helped to confirm the authenticity of the Qur'ān. Without such propagators as the Qur'ān has predicted, its validity would have been impaired. But those who have emerged and are trying to demolish man's faith in Allah and

His existence, thereby fulfil the Qur'ān's prophecy. In some divinely mysterious way, this invective against Allah has worked favourably to enhance Allah's commandments and faith, at the same time foiling the perpetrators' intentions. Such pseudo-scientific theories have proven unsubstantiated by empirical evidence. This failure of science to shed the slightest light on the secrets of creation has served to further the greatness of the Qur'ān.

Allah, in His wisdom, always provides clues to clarify the mind's dilemma in comprehending the Unseen. Thus when He says that He created man from dust or mud or baked clay, or clay like pottery, then breathed into him from His own spirit, He is in fact describing the progressive stages of the creation. When water is added to dust it turns to mud, which hardens when left to dry. Similarly, when mud is heated it becomes clay. It is the same process as that used by man in making pottery. Man is made from the same substance, or earth, which when analysed is found to contain all the elements of which the human body is made up. This information is strictly scientific and has nothing to do with proving or disproving the Qur'ān.

Allah has also given death as an example to explain the process of creation. If we considered life to be the final product of a number of constructive processes, then death could also be viewed as a reversed, destructive, process.

Both processes are analogous with the construction and demolition of a building. When, for instance, we construct a building we usually begin with the foundation before building upper floors. However, when we want to demolish a building we usually start with the top floor. Similarly, the last step we take on a journey is the first step we take on the way back. But although we know nothing about the process of creation, which has remained unwitnessed, we witness death (or the destruction of life) every day. The first thing that leaves the body is the soul which, according to the above rule, must have been the last step in the process of creation. Once it has left the human body a reversal of the process of creation begins; the body stiffens becoming like pottery. Then it decays; which duplicates the nature of hard baked clay. When mud loses its fluid it returns into being dust and earth. Thus the stages of destruction of the body seem to be nothing but a reversal of the process of its creation. In these stages, one sees the truth about the process of creation, the material used and the method of accomplishment as may be inferred from the process of destruction of the body and death. About the final stage God says:

> "So, when I have made him and have breathed into him of My Spirit . . ." (al-Ḥijr, 15:28)

When we are in doubt as to whether a person is dead or not, we usually examine his breathing. We deem him to be dead if his breathing has ceased. The same breath that gave him life causes his death when it leaves his material body.

Evidence regarding the divine creation of man can be drawn from the information which the Qur'ān has given us about conception and embryology. Although we have already touched upon this miraculous phenomenon it might be useful to point out that neither before the revelation of the Qur'ān nor for many centuries afterwards had mankind been in possession of such knowledge. It is only recently that science has been able to match what the Qur'ān had foretold fourteen centuries ago.

It is obvious that many of science's recent discoveries were laid down in the Qur'ān and will remain unchanged until the end of time. Those who inveigh against the Qur'ān overlook the fact that neither Muḥammad nor his contemporaries could have had the slightest notion of complex physiological processes or the composition of the human foetus. This information remained veiled until Allah decided that it was opportune for modern science to discover it, in order that mankind could benefit. It is indeed a challenge for those who have the intelligence to meditate upon Allah's might and providence and His message. If what the Qur'ān imparted was unfounded, science would, in time, have proved its falsehood, and the whole religion would have been destroyed. The Qur'an would have provided its enemies with the tools for its own destruction. But science has proved what has been recorded in it thus confirming beyond doubt that it is indeed Allah's scripture and speech.

The miracle of the Qur'ān is everlasting and constant. In the beginning it challenged the Arabs in the arts and linguistic skills for which they were renowned. It unveiled the barriers of the past and the future and revealed the inner human self by unveiling the malicious thoughts of the antagonists of Islam. It unveiled the near future by predicting the outcome of events many years ahead of their actual occurrence. It likewise removed the veil from some events in the more distant future, in order to give future generations portents of Allah's might and to give those who erred a chance to redress their ways and seek His mercy and forgiveness. If these portents had been described in detail to the early Muslims they would have produced adverse results. They were too complex to be believed or understood, and many would have deserted Muḥammad. (SAW)

The Qur'ān has, likewise, disclosed some aspects of the distant future by touching upon advanced theories intended for future generations as portents of Allah's might and the truth of the message. But because of the absence of appropriate scientific knowledge at that time, any attempt to describe in detail these phenomena would have been met with scepticism and ridicule, resulting in the desertion of some of the early Muslims. In view of their complexity and remoteness from issues that most concerned Muslims, these scientific phenomena were not dwelt upon, leaving them for future generations to explore and meditate upon them in depth and in doing so discover the truth about this universe and its Creator.

One should not, however, confuse the issue of foretelling events with the revelation of Islam's commandments. These commandments and precepts were delivered complete, devoid of ambiguity. They were fully explained and elucidated by the Prophet's speeches and directives in such detail that no room is left for doubt or uncertainty. In contrast, the exact meaning of Allah's portents concerning the universe and its phenomena were left open for contemplating, thus confirming the most miraculous feature of the Qur'ān: that of constant renewal and its ability to offer new meanings to successive generations.

The Qur'ān, as has been noted, challenged the Arabs to match its language, which they failed to do. Because it could not challenge the rest of mankind on similar terms, its challenge to these nations was based on science in which they excelled. The challenge was absolute, with no limit of time. They were challenged collectively to create one of Allah's smallest insects, and were given from now to eternity to accomplish such a task. About this Allah says to mankind,

> "O mankind! A similitude is coined, so pay heed to it: Lo! those on whom you call beside Allah will never create a fly though they continue together for the purpose. And if the fly took something from them, they could not rescue it from it. So weak are both the seeker and the sought!" (al-Ḥajj 22:73)

As this verse states, Allah challenges the whole of mankind. He says to them that the science which they worship and to which they give precedence over Him will never be able to create a fly. It is ironic that despite man's explorations in space and other fields he has not been able to create a fly's wing, which is indeed a very mediocre task in comparison with Allah's infinite might and creative power. Hence came His statement:

> "So weak are both the seeker and the sought!"

Then he adds,

> "They measure not Allah by His rightful measure, Lo! Allah is Strong, Almighty." (al-Ḥajj 22:74)

In fact, Allah is telling mankind that His capacity exceeds all imagination, and that they should not underestimate what He is capable of doing.

But the challenge continues when He says,

> "Have you observed the water which you drink? Is it you who shed it from the raincloud, or are We the Shedder?" (al-Wāqi'ah 56:68-9)

and again,

> ". . . He sendeth down the rain . . ." (Luqmān 32:34)

Here Allah reminds mankind that it is He Who sends the rain for the crops to grow and for all creatures to drink. Has man been able to control rain, or prevent drought and flood?

But the most powerful challenge is made to mankind in the following verse from Sūrah al-Nisā'!

> "Wherever you may be, death will overtake you, even though you were in lofty towers . . ." (al-Nisā' 4:78)

This challenge derives its magnitude from the great advance in medicine and man's ability to cure diseases or prevent them. For despite this immense leap forward, he is still impotent against death. He cannot escape from it or extend his life span by even one day, even by living in a germ-free cell or tower, away from risks and hazards.

Finally Allah challenges mankind with five unseen phenomena over which He alone has ultimate control:

> "Lo! Allah! With Him is knowledge of the Hour. He sends down the rain, and knows that which is in the wombs. No soul knows what it will earn tomorrow, and no soul knows in what land it will die. Lo! Allah is Knower, Aware." (Luqmān 32:34)

In the above verses, Allah tells us that there are things whose unveiling is far beyond our reach and knowledge, no matter how hard we try or how far we progress in learning, and they will remain veiled till the end of time.

Chapter 8

Allah be Glorified

Man, in his relationship with Allah, goes through a variety of situations wherein the nature of his interaction with the Unseen seems to change. For instance, in his daily life, when he is conscious and aware of stimuli coming at him from the outside world and of his own impressions, he can only see things in proportion to the level of this conscious awareness and the limits set on it by his physical body.

When we are awake all our actions are consciously governed by our minds. Yet this situation changes when we are asleep and begin to dream, for in this state we are no longer in control of what we do or wish to see, we seem to be able to perform acts that are physically impossible; we are able to fly and remain suspended in mid-air; we see strange creatures unlike anything on earth; we meet and talk to people who have long been dead. All this happens while our eyes are closed. What actually sees is not the eye, but rather the soul.

The soul must therefore have its own vision and be able to meet with those who have long since departed from this world. It is obvious that when we are asleep we are literally living in a different world wherein we are able to meet our ancestors and see and do things that defy reason and logic and the physical laws that govern our life in this world.

But what is it that allows us, when we are fast asleep, to see and to do things that are impossible to see or do when we are awake? What lets us visualize such unfamiliar places and meet such strangers in our dreams, which we find difficult to remember upon waking up: How can all this be explained? Anyone attempting to explain this phenomenon will be groping in the dark, because no mortal can pretend to possess knowledge of the laws governing the soul while the physical body is alive or dead. The soul is a phenomenon which Allah has kept outside man's knowledge. It is, therefore, wiser, in these cases, to admit our ignorance on such matters and be content to glorify Him and acknowledge His uniqueness and incomparability.

The following analogy may explain why it is better to remain silent on knowledge we cannot possibly possess.

If I tell you that one person struck another roughly without saying more, then I would not be telling you much, because the full implication of an act can only be in relation to its executor and when all the powers of the latter have been involved in the act. If I told you that a five year old child had struck me with all his might, you would hardly show concern. The same story would arouse more serious concern if the striker was a boxer, because whereas a child's blow would be harmless, a boxer's could be fatal. The identity of the striker is necessary for a complete assessment of an act and its repercussions.

If we considered the above analogy as a basis for comparison between Allah's power and man's power and placed the power of Allah under the expression "Allah be Glorified, and there is no other like Him", we would be better able to clarify many phenomena misinterpreted by sceptics in their attempts to beguile mankind.

There is no comparison whatsoever between the power of Allah and that of man, and it is sheer vanity for man to ascribe to himself powers beyond his limited capacity or to compare his acquired knowledge with that of Allah.

To maintain his faith, man has no option but to place all that he cannot comprehend of such divine acts under the only possible expression, "Allah be Glorified and there is no other like Him." By using this expression when we encounter those divine acts for which we have no explanation or which we can compare against our human limitations power, we may come closer to the meaning of many of those divine acts and what they truly indicate. Man, for instance, cannot conceive or imagine anything of this universe except that which he is able to perceive. But when Allah informs him of things that are beyond his vision or perception, he has no alternative but to exclaim "Allah be Glorified".

There is no way for man to come to an understanding of these acts on the basis of his restricted mental and physical powers. Thus when Allah says to us that He had taken Muḥammad (SAW) by night 'upon a celestial horse' to the Farthest Mosque in Jerusalem, we should not assess the likelihood of this miracle in terms of physical laws or our limited power and knowledge, since these laws are not applicable to Allah, nor is He limited to time and space. This miracle can only be appreciated and accommodated through the glorification of Allah and the and the acknowledgment that He is unlike any power on earth.

When Allah tells us about the miracles with which He in the past supported His messengers, or when He speaks about the worlds of the Angels and the Jinn, which are beyond our power to see, we should not doubt their existence.

For not only is the narrator Allah Himself, but He also possesses an infinite capacity to create such worlds. To compare with mankind's knowledge and power those of Allah is like comparing between one drop of water and the water of all the oceans, or between one grain of sand and the endless deserts. He creates that which is visible and may be perceived by man, and that which is spiritual and which, though at this point of time inaccessible to us, may one day be unveiled and made accessible to our knowledge.

But, as has been stated, Allah, being Gracious and Subtle, has set signs in the universe which bring closer to man's mind those spiritual phenomena that are too difficult to be fully comprehended without divine help, enhancing his faith in His all-compassing power and care for those who trust in Him.

This recognition of Allah's supreme power and the conviction that Allah, Who has promised to support, protect and ensure the safety of all those who hold firmly to Him, can also fill their hearts with hope and their minds with peace protecting them against the hypocrites and beguilers who would conspire to dislodge their faith.

We have already discussed the futility of man becoming involved in matters of the Unseen of which he has no direct knowledge, particularly the issue of matter and soul. In this chapter we will explore the evidence that indicates how, since the creation of man, those truths beyond man's senses and intellectual powers have eluded him until Allah deemed it appropriate for him to have access to such truths.

Although things that are beyond our vision and mental powers have certainly been with us since the creation of this universe, it does not follow that they have not been revealed to man at one time or another. For instance, no one in the eighteenth century ever thought that one day man would be able to travel in an aeroplane, stand on the moon, or communicate with one another by wireless or by telephone across the globe. If anyone had described such feats to the people of that century they would have accused him of insanity.

How did man accomplish such great achievements? Did he invent a new atmosphere to help him to fly? Has he conjured up a new medium, other than Allah's air, to carry his wireless messages across the continents? Of course not! The air that surrounds the globe is the same since it was first created. What has happened is that Allah has given man access to some of His knowledge, thereby removing the barriers which had in the past kept this kind of knowledge beyond man's reach. Thus Allah by simply uttering the word 'Be' enabled man to build an aeroplane in which to fly, stand on the moon and invent those devices which have enhanced his welfare and prosperity.

From this it is obvious that things do exist in this universe beyond man's perception. The human mind is not the ultimate limit of science and knowledge on this earth, and as time goes by Allah continues to impart gradually some of His knowledge to man to show him that there are things in this universe still beyond his intellectual powers to comprehend; man's ignorance of such facts does not mean that they do not exist.

As for things which are inaudible to the human ear, they are often experienced in everyday life. For example, when one sits alone in an empty room he hears nothing, yet once he turns on the radio, the room instantly reverberates with sounds and voices coming from around the world. How does this happen? The answer is that sound is a wave motion constantly vibrating in the air, but the human ear can only respond to a certain range of frequencies. Other frequencies cannot be heard without some mechanical aid or device. At present no one can predict what our ears might be able to capture when sophisticated devices are invented, what potentials these discoveries will provide man with, and what new secrets they may reveal to him. There may be other sound waves that are still beyond the human ear and the sound receivers we already possess. Surely, if the radio had not been invented we would not have known about the existence of such sound waves vibrating around us.

In addition to limitations on our mental power and hearing capability, there is also limitation on our vision. Indeed, there are things in this universe, including those which Allah has told us of in His Messages, that are beyond our vision and perception.

If, for example, one examines a drop of water from a pond or a stream, by the naked eye, one is not likely to notice anything unusual about it. If, on the other hand, you use a microscope you will soon discover that it contains hundreds of tiny moving organisms. Likewise, one cannot see anything unusual in a drop of an ill person's blood, but when it is examined under a microscope it will be found to contain many germs and blood cells. These tiny organisms and cells have always been with us, but they are too small to be perceived by the naked eye.

Until the invention of the microscope, no one could see or believe in the existence of such micro-organisms. In fact, until recently, the ordinary microscope was itself not good enough to reveal many kinds of micro-organisms, particularly viruses. This only became possible when the electron microscope was invented. The same thing could be said about television and the telescope, for they too have enabled man to see aspects of Allah's universe which were once beyond his wildest dreams and normal vision. But all these inventions could not have been made without man's making use of Allah's already-created physical conditions which were created at the same time as the rest of the universe. These are namely; air, light, electro-magnetic waves and their corresponding laws.

All this knowledge has not been discovered accidently by man, but rather by the will of Allah, and only when He deemed that mankind was ready to have access to this kind of knowledge. In fact Allah has released this knowledge to man to convince him that what is beyond his intellect, vision and hearing does indeed exist, so that when he is told about an unseen or hidden phenomenon he should not doubt it, but should accept as true what is being conveyed to him. What is beyond man's power and senses does exist, and on such an unimaginable scale that it can be understood only if we appreciate the limitless difference between the power of the Creator and that of man. But the issue of the Unseen – which is basically an issue of faith – should not be exploited by misleaders for beguiling mankind and alienating it from Him. He therefore allowed human knowledge to develop and progress gradually according to His will and design from one generation to the next, so that what was once difficult to perceive might become less obscure and easier to grasp. Thus, the eye was able to see, the ear to hear and the mind to comprehend what had once seemed to be beyond the reach of faculties. Certainly, Allah could have furnished man with all this knowledge and power on the first day of creation, but He withheld it until the time He deemed that mankind needed to be reminded of His infinite capacity, and as a confirmation of the existence of the unseen world, despite its invisibility and man's inability to perceive it.

Human Knowledge

Human knowledge is acquired from two cardinal sources. The first source is through experimentation with concrete matter in specialised laboratories, wherein human influence is totally eliminated. This is the world of knowledge and exploration which Allah has made accessible to man and allowed him to explore. He has promised this knowledge to those who have the motivation and perseverance to look into the operation of this universe to discover how nature works, thereby coming closer to Allah's design. The second kind of knowledge involves such issues and theories as cannot be subjected to empirical experimentation, or tested in laboratories. This kind of knowledge, whether philosophical, political or otherwise, is often subject to the conflicting ambitions and covetousness of the human race. This knowledge is most likely to develop in the absence of concrete and purely objective material to experiment with, and because of the openness of the theory or doctrine to human bias, desires and lusts.

In the first kind of acquisition of knowledge, the learner or researcher never rests, and may spend years patiently working before achieving success. When success is accomplished, its benefits are shared with the whole of mankind.

As for the knowledge in which ambition figures significantly, the theorist himself and his advocates and followers are the ones who benefit the most. The reason is that they postulate their theories and philosophies along lines that are more convenient to their own ideas and desires than to the needs and hopes of those who are compelled to abide by these policies and philosophies, willingly or otherwise . . .

What has science offered to mankind?

No one can dispute that the resources, or elements, which sustain life on earth have not changed since their initial formation by the will of Allah, nor has science found alternatives to these basic natural elements. All science has done so far is to make life easier and more comfortable, but it has not been able to create or provide us with the elements that make life possible. Allah, being aware of man's shortcomings, ambitions and lust, has barred him from acquiring this knowledge and the power to manipulate and have control over these elements that are essential for the survival of life on earth. He was careful not to give man access to more than what was needed to maintain his life, and kept out of his reach the secrets of the process of creation lest he use it for the destruction of mankind itself.

The main resources of life in this universe consist of our planet Earth, and a cosmic and solar system which man cannot control, nor through his available knowledge, reproduce or match. They have been created by Allah and are ordained to operate according to the pattern He has prescribed. If science could only discover the divine signs and portents by which Allah reveals Himself and His infinite powers to man, it would have made a great deal of progress. But science, no matter how it tries, and despite all its resources, has so far been unable to add to the elements of nature or alter their divinely-instigated pattern. The mere fact that we are already living in the glorious years of the age of science leaves not the slightest doubt about the foregoing reality.

We come next to the three main requirements essential for maintaining life on earth. They are: air, water and food. Man cannot stay alive without air for more than a few short minutes. This is one of the reasons why Allah has not allowed him to have control of it. He has made it free for all living things, and no one has been endowed with the power to control its movement, change its composition or prevent it from reaching all organisms without discrimination.

Equally important is water, which no man can live without for more than a few days. Here we may remark that man's control over its free flow is somewhat limited; so is his power to prevent rain from falling or to control its distribution over the surface of the globe.

The third requirement is food. Here man's capacity to have control over its production and storage is considerably greater than is the case with air and water. This allowance has been made because man can live without food for longer periods of time and sustain life with very small amounts.

These examples illustrate Allah's wisdom and providence and the perfect order which governs this universe and ensures the survival of all His creatures. He provides for all according to their real needs and requirements and to His perfect knowledge and understanding of man's shortcomings and the likelihood that he might abuse the pattern He has prescribed for the operation of the forces of nature.

The processes from conception to childbirth are synonymous with present day medical descriptions for the stages; Zygote, blastocyst, uterus, (in the wall of which the blastocyst embeds itself), embryo, foetus until finally the birth.

The Qur'ān has also dealt with the anatomy of the human body and the functions of its different specialized systems and organs.

It is frequently remarked in verses touching upon the functions of the eyes and the ears that hearing is always given precedence over seeing. Not once has this order been reversed. This consistent preference may seem baffling because, in man's reckoning, the loss of sight is regarded as a more severe and incapacitating handicap than the loss of hearing.

This assessment of the significance of these two sense organs is not without reason. If Allah has deemed hearing to be more important than seeing, it is because the ear is the first sense organ completely functional at birth. It takes the newly-born infant approximately three months to control the movement of his eyes and to focus them on the objects and persons surrounding him.

Moreover, unimpaired hearing will be essential on the Day of Judgement when mankind will be called before Allah; and the ear never sleeps. A sleeping person will not wake up if you move your hand near his eyes, but he is sure to wake up if you make the slightest sound in the room. In short, the ear is man's link with the outside world.

When Allah ordained that the 'People of the Cave' (Ahl al-Kahf) should go to sleep for hundreds of years, He simply blocked their ears, as is stated in the following verse;

> "Then We sealed up their hearing in the Cave for a number of years." (al-Kahf 18:11)

They slept undisturbed for three centuries. It is a fact that noise disrupts sound deep sleep during the day. In contrast the absence of noise at night is an essential condition for uninterrupted sleep.

It is also noticeable that although Allah consistently uses the singular form of the word hearing (*sam*ʿ), He always uses the plural form of the word seeing (*abṣār*) whenever He refers to that sense organ, as in the following verse:

> "You did not hide yourselves lest your ear (hearing) and your visions (eyes) and your skin should testify against you . . . " (Fuṣṣilat 41:22)

Why did Allah use the singular form *sam*ʿ ('hearing', or 'ear') and the plural form *abṣār* ('vision' or 'eyes')? One would expect Him to have used the plural form in both cases in conformity with correct usage. It is also logical to argue that there is but one 'seeing' and one 'hearing'. This peculiar usage illustrates the unique accuracy and meaningfulness of the language of the Qur'ān.

Vision is naturally one of the sense organs that is entirely controlled by man's own volition. He has the freedom to look at things or shut his eyes when he wishes to avoid them. In contrast, he cannot shut his ears to incoming sounds or vibrations around him. One cannot inhibit one's ears from hearing the noise coming from the street or from a crowd of guests in a room. Whereas seeing is optional and selective, hearing, in contrast, is a compulsory and non-selective process. It is forced on the listener whether he likes it or not and without discrimination. When a loudspeaker is blaring in the street, all those who live close by can neither avoid hearing it, nor ignore it. In contrast one can avert one's eyes or shut them to avoid the sight of a bleeding man who has been hit by a car, or any such painful scene. This multiple and selective function of the eye (or seeing) underlies the consistent use of the plural form of 'vision'. This usage could not however, be applied to hearing, because it is forced upon us and we cannot be totally impervious to sounds if we happen to be within their range.

The ear was given precedence over the eye possibly because it is always active. Moreover, with regards to the creative process, the organ that is constantly active and is never dormant is considered to be more significant than, and superior to, other sense organs. This superiority pertains to the fact that the ear is the only sense organ that is completely developed before birth and is perfectly functional at birth. Other organs may take months or years before they are fully developed and able to perform their biological functions. When we are asleep all our other sense organs also go to sleep. The ear is the only sense organ that remains awake and alert to incoming stimuli, ready to signal to the brain so that it, in turn, signals to the other sense organs, including the eyes, to resume functioning. Unlike the eye, which does not function unless light enters through its lens, the ear works in both darkness and daylight. As for the skin, it is known to be the main source of bodily sensation, with a variety of nerve endings located in it. This scientific fact has been touched upon in the Qur'ān, as can be seen in the following verse from the Sūrah 'al-Nisā', wherein Allah gives a description of the torture which unbelievers are doomed to suffer.

> ". . . As often as their skins are consumed We shall exchange them for fresh skins, that they may taste the torment . . ." (al-Nisā' 4:56)

Allah has emphasized the skin because of its extreme sensitivity and response to pain. The changing of the skin is in itself an indication that those parts (or nerves) which respond to pain are laid down in and under the skin, as detailed by modern neurology.

Test-tube Babies

A word should also be said about the scientific accomplishments regarding test-tube babies, the determination of sex of the unborn foetus and the assumption that these accomplishments demolish all that has been established about them in the Qur'ān and particularly those verses in which it is stated that only Allah knows what is in the womb, as is stated in the following verse from the Sūrah 'Luqmān':

> ". . . and knoweth that which is in the wombs . . ." (Luqmān 31:34)

To say that the above verse means that Allah alone knows the sex of what is in the womb is to misinterpret it. In fact it is referring to characteristics and features such as colour of eyes, in short, all that involves the unborn child. This divine knowledge was demonstrated when Allah informed Zachariah of the prospective birth of his son, and gave him an entirely new name not previously known or used by his people. He informed him of his son's future role as one of His Apostles. This information was imparted to him in the temple long before conception had occured, as is indicated in Sūrah Āl 'Imrān:

> "Then Zachariah prayed unto his Lord and said: My Lord! Bestow upon me of Your bounty goodly offspring. Lo! You art the Hearer of Prayer. And the angels called to him as he stood praying in the sanctuary: Allah gives thee glad tidings of (a son whose name is) John (Yaḥyā) (who comes) to confirm a word from Allah, lordly, chaste, a Prophet of the righteous. He said, My Lord, how can I have a son when age has overtaken me already and my wife is barren? (The angel) answered: So (it will be). Allah does what He will." (Āl 'Imrān 3:38-40)

Thus the prophecy concerning Zachariah's child and his decreed future had been enunciated long before the child was conceived and created in his mother's womb. His name, sex and role as one of Allah's Apostles were all imparted to Zachariah in the temple. They were all fine details denoted by the pronoun *mā* ('that which'), and were more of a biographical characterisation than a determination of sex. The assumption that the pronoun *mā* ('that which') entails the determination of sex is unfounded as far as both usage and meaning are concerned.

Nevertheless, the determination of sex cannot be considered an established scientific fact unsusceptible to error, because of the equal rate of probability. An unborn child could be either male or female. In each case the probability coefficient is fifty-fifty and either prediction has a 50% chance of being correct irrespective of scientific theory.

The scientific achievement of uniting a sperm cell with an ovum (egg) has aroused a certain controversy due to its closeness to Qur'ānic facts. However, those who would equate this feat with creation must understand that it is but a simple experiment in which human substances have been united artificially by man, using a medium other than the womb. All science has done is to use knowledge bestowed by Allah to devise a new way to advance and fulfil Allah's purpose and overcome the physiological defects that may impede conception and pregnancy.

There is no creation of any sort involved in the production of test-tube babies. The whole process does not go any further than the discovery of a new method to cure some physiological abnormality, for in order to create a living organism science must first create the living human cell.

In conclusion, one should bear in mind that the miracles of the Qur'ān have not come to unfold the secrets of the universe or touch upon its more complex phenomena and established facts. The Qur'ān has come as a challenge to mankind. It challenged the Arabs' excellence and mastery over language. But as Islam is the religion of all mankind, its challenge was not restricted to the Arabs alone. It also challenged other peoples and races. The challenge still exists and will continue to exist until the Last Day.

The Qur'ān has unveiled the secrets of the past, the present and the future. It has unfolded intricate factors governing man's emotions and self. It contains signs which point to facts which may one day be illuminated and their knowledge made available to man, as will be discussed in the next chapter.

PART II

Chapter 1

Allah and the Universe

When lecturing about Allah, I sometimes encounter misinformed and arrogant persons who seem to be all too ready and willing to dispute His existence and sovereignty over this universe. In their vain attempts, they invariably support their case with unfounded hypotheses, based on dubious logic, that are flagrantly lacking in empirical evidence and valid proof.

It is necessary to point out that persons whose most desired goal is to cast doubt about Allah's existence and His discipline are but heretics whose main dilemma lies in their lack of faith in the divine messages. They have willingly embarked on a path of disobedience to, and resentment of, Allah's laws and decrees. This rebellion against Allah provides them with an outlet for easing the pangs of their troubled souls and alleviates their agonizing apprehension of the Day of Judgement when they will be asked to account for their deeds. This fear and anxiety are, in fact, the driving force behind their persistent denial of Allah and their futile self-deception.

Philosophers have tried for years to cast doubt upon Allah's religions, using all sorts of reasoning and distorted facts, sometimes drawing a parallel between religion and slavery and at other times postulating that to free oneself from religion is the essence of freedom itself.

Belief in Allah and His existence has always been, and still is, one of the most contested issues engaging the thoughts of mankind since time immemorial. The debate however, has failed to settle much and does not seem to have an end in sight. This perseverance in seeking evidence for the existence – or absence – of a supreme power behind this material world, is indeed a clear indication that we know Allah by instinct and that there is something inside each one of us which confirms His existence. If this was untrue, mankind would not have exhausted itself seeking answers to this question. The human mind would have felt secure, happy and satisfied with its limited knowledge about this material world and the sciences created for his welfare by Allah.

If we look at those people who worship this material world we find that, despite their material success and accomplishments, they are always perturbed by an inward feeling of anxiety and uncertainty. This anxiety and stress are believed by psychologists to be one of the main factors behind the high and ever-increasing rate of suicides which take place in the most affluent and materially-orientated nations. It is not uncommon to find that most of the people one may envy for their material success are often troubled by a nagging and distressing feeling of disharmony with Allah's universe. This is because harmony between the self and Allah's universe cannot be restored without complete faith in Him and adherence to His discipline and His way.

This issue of faith in Allah is well defined in the following verse which is frequently recited by all the faithful whenever they are distressed and wish to draw near to Allah:

> "Allah! There is no God save Him, the Alive, the Eternal. Neither slumber nor sleep overtakes Him. Unto Him belongs whatsoever is in the heavens and whatsoever is in the earth. Who is he that intercedes with Him save by His leave? He knows that which is in front of them and that which is behind them, while they encompass nothing of His knowledge save what He will. His Throne includes the heavens and the earth, and He is never weary of preserving them. He is the Sublime, the Tremendous." (al-Baqarah 2:225)

The word 'alive' means that He is the only one true living God, Who is self-subsisting and never dies because He has created life and death. His life does not depend on other beings and He is not limited to time and space. The word 'al-Qayyūm' includes not only the idea of 'self-subsisting', but also the idea of keeping up and maintaining all life and ensuring that the laws governing this universe are kept operating according to its established order and that not for one brief moment since its creation has this universe been left to operate unsupervised by Allah. He knows all things and observes all that happens in it.

But what is the underlying meaning of all this? Actually Allah is teaching us not to succumb to despair in our moments of distress. It was He Who established the laws of this universe and commanded that we follow them and accept their outcome no matter how distressing or hopeless they may seem, or how helpless we may be. He is always nearby, keeping a vigilant watch over all His creatures in their daily activity and practice of His commands, always wishing to lend a hand to the distressed by bending the established laws and forcing the elements of nature and the course of events to work in favour of the distressed. Man knows this by instinct. He is aware of Allah's sovereignty over His universe and all that moves within it. This is the reason why we, believers or otherwise,always seek His intervention and help when no other help is within reach. He alone can turn despair into hope, hardship into comfort, restore the rights of the aggrieved and punish the unjust.

An example of this divine authority over the laws of nature and Allah's care for His creatures is illustrated in the story of Hagar and her infant child Ishmael, who were left helpless in the parched desert. When all her efforts of finding water failed, her hopes dashed, on the verge of dying, she turned to Allah and prayed for His help. At this moment, when nature's laws worked without regard to her plight, Allah inspired her helpless child to dig his foot into the sand, whereupon a spring of water gushed to the surface.

Muḥammad (SAW), too, underwent a similar experience during his call to Islam. In his decision to leave Makkah to avoid persecution he sought sanctuary in al-Ṭā'if. There, however, he suffered humiliation at the hands of young fools and old antagonists who resented his call. Just as things were looking the bleakest, Allah sent His confirmation to Muhammad in the form of the sacred Night Journey from the Sacred Mosque (in Makkah) to the Farthest Mosque in Jerusalem. As a result of this, Muḥammad (SAW), faith was consolidated, and he resumed his mission, beginning with the people of Makkah and visiting traders and pilgrims who also resented him. Then a delegation from Yathrib came to declare their allegiance to him and to confess their Islam, and thus began the Hijrah (migration) and the victories that followed it.

If each one of us reviewed the experiences of his life he would soon discover that he had undergone situations wherein natural laws seemed to forsake him and leave him in helpless despair. When all attempts at solving these problems have been foiled, suddenly, in some mysterious way, a solution is found. But this solution has not come out of the blue, but because Allah is always watching over us, ready to answer our pleas, alleviate our distress and fill our hearts with peace and tranquility. For Allah hears every voice, sees every movement in His universe, and is always ready to answer the pleas of those who acknowledge His sovereignty and submit themselves to His will in their moments of distress and helplessness.

The verse goes on to assert that "Neither slumber nor sleep overtakes Him". This means that He is constantly watching over us and that all man's deeds are known to Him. Allah wants to assure us and consolidate our faith in His uninterrupted care, and to dispel our apprehension of what might befall us in the course of our daily life. He wants to assure the believer that nothing in this universe escapes His attention, and that he can go about his daily activities unperturbed by his enemies' evil intentions and intrigues. A believer need not fear his oppressors or seek any protection other than that of his God Who created him and has taken in His hands the task of shielding him from hazards. It is this faith in Allah and His concern about the welfare of His worshippers that keeps their hearts filled with hope and peace, even in the bleakest moments when hope and salvation seem far away.

The verse goes on to consolidate and enhance the harmony between the human self and Allah's created universe in saying that "Unto Him belongeth whatsoever is in the heaven and whatsoever is in the earth." Here again, Allah puts man's mind at rest with regard to his sustenance and the means of making a living. He reminds him that this universe and all that it contains of material wealth and provision belongs to no one but Him; and He is the Sustainer and Provider for all creatures according to their needs and capacities. To some He grants sustenance in abundance; to others He gives it in strict measure. The righteous man should not, therefore, fear poverty or hardship or feel that he stands alone in this world uncared for or unprotected by his Creator, Who never sleeps but is always listening to the cries and pleas of the helpless, the aggrieved and the oppressed.

The verse then states that no one could intercede in His presence except as He permits. How can any creature stand before Him as of right, and claim to intercede for a fellow creature, when both are His, and He cares as much for one as for the other, and both are dependent upon His will and command? Nevertheless, in His wisdom He may place His creatures and give one superiority over the other. Then, by His will, such a one may intercede or help according to the laws and duties laid on him. In other words, Allah is telling His devotees not to fear any other being no matter how mighty and oppressive he may be, because such malicious persons have no authority to intercede on another's behalf, because their wrongdoings have barred them from His court and alienated them from His grace. Only the righteous who are highly esteemed by Him may intercede for others.

The verse goes on strengthening the believer's faith and warding off his fears of evil-doers. He is assured that Allah "knows that which is in front of them and that which is behind them." Here again Allah enhances the believer's faith in Him and comforts his anxious heart by assuring him that He is well aware of all the actions and secrets of wrong doers, whether they are deeply buried in their minds and hearts or are revealed; that he alone can penetrate the deepest recesses of man's inner soul and heart and is capable of foiling whatever malice they plan for the unwary. With such protection the believer has nothing to fear, as long as his faith in Allah is deeply rooted in his heart.

The verse also speaks about Allah's absolute knowledge and what He imparts of it to mankind. In this context he says ". . . while they (mankind) encompass nothing of His knowledge save what He will . . ." From this we may glean that Allah's knowledge is absolute and is not restricted by time or space. There is no comparison between Allah's knowledge and ours: they are of different categories. We only see a reflection of reality when it accords with His will and design.

There is some knowledge which Allah bestows on select servants. There is also knowledge which He grants freely to the whole of mankind irrespective of creed. The third kind of knowledge is confined wholly to Him and is not shared with mortals. The first kind of knowledge is granted to His Messengers and chosen Apostles. It is a personal kind of knowledge exclusive to the servant and is not to be imparted to any other person or be made an object of discussion. The second kind involves the whole of mankind and is systematically revealed to succeeding generations. This kind of knowledge has a predetermined date of discovery. If it coincides with scientific research being conducted by a particular scientist Allah usually gives it to him. However, if He deems that the welfare of mankind requires this knowledge, when no one is actively seeking it, He decrees that it should be discovered accidentally. Examples of this accidental imparting of knowledge from Allah to mankind were the discoveries of X-rays and penicillin. These chance discoveries happen because their predetermined dates of discovery have arrived. It passes into mankind's repertory of knowledge with the utterance by Allah of the word 'Be'. This is why we frequently hear scientists announcing the discovery of cures of diseases or of new phenomena, completely unrelated to the study or research in which they are engaged. In these situations we usually say that the accidental discovery was the work of chance, whereas, in truth, it has been revealed to mankind because the date of its discovery, which was predetermined since the beginning of creation, has finally arrived.

The third category of knowledge is, however, strictly confined to Allah. It is neither accessible to man, nor can he, with his limited intellect and mental capacities, comprehend it or manipulate it.

It is obvious that the main theme in the above verse is one of reassurance to the believer in Allah's absolute power and His all-encompassing knowledge. He is asked to put his trust in Him and not to fear malicious and unjust persons plotting against him, for He knows them well and is aware of their covert plans and is able to defeat their purpose. Nor will He allow them to abuse the little knowledge which He has imparted to them, or enable them to use it for their own destruction, or to inflict misery and hardship on others.

With all this protection and care the believer should therefore feel safe, secure and unperturbed as long as his faith in Allah's superiority and mastery over His universe is firm.

It might be useful to clarify the fact that Allah's gifts to mankind are of two kinds. The first involves those gifts which He grants to the whole of mankind in His attribute as Lord (*Rabb*), Sustainer and Cherisher of all people. The second kind are spiritual gifts which He bestows on the righteous and the believers. The first kind is defined in the verse from the Sūrah 'al-A'rāf (7)', in which He says:

> "And (remember) when thy Lord brought forth from the Children of Adam, from their reins, their seed, and made them testify of themselves, (saying): Am I not your Lord? [or: Sustainer] They said: Yes, verily. We testify. (That was) lest you should say at the Day of Resurrection: Lo! of this we were unaware."
> (al-A'rāf 7:172)

Why has not Allah said, "Am I not your God (ilāh)?", and made them testify as to His divinity? The reason here is that the giving is due to the attribute of lordship; a kind of giving that is given equally to all believers and non-believers alike without discrimination between them. For instance, Allah has created the universe and commanded it to serve man, thus making it possible for him to harness some of the elements of nature for his prosperity and development. Although such forces are immensely more powerful than man, they have been subjected to his control. The Sun for instance, could burn to ashes all that exists on this planet and turn it into cosmic dust; the slightest imbalance in the Earth's revolution would result in the destruction of all life; water could, without divine control, inundate the planet, and life would end if rain ceased. All these forces are much greater than man's power and beyond his control, but because Allah has ordained that they should operate according to a prescribed pattern, they have no choice but to obey His eternal decrees. Therefore, the Sun cannot change its celestial cycle, nor can rain fall or cease haphazardly. These forces have no volition of their own. They all operate according to the laws set by Allah, and have been commanded to yield their benefits to man's service and contribute to his needs.

Allah does not discriminate between believers and non-believers when bestowing these gifts on mankind. Thus, the Sun shines and divides its energy equally among all, and the Earth yields its crops to those who are willing to work to tap its varied resources, regardless of their faith or creed. It will yield nothing to the idle no matter how righteous he is or how strong his faith. In contrast, he who invests the knowledge imparted to him by Allah to establish a new industry or participate in any way in promoting the welfare and prosperity of mankind, is sure to be rewarded. Thus, with regards to the first kind of gift, Allah does not favour one particular group or nation with His bounty. They avail themselves of it on equal terms according to each one's endeavour. This is the reason for Allah's saying "Am I not your Lord?" and not "Am I not your God (ilāh)?"

The second kind of bounty is confined exclusively to those who believe that there is only one true God. This faith binds man to Allah and constitutes a covenant between them. So crucial is this question of faith that it is emphasized in the introductory verses of Sūrah al-Baqarah in which Allah states,

> "This is the Scripture whereof there is no doubt, a guidance unto those who ward off evil; who believe in the Unseen, and establish worship, and spend of that We have bestowed upon them; and who believe in that which is revealed unto thee (Muḥammad) and that which was revealed before you, and are certain of the Hereafter. Those depend on guidance from their Lord. Those are the successful." (al-Baqarah 2:2-5)

Throughout the whole of the Qur'ān, Allah always addresses the faithful with the words "O ye who believe", making it obvious that true faith is a fundamental prerequisite to gaining His spiritual gifts which are embodied in the Qur'ān and which are explained as being belief in the Unseen, Resurrection, the Day of Judgement and the right path to a secure, peaceful and prosperous life as laid down by Allah in His divine scripture for all steadfast believers. A peaceful life in this world and in the Hereafter is Allah's reward to sincere believers who strictly follow His way and discipline as defined in the Qur'ān. In this way discipline is the cure for the ills of life. It ensures the regulation of a healthy and sound society enjoying all Allah's providence and blessings.

One may often wonder at the misery and hardships which plague us. The reason is that not infrequently we ignore Allah's laws and His prescribed way, and substitute for them our own man-made laws and legislations, despite the fact that in Allah's laws is laid the foundation for the building of a perfect society. For Allah, being the Creator of this universe and of the human self, knows best what is good for man's welfare and happiness and how his life ought to be organised.

It is no wonder that the believer, whose heart overflows with faith in Allah, and who adheres strictly to His prescribed path is always aware of Allah's spiritual gifts bestowed upon him, and is, therefore, in a constant state of bliss and contentment. When the verse ". . . Allah will protect you from mankind . . ." (al-Mā'idah 5:67) was revealed to Muḥammad, he instructed his followers, who had gathered around him to defend him against the hostile disbelievers and the hypocrites, to disperse and leave him alone to face his antagonists. He acted so because he knew that he was fully protected by Allah's power and providence. With such power on his side he needed no assistance from anyone else. He was sure that no one could come near him or inflict any harm on him. Similarly, 'Umar ibn al-Khaṭṭāb, armed with the faith that Allah never slumbers or sleeps, used to sleep in the open, under the shade of a tree, unafraid of his enemies, believing that Allah's cherishing care is safer than the protection of any guard.

The focal point in the issue of faith is whether one sincerely believes in Allah or not. To believe in Allah is to believe in the existence of a supreme power purified of all desire or lust; to believe that this unimaginable Power is behind the creation of the universe and that It is incomparable in Its scope of knowledge, creativity, mercy, punishment and all the other features attributable to Allah. Once this faith has taken root in the heart of the believer, he becomes aware of the fact that man should not assess Allah's power and absolute knowledge in terms of his own limited knowledge and physical powers, and that if Allah commands him "You must do this", he is not qualified to question His authority and ask for reasons or motives, for dialogue is futile and will not serve its end unless those taking part in it possess equal mental ability and logic. But man's mental and physical limitations make him no match with Allah, no matter how knowledgeable and powerful man may be. Yet we still meet some unfortunate and vain persons who pretend shamelessly to be qualified to argue with Allah over His knowledge, the standards of living and the way He has prescribed for mankind. This recognition of Allah's supreme power and sovereignty over His universe and mankind, and His all-encompassing knowledge, establishes the route through which faith enters mankind's heart where it lodges and grows. But this route does not open without prior contemplation and musing about this universe and the signs through which Allah reveals Himself to us.

Some sceptics describe as bondage our devotion and submission to this supreme power and to its divine commands and law's, and religion as another form of slavery. In answer to these heretics we say that although religion is indeed bondage to Allah, there is an immense difference between being a slave to another mortal and being a slave to Allah. In the former case, the purpose of the master is to exploit the capacities of the slave to promote his own welfare and prosperity, thereby depriving the slave of self-fulfilment and material rewards. Thus the slave tills the field and the master reaps the crop; he toils and labours so that the master can possess and enlarge his wealth. This kind of human slavery, the ultimate goal of which is to rob the slave of any worldly rewards which he could have achieved if he had been a free man, is strongly condemned in Islam.

In contrast, slavery to Allah is meant to enhance the slave's capacity and welfare and increase his share of Allah's bounty, both materially and spiritually, for Allah is Self-subsisting and in no way in need of mankind's assistance;

It is not only the wife and children who have a share of what the husband makes, but also many others who may not be related to him. This divine social justice is clearly defined in the Sūrah al-Nisā' (4) where it is stated that men get only a share of what they earn: ". . . Unto men a fortune [or share] from that which they have earned . . ." (al-Nisā' 4:32)

Sometimes we wonder why a covetous and miserly person is always afraid to spend of his money or enjoy life. The reason is that this earned money, which he strived hard to save, is not actually of the share of sustenance allotted to him by Allah. It will finally reach the hands of the person for whom it was initially granted. The miser is but the keeper and guardian of this money, and the wealth, by the will of Allah, is ordained to remain intact until handed over to its rightful owner, the miser having no power to use it for his own benefit.

Slavery to Allah is, therefore, a state of receiving rather than of giving. In it, Allah gives and never takes. He commands us to worship Him, not because He is in need of our efforts or He wishes to exploit them, but rather to make us eligible for His favours and support, and to give us access to His material and spiritual bounties. Slavery to Allah is always favourable to the slave, and it something that is fervently sought by him, because in it lies his security and prosperity and at the same time it is his shield against the hazards and vanity of his material lust and ambition.

Allah has truly promised those sincere believers among his slaves a good and fruitful life. His commands are, therefore, intended for the benefit and welfare of him who believes in this life and in the Hereafter. Man's obedience and submission will not benefit Allah in any way or add to His bounty, nor will his defiance and disobedience detract anything from Allah's kingdom. But a sincere believer who follows Allah's way chooses the good life, not only on the basis of his own potential, but also on the basis of his awareness that Allah's might surpasses all human powers. In contrast, a person lacking in faith is always ready to argue, hypothesize, philosophize and decide in terms of his own capabilities. In fact, the distinction between belief and non-belief lies in the choice of a way of life planned by the will of Allah, the acknowledgement of His limitless powers and His unreachable knowledge and the adherence to the way of life prescribed by Him and not by man's restricted mental powers and imperfect knowledge which can never be purged of human desires and lusts.

Allah in all His divine messages to mankind commands us to contemplate His universe and seek His signs and portents. Why does He command us to do this? Certainly, He would not have asked us to do so, if He had known that there was a single sign in the universe that could testify against His unity and His supreme powers. Surely, a person who is doubtful about what he designs or makes does not insist on your inspecting it thoroughly and will try to distract your attention from discovering its faults. In contrast, a person who is sure of his skill and the perfection of his work will be only too eager not to hide anything. This is the case with Allah's universe. He commands us to look into it and explore its harmony and flawlessness because He is sure of its perfect order.

We are told in the Qur'ān to contemplate creation and the universe, because in them are signs and portents in which

Allah reveals His unity and His all-compassing power. As there are signs in the creation of man, so are there portents in the creation of the earth and the heavens. About these portents Allah says:

> "We shall show them Our portents on the horizons and within themselves until it will be manifest unto them that it is the Truth . . ." (Fuṣṣilat 41:53)

If Allah were not truly the architect of this universe and did not know its secrets and how it functioned, or if He were uncertain about its perfection, would He have commanded us to examine it and explore it? But, being its Creator and being certain of its perfection, He challenges mankind to find any flaws in its structure and functions.

This challenge to mankind to ponder on the process of creation could not have been made unless the challenger were Allah Himself, Who has wisely and purposefully put these signs into the universe, and is manifested in the obedience of nature to His eternal will.

When we ponder on this, we soon come into contact with Allah's greatness. This, indeed, should be the ultimate goal of man: to let his searching and inquisitive mind explore the marvels of Allah's universe and to try to discover for himself his inability to harmonize with it without surrendering himself to his Creator. But man has willingly accepted the trust. About this Allah says:

> "Lo! We offered the trust unto the heavens and the earth and the hills, but they shrank from bearing it and were afraid of it. But man undertook it. Lo! he has proved a tyrant and a fool." (al-Aḥzāb 33:72)

What is meant by this verse is that all other creatures, except man, declined to undertake the responsibility of the trust (the free choice between good and evil) and were wise enough to surrender their will entirely to Allah's perfect will. They knew that submitting their will and freedom of choice to Him would give them more happiness and spare them the pitfalls of choosing between good and evil, lest they betray the trust. But man, being audacious and ignorant, failed to realize this, and in his foolhardiness accepted and betrayed the trust. The result is that a portion of mankind have become hypocrites and non-believers, thereby bringing punishment upon themselves. Thus man, because of his audacity and ignorance, wronged himself when he volunteered to bear the burden of the trust and accepted the freedom of choice offered to him by Allah.

To explain the above, let us suppose that an acquaintance has come to you at the beginning of each month and deposited with you a certain sum of money and asked you to keep it for him in trust for a certain period of time. When he comes at the end of that period to claim his money he discovers that you have squandered it on your pleasures and have nothing to give him. This is what man has done with Allah's trust. For He had bestowed upon him of His bounty in abundance and told him to enjoy what He gave him, but at the same time had cautioned him not to use His trust to corrupt the world. Thus man was told not to steal, not to disobey His commands and not to be unjust. But man was too foolish to assume the trust and freedom of choice. Satan has found in man's freedom of will a convenient access to his soul, and has been able to corrupt it. With this freedom of will man was also made accountable for his decisions to Allah, for any breach of the trust carried its own punishment.

All the divine messages which Allah has conveyed to mankind have laid down the right way which is to be followed. But the trust which man alone from Allah's creatures has willingly undertaken has given him the option to do or not to do, to obey or to defy the will of Allah, because when Allah said to man, "This you must do, and this you must not," He did not force him either way, but left him to make his own decision. None of Allah's other creations have been given this free will. The sun for instance, is not free to set or rise as it pleases, nor are the moon and the stars. Even the angels have not been granted this freedom of choice and will.

How did man exercise this freedom? Indeed, as Allah

predicted, man failed to honour the trust. In his ignorance he missed the right path, denied his Creator and substituted heavenly bodies, stone idols, beasts and all other things which he thought were capable of helping him or influencing his destiny, thereby surrendering himself to the devil. In his ingratitude, he spurned the divine messages which were sent to him to show him the right way to the good, secure and rewarding life. Instead he began setting down his own laws to suit his own ambitions and desires and, as a result, disrupted his own life and subjected the human race to misery, hardship and Allah's wrath.

Allah has vividly summed up in the following verse how Satan is able to infiltrate man's soul and tempt him into surrendering it to its volition:

> "But the devil whispered to him, saying: O Adam! Shall I show you the tree of immortality and power that wastes not away?" (Ṭā' Hā' 20:120)

In fact, Satan has used the two things that are most tempting and alluring to man, which are eternal life and inexhaustible wealth. Man has always longed to live forever, to maintain his youth and never grow old, and to amass all the wealth his hands could seize. It is through these two desires that Satan finds easy access to man's soul. In fact it was this lust for eternal life and endless wealth that prompted man to invent his own idols, hoping that they would ward off evil and sickness and guarantee him wealth. It is this same avarice which stirs man's hypocrisy and idolization of authority, power and human talents, in the hope of maintaining sustenance and health. The truth is that these man-made idols are incapable of inflicting any harm or doing any good to any one of Allah's creatures. It is the fear which Satan sows in the hearts of the unfaithful that renders them so weak and so insecure that they begin to seek the assistance of other creatures, or for the same reason to believe that their destiny is governed by someone other than Allah.

Indeed this false belief in powers other than Allah is the result of fear that can only dwell in the heart in the absence of faith. A person whose heart throbs with faith in Allah's incomparable power knows no such fear, nor seeks any help other than that of Allah, Whom he knows is always watching over him, ready to answer his pleas and protect him. In contrast, only those who are enticed by lust and ambition which they cannot satisfy by legitimate means are always eager to seek ways and means other than those that are decreed by Allah.

To explain this, let us imagine that I am a rich man who covets someone else's fortune and plans to possess it by illegitimate means despite my conviction that such an act breaches the standards of a virtuous and happy life as decreed by Allah. This forbearance is intended to protect me, because I am only one member of a whole society, and if I allow myself to defraud someone else of his property, and I make a habit of it, then every other member of the society should be allowed to defraud me. This is the reason why Allah has disallowed such practices. If I reflected on these divine injunctions for a few moments I would soon reach the conclusion that they were decreed to spare me Allah's wrath and damnation, and to protect my own possessions. But Satan knows of my lust for wealth and how much I long to possess the other man's property and is ready with his soul-stealing stratagem. Yet though Allah has warned me and informed me of Satan's strategy and the way he enters the souls of men, so that I may guard myself against his tempting tactics, I knowingly disregard His cautioning, give myself up to my ambition and lust, stifle my conscience and defraud the unwary man. But as soon as the deed is done and my hunger for the other man's property is satisfied, my inner soul, which has seen Allah and known Him well, suddenly awakes, begins to torment me and displays before my mind's eye the magnitude of the misery I have brought upon myself in this world and the awesome damnation that awaits me in the Hereafter. I might try to look for reasons to justify my wickedness and ease my anxiety and stifle it by clinging to some made-up excuse, or dismiss as improbable any divine punishment.

The following example may explain what is actually meant

in the above lines. If we introduced a youth to a very pretty woman and told him that she was his for the night, but at the same time showed him a burning furnace in the backyard and told him that in return for that night's pleasure he would be hurled into the furnace, would he accept the offer? Of course not!

Divine punishment is hidden from us, being one of the unseen truths, so Satan makes use of this to gain access to our souls. By persuading us that there is no punishment for the rebel, nor reward for the righteous, we are tempted to embark on the road to sin. Once man has embarked on this path he gives his lust full reign and becomes obsessed with the glitter of the world and all its material wealth and power, heedless of what awaits him at the end of his journey. Such a miserable traveller finds his only support and ease of conscience in his denial of Allah's existence. But the mere fact that he is in constant struggle with himself and attempts to cultivate his doubts is, in itself, the unconscious proof of the existence of Allah, for no one can deny what does not actually exist.

Chapter 2

Doubt and Existence

Islam is either a belief, and hence a religion, or not a belief, and therefore hypocrisy. But before we begin our discussion we must first define the meaning of the word 'belief'. In essence, belief is a cause that develops steadily in the heart until it reaches full maturity and turns into a firm faith and certainty. Once it has reached this stage, it never emerges to the mind to be discussed or reviewed anew. If we ever recall it to mind, then something is amiss with our faith. This lack of sincere faith is pointed out in Allah's comment about the desert Arabs who professed Islam only to gain some favours, as is revealed in the following verses:

> "The wandering Arabs say: We believe.
> Say (unto them, O Muḥammad): You
> believe not, but rather say 'We submit',
> for the faith has not yet entered into your hearts . . ."
> (al-Ḥujarāt 49:14)

It appears, therefore, that true faith entails a firm conviction so deeply entrenched in the heart and soul that it can never re-emerge to our conscious mind to be discussed, or subjected to our senses. Its place is not the various areas of sense faculties or the material world in which it lives; the true realm and test for faith is the world of the Unseen. It is a world which is invisible and cannot be reached by our physical senses. We therefore customarily identify faith with innate certainty, as if we actually saw the object of faith.

An example of this innate certainty is expressed when one

sometimes says, "I am sure such-and-such is going to happen tomorrow" or "I believe that such-and-such will happen." You seem to see the event as clearly as you see your image in a mirror. But what you predict is hidden from you and could materialize or not, and you cannot guarantee its occurrence. But trusting your faith, your prediction seems to be as real as the world you can actually see and feel. If this is how far you are willing to go in your faith about trivial worldly matters, then surely your faith in the existence of Allah ought to be much greater, and you must worship Him as if you actually saw Him. It is not important if we do not actually see Him, because He sees us. And if we consider worship to be synonymous with seeing Him, then seeing is no longer a controversial issue, for once faith is subjected to controversy and mental debate it loses its true meaning and essence. In as much as it is debated in the mind, it is imperfect and incomplete.

The main objective of these debates is to confirm or deny the existence of Allah. Yet, if you ask anyone who supports the case for the existence of Allah about the motives which prompted him to seek such evidence and why he became involved in such a painstaking task, requiring a great deal of mental energy and dedication, profound reflection and insight, he would certainly say that he was propelled by an inborn and persistent feeling that Allah was inside him.

Indeed Allah resides naturally in those who believe in Him, obey Him and follow His right way, as well as in those who, though they wallow in wrong-doing and self indulgence, can nevertheless feel Him in them, and are constantly perturbed by the awesome penalty they know awaits them on the Day of Judgement. They are in constant terror of that Day, which they instinctively know will come, and try desperately to ease the torment of their souls and to escape their dilemma by inveighing against Him and His divine Justice, and disputing it with vain argument.

It is obvious, therefore, that those who try to provide evidence as to the existence of Allah have in fact confirmed it without the necessity of any concrete proof. For in their striving to find proof lies the proof. The quest for this evidence and the mental effort that is expended indicates that their inborn faculties are in no doubt of His existence. We can sense Him and know that He is all around them. Surely the awareness of Allah's existence must have been present when the attempts for confirming evidence began. In these attempts, which are likely to continue till the end of time, is embedded the implicit acknowledgement of His existence. Man, by nature, can only produce evidence within his mental capacity. If we therefore thoroughly study the divine messages we will soon discover that the most important and significant evidence concerning Allah's existence is presented in a way that is most commensurate with mankind's past, present and future mental capacities, with surpassing accuracy and detail.

If we investigate Allah's knowledge, we will find that it is imparted to man through the association between words and their meanings in the mind, as stated in the verse, "And He taught Adam all the names . . . " (al-Baqarah 2:31) i.e. that Allah has taught Adam the nature of all things and their names. Afterwards, He called the angels and asked them to inform Him of these names, but they could not and replied that they had none except that which He had taught them.

We infer from the above that meaning ought to be defined first, or that a thing should be found and clearly defined and perceived by the learner or listener, before it can be given a name which consolidates its shape in his mind. Thus, when we say the word 'house', there is a meaning for it in our memory. If, for example, you mentioned the word 'mountain' to a man who had never seen a mountain, he would not understand what you meant, no matter how hard you tried to explain it to him. The nomads who live in the deserts, isolated from the modern world, can never understand, or even imagine, what a television looks like. Yet there is no man on earth who does not know the meaning of the word "Allah", no matter how ignorant and isolated from civilisation he is. He understands it as the mighty power that created this universe and exercises total control over man's activities and fate. But how can man understand the meaning of the word when he has not seen Him? The answer is that if his inborn instincts did not tell him that Allah was lodged in his heart and soul he would never have understood the meaning of the word, nor would it have acquired that universal meaning which lives in harmony with mankind. It is, indeed, our faith in His existence which makes us understand the meaning of the word 'Allah', for, all those things that are not registered in our memory and mind are meaningless.

If we consult the different dictionaries of all languages we will find that they contain only words which name well-defined and existing objects. They are revised periodically so that new words for newly-found objects are added. It is therefore essential that a thing must be found before a new name for it is devised. In fact there is in every country a body of professional linguists whose main task is to revise their language and supplement it with new words and terms for newly-discovered things and meanings. But the fact that the word 'Allah' (or its equivalent) is found in all languages is a clear indication that He has never been far from man's thought; it provides the indisputable evidence that His existence preceded all His creation, as well as the development of any language. This universal agreement by all languages and all peoples about the meaning of the word 'Allah' and what it implies shows that the human mind knows Allah by instinct, even though it is beyond his power to see Him. This takes us back to the divine messages and the verse in which Allah says,

> "And when thy Lord brought forth
> from the Children of Adam,
> from their reins, their seed,
> and made them testify of themselves,
> (saying): Am I not your Lord?
> They said: Yes, verily. We testify.
> (That was) lest you should say at the
> Day of Resurrection! Lo! of this we
> were unaware." (al-A'rāf 7:172)

The above verse shows how Allah lives within us, although it is beyond our ability to see Him. This is the reason why

His name never sounds unfamiliar or meaningless when we hear it spoken. We are always sensitive to its sound and can feel its echo within us; we are quite aware of the power it signifies, and know that life cannot be harmonious without our feeling that He is close to us. There are millions of illiterates who have very little worldly knowledge, and will accept with doubt and scepticism any explanation you may give about them, but there is not one single person in this universe, young or old, literate or illiterate who is ignorant of the meaning of the word 'Allah'.

It is not uncommon for people to disagree about an issue or fail to understand its meaning, but not once has there been any discord among all people about the existence of Allah and His mastery over this universe. They all acknowledge His sovereignty and worship Him. This is the reason that when you enter one of Allah's houses you find men of all walks of life, who may be different in age, social class, education, customs and habits, sitting together, or engaged in worship glorifying Him in harmony and submissiveness. All these worshippers could not have gathered in this way unless they were motivated by their instinctive feeling that Allah truly resided in them.

As for those who try to deny Allah's existence, we say to them that their mere attempt to deny Him is in itself an acknowledgement of His existence. That is because no one need deny something that does not exist. For instance, a few centuries ago, some people asserted that the earth was flat, while others believed that it was spherical. If the earth did not appear to be flat for some, or if science had not proved it to be a sphere, no argument would have arisen. This dispute developed, in the first place, because of the conflict between what was actually visible and the scientific theory before it has been proven, otherwise we would be debating nothing. It is, therefore, logical to say that the attempts to deny the existence of Allah must have begun when it became evident that He truly existed; otherwise, why should any non-believer try to deny Him? If Allah was not truly there, whom, then, were they trying to deny?

To cast any doubt about Allah is tantamount to admitting

His existence, and those who try to dislodge or weaken our faith in Him have unintentionally provided the evidence of His existence and defeated their own purpose. For looking for such evidence must necessarily bear an implicit acknowledgement of His presence, and all mental effort expended in its confirmation or denial could not have emerged out of nothing.

If we accept the conclusion that Allah is in us naturally and that all believers and non-believers alike can sense His presence in their hearts and souls, then it follows that those who deny Him do so because they fear Him and are apprehensive of His wrath, and therefore try to alleviate their anxiety by convincing themselves that heaven and hell, reward and punishment are but the invention of man's own thoughts, and are non-existent. Despite this defiance and self-deception they are constantly haunted by their subconscious fear of the Hereafter and the Day when they will stand before Allah and give account of all their deeds. They know no peace of mind and are always miserable and scared, no matter how secure and confident they may seem about the present.

This would all be incomplete without reflecting upon Allah's discipline and His right way to discover the reasons which make some people avoid them, and whether or not they do so because His way does not provide equal justice and happiness for all men.

Why does man always try to seek a different way, which he sometimes describes as contemporary thought or modern theories? Why does he run away from Allah? Allah has set restrictions upon human desires. These limits have not been set forth in favour of one specified group or another, but rather for the welfare of the whole of mankind. But human ambition and desires know no bounds. Man wants to give full reign to his instincts, despite his knowledge of their harmful repercussions on himself and on the society. For example, he is obsessed with a desire to possess everything. His greed drives him to possess the riches of the world if he could, and always to covet other people's possessions. He seems oblivious of the fact that his life on this earth is temporal and that no one could ever make use of all his amassed wealth in that short period, nor take one little bit of it with him when he leaves it. But why does man struggle to hoard wealth for its own sake? The reason is that his greed makes him oblivious to the certainty of death; he is hopeful of cheating death at least until he has satisfied all his desires. This false hope is referred to in Muḥammad's (SAW) ḥadīth wherein he says:

> "I have not seen a conviction that is equal to doubt as the certainty about death."

In His wisdom and cherishing care, Allah has been careful to curb the lust for possession, by condemning the acquisition by unlawful means or false pretences of another person's properties and possessions. He established these laws to protect every member of society, and to teach us to observe the rights of others. Thus He forbids us to acquire wealth by unlawful means, to touch an orphan's property or to take personal advantage of it if we are appointed as guardian over him, and so on. Through these laws, Allah safeguards the rights of both the weak and the powerful. This balance, although it may appear paradoxical, is unequivocally sound, because when Allah has forbidden us from coveting the property of others, He has also forbidden society as a whole from transgressing against its members or abusing their rights. He has protected the lawful rights of the weak from the strong. If Allah had permitted the strong to wrongfully seize the property of the weak, He would have given society access to the weak man's money and wealth. Here we see Allah's justice. He protects the weak and shields the strong from the bias of society. The legislation has been made to enhance the welfare of the whole of society and ensure its harmony. He has also decreed that the rich should be charitable and allot some of their wealth to the poor so that the whole society can enjoy a peaceful life, purged from envy. Only in a healthy climate of this nature can fellowship, co-operation and concern for one another grow. This is only one example of Allah's legislation. It has been set forth as a barrier against the greed of those who are obsessed with the uncontrollable desire to hoard wealth, regardless of the means of its acquisition or the persons they acquire it from; these laws have come to protect these same persons from their own shortcomings and lusts.

Regarding physical lust and the physical relationship between man and woman, we find that God has also established certain rules which ensure that this relationship does not become a source of corruption in society.

It is told that a man once came to Muḥammad (SAW) and, after declaring his allegiance to him and professing his Islam, added that he was fond of women and could not restrain his desires, and asked the Prophet (SAW) if he was free to pursue this habit. Muḥammad (SAW) did not feel offended, nor did he chastize him. Instead he calmly and wisely explained to him the underlying purpose of the rules decreed by Allah on that issue, in a clear and instructive way that could be fully comprehended by the man. He asked him if he would accept that his lust be practised with his mother. This question seemed to offend the man and he said, "No". The Prophet (SAW) continued, "would you accept it to be done to your sister?" This second suggestion seemed to increase the man's anger and he vehemently answered, "No". But Muḥammad ignored his outburst and said, "Would you allow it to be committed with your wife?" The man could not control his anger and shouted, "Never, never!" Then Muḥammad (SAW) concluded "Neither do any of us, my Arab brother". With this simple dialogue Muḥammad (SAW) was able to make the foolish man realize that Allah's legislations were made to protect his mother, his sister and his wife from an act that no honest man who had any pride in himself would approve of. If anyone paid heed to this dialogue before committing any act of adultery he would never indulge in such sin. The legislation has therefore come to refine our instincts and to protect the individual himself as well as his own kin. Through this legislation, Allah has shown us that all men are equal before Him and that His justice knows no discrimination or bias. No one escapes His punishment if he breaks His laws; anyone is chastized if he embarks on a way of wrong-doing and corruption that endangers the fabric of society.

But there are persons who have no concern for others' interests and rights. They feel no remorse for cheating others and yet do not accept to be themselves cheated; they feel free to slander them, yet are immensely offended if they are slandered, forgetting that when God set forth His guiding laws, He made no allowance for one over the other, no matter how strong and wealthy the former, or how poor and deprived the latter. His justice is even-handed and its primary aim is to ensure the welfare of society as a whole, and to protect mankind from its own destructive desires.

When Allah decrees anything, His ultimate purpose is to educate and refine the human self, to nurture its inner spiritual values and to inculcate in it the values of justice and concern for the rights of others, thereby elevating man above all other creatures, and at the same time laying down the foundation for a healthy society that is guided and governed in its interactions by these divine laws.

In His discipline, Allah lays down the foundation for the kind of society that can live in harmony on earth. He alone has the power to do this because His power transcends all human power and knowledge. He has created this universe and harnessed its forces for the service of man. If Allah has created all these forces for the benefit of man, whose mental and physical powers are greatly limited, then He is better qualified to plan for him the perfect order for a righteous and happy life on this earth. Man, no matter how far his knowledge may reach or how vain and ambitious he may be, cannot pretend that he is better qualified than his Creator, nor can he match His skill in planning his own right way. Man is not without ambition and desires, and these shortcomings are likely to leave their mark on any plan he might set out for himself or for others. In contrast, Allah is without ambition, and as His ultimate purpose is the welfare of the whole of mankind, His plan is sure to be perfect and just.

If you were to meet a group of misguided persons who have avoided Allah's discipline and His right way, and you were to ask them to tell you who created this universe, they would unthinkingly say, "Allah". If, however, you pursue this dialogue a little further and ask them about their reasons for not adhering to His discipline or for resenting His decrees, you are mostly likely to get no answer from some of them, while others will challenge you with a man-made discipline which they equate with that of Allah, and are only too enthusiastic to convince you of its merits.

These unfortunate persons are indeed contradicting themselves. On the one hand they seem to acknowledge that the government of the whole of creation and the maintenance of this universe is in the hands of Allah and that it was He who established the laws for their operation and function; yet on the other hand, they are ready to reject those laws which He has established for the guidance and welfare of mankind. How can they turn away from this divine gift and substitute for it something which is marred with man's ambition and desires, exchanging Allah's perfect knowledge for the limited and inferior knowledge of man, thus equating the Creator with the created?

Faith must necessarily precede following Allah's discipline. Thus we find that when speaking to mankind, Allah always begins with the phrase "O ye who believe". It is repeated over and over again throughout the Qur'ān. This emphasis is made to show that following Allah's discipline cannot be realized without a solid foundation of faith in Him and His messengers, and that without this faith there is no spiritual value or gain in all we do, even if we strictly obey His commands. For instance, Allah has commanded us to give charity and help the poor. But charity whose purpose is to gain publicity and whose motivation is ostentation and not pure faith is worthless and gains no heavenly or spiritual rewards. The chief motive in charity should be Allah's pleasure. It follows, therefore, that the mechanical exercise of all deeds and acts of worship has no spiritual benefit unless they are based on an unshakable and deep-rooted faith.

Allah, in His glory, has no need for partners and approves of charity whose only motive is to seek His pleasure and nothing else. He does not accept it if, for the charity given, the giver obtains the slightest worldly benefit or gain.

The acceptance or rejection of charity and deeds is clarified in the ḥadīth of the Prophet (SAW) in which he says that deeds derive their worth from the motive behind them and that man's deeds will be judged in terms of his intention ('actions are but by intention'). For the seat of intention is in the heart, and Allah knows perfectly every hidden thought and motive in our minds and what our hearts conceal. But some foolish persons believe that they can beguile Allah. This arrogance is the core of mankind's dilemma.

For years, philosophers have been striving to find an answer to the question of Allah's existence. But in all their efforts they have relied on reason and their own mental resources and ignored the divine messages, thereby asking the mind to yield something for which it was not made. That is because the human mind was endowed with limited intelligence, sufficient to perceive and understand this material universe. It was, therefore, beyond man's ability to secure any evidence pertaining to the existence of Allah by using only his limited mental capacity and without the help of the divine messages in which He had imparted signs that are perceptible to the limited intelligence of man, and in which He gives him a reflection of His reality. But philosophers seem to be intent on overlooking this fact and continue to burden the human mind with a task beyond its reach.

In his messages to mankind, Allah has shown them the right way to worship Him. He explained it fully, and set down the spiritual rewards for righteousness and the penalties that wrong-doers must pay. The establishment of these laws is in itself a manifestation of Allah's sovereignty and presence. It would be difficult to imagine idols or any other man-made gods capable of sending messages to their worshippers explaining the rules of righteousness. We have never heard of a messenger being sent by the sun to teach the ancient Egyptians how to worship it. All these man-made gods were worshipped according to rules established by the same people who invented them.

Both logic and reason suggest that we should not delve into things that are beyond our reach and capacity. But despite his limitations, man, enticed by vanity and ignorance, still tries to penetrate this barrier of the Unseen. Not once, therefore, have any of the schools of philosophy which look beyond the material world been able to produce conclusions that agreed with what the other schools have been able to postulate. Each theory has contradicted the other, and none of them has produced anything acceptable to all minds.

We, as human beings, perceive this world through the five senses with which Allah has endowed us. It is through these senses that we are able to understand the world, give names to its varied elements and appreciate their properties. Thus we are able to distinguish between colours, between the ugly and the beautiful, between that which is bitter and that which is sweet and so on. But these faculties are virtually impotent where the world of the inner self, motives and emotions is concerned. How, then, can man make contact with this inner world? Some may say that contact is made through inspiration, or through nature, and so on. Nevertheless, the only certainty on which there is unanimous agreement is that what goes on within the self cannot be felt or perceived through our senses, even though we might be aware of them, and man can only be conscious of their existence. Thus, although we may be fully aware of our hunger, sadness, happiness, anger, and so on, we can neither touch, see, taste, smell, nor hear any of these feelings. A man may like, or dislike, a person for no logical reason at all, and no one has so far identified the faculty that could sense these feelings.

There are certain emotional reactions which cause us to be aware of certain feelings, and yet they are totally beyond the grasp of our senses. All our efforts to define and explain love and hate and how they are sensed have been in vain. Both feelings are completely independent and have no link with the other senses which connect us with the outside world. Scientists are always careful not to link these senses with the other internal endowments such as feeling, inspiration and all the other spiritual gifts which connect cognition with the realm of the inner self and influence it.

Thus, although a person who does not submit his thinking to the dictates of logic tends to deny the existence of these internal faculties, he is never able to produce a plausible explanation as to how these internal sensations are identified and processed. A remarkable fact about inspiration and its recognition is that it always arises before previous sensation about the external world. This is one of the wonders of creation. A hungry infant cries first, and then uses his senses to get in touch with the external world. He is born with an instinctive need for warmth, love and security, and can sense cruelty, aversion and anger. But whereas all these feelings are fully developed at birth, all the other senses may take months to reach their full development and efficiency.

If we study these internal feelings in a grown person, we realize that his feeling of the presence of Allah is most prominent in his awareness, despite its haziness and the numerous facts that need to be accommodated and the mystery that clouds them and makes them seem unintelligible to man's limited intelligence. This feeling affirms the existence of an inward power which compels us to sense and feel the presence of Allah.

Although our senses do not operate or respond in any way when the name of Allah is pronounced, His name is spontaneously sensed inwardly by an invisible faculty. Thus the overall meaning of the word 'Allah', whose perception is outside the capacity of our senses, is unmistakably grasped by these inward senses in some mysterious way which, although too difficult to be grasped and analysed, seems to be quite familiar and identifiable to these inner and non-physical faculties. Thus whenever the word 'Allah' is enunciated, the notion that emerges to our conscious mind is that of a mighty and all-encompassing power which is responsible for the creation of this universe and its order, and the perception of which is far beyond our senses and mental powers.

Though the ear is able to hear and register the word 'Allah', it nevertheless has no capacity to elucidate its meaning or its overwhelming connotations or give meaning to something that has not previously been identified, processed and preserved in memory.

How can we recognize this force? Why does Allah's name sound so familiar to us despite being beyond our senses, as well as our intellect? The answer to these questions comes from within us in the form of inspiration or feeling which tells us that this force, despite its invisibility, does indeed reside in us, and can be sensed and understood by the inner self.

In ancient times, Greek philosophers began to study phenomena beyond matter, or beyond the natural world and the power that created it. Here one may ask: what prompted them to search for such knowledge? How did they come to the notion that there was indeed some force behind the creation of all matter and that our senses are not the ultimate test for obtaining knowledge beyond this material world? We are not discussing the merits of this philosophy. What concerns us here is to seek out the reasons that prompted them to look beyond the immediate physical world, or beyond that which was perceptible only to their limited physical senses.

Since the dawn of history man has never ceased to search for something beyond the material world, perhaps as a way of expressing his submission and humility to this majestic, supernatural and spiritual power. What is important is that man since his creation has always inwardly felt that there was a power behind this visible universe. Indeed, there is an inborn feeling in all of us that tells us that Allah exists, and that He is the true power behind this universe. It is this same intuition that makes us believe that this universe cannot function without the government of that glorious and unimaginable power.

But this material world cannot by itself create in us this feeling, nor can our senses alone reveal to us the nature of this power. It follows, therefore, that a power other than this material world must have endowed us with this feeling and inspired us to look for it beyond the immediate material world. This is how the quest for this power, and our surrendering ourselves to it, began.

Man does not usually begin to think profoundly and purposefully about Allah's existence before he has reached the age of twenty years, or even later, when his intellect and reasoning ability have reached an appropriate degree of maturity capable of contemplating and discussing such intricate and unseen phenomena. The question that forces itself upon us is: How did people condition themselves to worship Allah before reaching this stage of mature thinking and what was their guiding logic? How did they comprehend this complex philosophy and come, with their limited resources of insufficient education, knowledge, logical reasoning, and insight, to realize that there ought to be another power, beyond this material world? But we also notice that simple people who have no education, who know nothing about matter and have never been tempted to discuss this issue, seem to take for granted the existence of Allah, and worship Him, never finding any conflict between this material world and the existence of its Creator. Most of them feel an inborn and natural certainty that the material world and Allah cannot be separated, and cannot be understood in isolation from each other.

If we are inwardly convinced of Allah's existence, what then is the true cause of this anxiety which grips mankind and has given rise to modern doctrines and theories aimed either at confirming Allah's existence or denying it? What are the true motives underlying this paradoxical attitude which defies our inborn faith in His existence? All evidence points to man's desires and ambitious lust. The human mind, in its attempts to undertake a task far beyond its capacity and natural endowment, and failing to come up with any logical conclusion, resorts to imagination and conjecture.

The following example may clarify what is meant here. If I were sitting in a room with the door shut and heard someone knock at the door, my senses would tell me that someone was standing outside. This is something that is within their power. Yet these same senses cannot reveal the identity of the person who is knocking. If I try to guess his identity my imagination may furnish me with a number of guesses, none of which may be true.

Some philosophers have done just this in trying to identify Allah or get a glimpse of Him. This is not possible however, for the human mind to grasp, for in order to imagine something, its form and substance must be capable of assimilation. For example, when you try to explain to someone the form or shape of a certain object he will never be able to grasp it until you give him a comparison. You may say to him "it looks like a ball". Only then will he understand that you are talking about a spherical object. In fact, you have moved the notion from the realm of imagination to the realm of reason, making it possible for the person to visualize the object. But Allah is unlike anything we know in this material world. It follows, therefore, that all that the philosophers said did not go beyond the realm of imagination and could not in any way be conceived by the human mind or appeal to logic. If they had resorted to logic, they would not have deviated from the truth, for Allah has informed us clearly and precisely of what He wants us to know about Him and how to worship Him. But man's vanity and folly urge him to fly beyond the places he could reach, resulting in total perdition. If we adhered to what He has planned and ordained for us, we would never stray from sound logic and reason, for with logic and reason we will come to realize that Allah resides naturally in all of us. Both will guide us as to the best way of worshipping and obeying Him. For whereas logic urges us to follow the heavenly messages, imagination entices us to search for something that is beyond all human mental powers, and causes us to lose our bearings. Indeed in these divine messages is laid down the most valid evidence about the nature of Allah and His existence.

Now let us examine the deeper meaning of the word 'horizons' (āfāq) in the following verse:

> "We shall show them Our portents on the horizons and within themselves until it will be manifest unto them that it is the Truth . . ." (Fuṣṣilat 41:53)

Why has Allah said 'horizon' (āfāq) and not 'earth' (arḍ)? We know that the Qur'ān is truly Allah's diction, and that every word spoken is carefully and accurately selected to fit the precise meaning desired. In fact, Allah is saying that He will unfold to future generations, in His own time, some more portents ('horizons') of His existence, which until now

He has not disclosed. Perhaps man's landing on the moon and his attempts to explore the other planets and uncover the secrets of the horizons around the planet Earth may conform with the information imparted in the above verse. But some people are fascinated by their petty scientific knowledge and seem to forget that all knowledge comes from Allah at His will and in His own time. They try to philosophize in matters of worship regardless of their limited knowledge and mental capacity. Thus we find that some orientalists attempt to cast doubts upon the divine origin of the Qur'ān. For example, they single out the verse in which Allah says:

> "Unto Allah belong the East and the West, and whithersoever you turn, there is Allah's Countenance . . ." (al-Baqarah 2:115)

They argue that, despite the clarity of this verse and its indication that Muslims can face in any direction when praying, they are elsewhere, told to face the Inviolable Place of Worship in Makkah, and that failure to do so cancels prayer. They also demand why, if Allah is present everywhere, worshippers should be forced to face the Ka'bah when praying.

Any answer to this presumption must take into consideration man's faith in Allah and His all-encompassing knowledge. Once a man has reached this unwavering faith, he will soon realise how far from perfect is his judgement in matters of worship. He will be anxious to commit himself into the hands of this All-Wise God, knowing that He is the best judge as to what is good for him and how he should conduct his duties of worship. This is, in fact, the core of faith, for there is no comparison between the power and knowledge of Allah and that of man. In fact, belief in Allah is the prelude to faith.

Indeed, man's facing the Qiblah (the direction of the Ka'bah) does not imply an extra duty to worshippers or involve any more effort than they would otherwise exert when facing any other place on the globe.

Now let us contemplate the following verse:

> "The foolish of the people will say: What has turned them from the Qiblah which they formerly observed? . . ." (al-Baqarah 2:142)

One should be aware here of the use of the future tense (sayaqūl) which is used to indicate future events. This verse indicates that the act had not yet happened but would come to pass at some time in the future. Thus Allah says "The fools will say". He already knew that they would be critical when the first Qiblah was changed. But Allah, Who knew all the plans of the enemies of His faith and what they concealed, revealed to His messenger the criticism that would result, long before it actually did. But this verse, in revealing to these critics their secret plans, challenged them either to desist from making the criticism or to carry it out. This challenge in itself is seen as a miracle, in that it told those heretics what they would do, described them as foolhardy and gave them freedom of choice. But Allah knew that they would not change and, therefore, passed His judgement on them in this divine verse. But the Qur'ān is Allah's Word: it will not be changed and will remain intact until the Last Day. What would have happened if, when these heretics heard the revelation, they had decided not to question the change of the position of the Qiblah, and had remained silent? If they had devised such a plan, they would have damaged the whole religion by challenging the authenticity of the verse and by accusing Muḥammad (SAW) of concocting the whole message.

Because Allah was the speaker and designer, He foiled their scheme by using their allegations against the Qur'ān as supporting evidence for its validity and confirmation. He predicted in His own divine words, that some foolish people would emerge who would mock the changing of the Qiblah from its previously established direction towards Jerusalem to the Inviolable House of Worship in Makkah. As Allah predicted, they indeed came and repeated Allah's words, thereby confirming the authenticity and miraculous nature of the Qur'ān.

The change of the Qiblah represented a worthy miracle, for through it Allah has challenged the enemies of Islam in an issue in which they had freedom of choice. When the Qur'ān states that "Unto God belongs the East and the West" it is likewise manifesting this miraculousness. For it disclosed that Islam would eventually spread throughout the whole world, and that all believers would turn towards the Ka'bah in their prayers. In reality, one direction or another does not matter, because in order to face the Ka'bah one worshipper may have to turn to the west, another to the east or to the north and so on, despite the fact that they are all facing the Qiblah. Furthermore, prayer is correct and accepted if a worshipper fails to find the right direction and chooses a direction which he considers to be as near as possible to the correct direction. Similarly, prayers can be practised wherever we are, in whatever circumstance, at whatever time and at whatever place. Thus, prayers may be practised on a plane or ship regardless of their constantly changing course. The Qiblah stands as a symbol of unity for Muslims and their submission and humility to Allah.

During the pilgrimage, pilgrims are commanded to kiss one stone, and to cast pebbles at another. Both actions are done without questioning the motive behind these acts. The pilgrims do them because Allah has commanded them to do so. They know that He has His reasons and purpose. In this situation, a person is either completely governed and motivated by his faith in Allah, both as a worshipper and a slave who strictly obeys, executes and carries out contentedly and humbly all that which He has commanded him to do; or he acts as a faithless heretic who scoffs at all divine directives and behaves like a man who follows the dictates of his own mind and reason, hoping to rival Allah's knowledge. Such a man is prone to steer clear of Allah's way with the ultimate result of bringing upon himself His condemnation and wrath. He is like a sick man who ignores his doctor's orders, thereby endangering his own life.

Allah has put man's mind at ease, and spared him a great deal of anxiety and misery by providing him, in His divine messages, with the guidance and knowledge which illuminates his path and shows him the way to the good life. But some people reject this guidance and care, and prefer to embark on a path that leads to nothing but weariness of mind and damnation of soul.

Allah has chosen the areas of belief in Him and of worship as the most reliable test of man's sincerity of faith and devotion. He did not extend this test to any other area. He made them a test of the human self and soul by showing man the right way to worship Him as the one true God and by asking him to prove his sincerity of faith by following what He has permitted him to do, and desisting from what He has forbidden him. For obedience and sincerity are but the sum and substance of faith, and sincere faith dictates that man should worship Allah according to His divine law and not according to his own man-made law.

Perhaps the changing of the direction of the Qiblah was meant to be a test of faith for the Muslims. Surely to turn east or west does not require any effort. But God says:

> ". . . And we appointed the Qiblah which ye formerly observed only that We might know him who follows the messenger from him who turns on his heels. In truth it was a hard test save for those whom Allah guided. But it was not Allah's purpose that your faith should be in vain, for Allah is full of pity, Merciful toward mankind." (al-Baqarah 2:143)

Those who dispute the cause of faith have never been able to come up with any valid evidence in support of their case and always tend to avoid any discussion about the sum and substance of the message and the way which Allah established for His worshippers. Although they are always ready to contend that the Qur'ān cannot be Allah's word, they never seem to be able to disprove it on empirical grounds. In fact all their logic and reason is motivated by vanity and ambition which they try to satisfy and realise by substituting Allah's law with their own laws, in the hope of securing for themselves more rights than those initially granted to them by Allah, and at the same time robbing others of these divine rights.

Moreover, those heretics, in their attempts to beguile the unwary, resort to unfounded scientific hypotheses which have never been tested or proven. Darwin's theory on the origin of man is one such example. In this theory Darwin speculated that man belonged initially to the ape species, yet neither he nor anyone else throughout history has seen an ape change into a human being.

If the theory of evolution is true, how can those who expound it explain the reasons why we cannot distinguish between one bird and another, or between one horse and another of the same species? Despite the fact that the whole human race shares identical features which distinguish it from the animal species, each individual has his distinct features that make him unique and unlike the rest of the whole of mankind; and although we are the same in terms of physiological structure, each one of us has his own distinguishing features. Thus each individual is easily recognizable from among millions. You will instantly identify your own son from among all the other children in the school. There are 12 million people living in Cairo, yet you will be able to identify a relative or a friend without the slightest difficulty. In contrast, one will find it very difficult to single out a certain cow from a herd of cows. The task will be almost impossible if the herd contains a hundred or more cows. The same thing applies to all other species. Allah has given every man distinctive features so that he can live according to the way He has planned for him. He has distinguished him so that he can be judged in the Hereafter. Without such a distinction man's life would be difficult, and it would be impossible for him to be a witness against himself on the day of Judgement. In fact, this differentiation among men is so exact that there is no one on earth who has the same finger-prints as another. This feature will continue to be so until the end of time. Man is an image that is never repeated. This is exemplified in the portraits and statues of ancient kings who died centuries ago. Thus we can easily identify the features of Cleopatra, Rameses and Napoleon from the statues and portraits which were made of them, hundreds or thousands of years ago. For each man stands unique and different from all other men. His own features and identity can never be reproduced, regardless of the continuous generations. In this way, each man is identified and singled out to give account of his deeds and be judged. This individual differentiation has not come about accidentally or through evolution. It is the wonderful work of Allah. About this Allah says:

> "We will show them Our portents on the horizons and within themselves until it will be manifest unto them that it is the Truth . . ." (Fuṣṣilat 41:53)

The human brain, which is encased in a small area in the skull, consists of 23 billion cells whose function is to interpret the outside world and give it meaning. It transmits signals to every other cell in the body, telling them how to protect this body and enable it to exercise its functions. There are three thousand taste buds on the tongue, whose task is to distinguish between tastes. All these complex and highly specialised physiological cell structures and their functions could not have developed by the mere process of evolution. The immense developmental gap between man and the animal kingdom can only be the work of a supreme divine power.

Within man are inborn endowments unknown to him. Allah has left them latent and outside his conscious awareness. As a result, not infrequently he seems to be incapable of understanding some of his own reactions and motives, or what goes on deep within his inner self. In fact, human behaviour has not, until the present, been fully explored or completely defined. There are many laws which govern our behaviour and reactions, over which we seem to have no control. For instance, when man likes or loves a person he does not know why he likes him, while to others he may appear loathsome and unworthy of friendship or love. Hate and love are, therefore, two emotions for which the human mind has no conceivable laws. In fact, there is much in these feelings that seem to defy reason and logic in many cases. The human self is rather a combination of both reason and irrationality, self-denial and selfishness. It will remain as such until the Last Day.

Chapter 3

Thoughts on Sūrah al-Kahf (the Cave)

In discussing the meanings embedded in the Qur'ān, one should be aware of the implicit and underlying wisdom of its verses. It is not uncommon for the reader of the Qur'ān to miss certain meanings which Allah intended us to contemplate. This does not mean however, that one should ascribe to the words of the Qur'ān any meaning other than that which they actually possess. Scholars, in their attempts to keep pace with modern trends and meet the challenges they face from science and sceptical doctrines, may try to find a common ground between some of the spectacular new scientific theories and the miraculous portents revealed in the Qur'ān, or to try to find evidence to support the Qur'ān with these theories or these theories from the Qur'ān. The danger of such practices lies in the fact that scientific theories are susceptible to modification and misinterpretation. Indeed, the situation would be precarious and damaging to the whole religion if it so happened that we used one of these scientific theories to validate some Qur'ānic facts, only to discover, later, that the theory was false. It is, therefore, neither wise nor desirable that our enthusiasm cause us to search the Qur'ān for facts which accord with any modern scientific hypothesis or discovery. The Qur'ān is, in the first place, a religious scripture and not a textbook and as such should never be used as source material for explaining science. In fact, Allah explicitly defined the main purpose of the Qur'ān when He said:

> "This is the Scripture whereof there is no doubt, a guidance unto those who ward off evil; who believe in the Unseen, and establish worship, and spend of that which We have bestowed upon them."
> (al-Baqarah 2:2-3)

In these few words, Allah defines the whole purpose of the Qur'ān as being a guidance for believers.

As has already been mentioned, those who study the Qur'ān should be sensitive to the meanings implicit in the Revelation. For Allah has placed within the Qur'ān many signs that are worthy of profound contemplation and thought. Sūrah al-Kahf serves as a great indication of this because of the many mystical facts it contains and the challenge it offers to the inquisitive mind.

As we all know, a cave, or kahf in Arabic, from which the Sūrah derives its name, is a cavity found on the side of a mountain. Allah has created these caves in nature so that we can discover for ourselves how they look and what impression they make upon our senses.

No one can truly know how impressive a cave is unless he has had the opportunity to explore one. Therefore the title of the passage should not pass without some thought. If we do skim over it, we will soon come to realise that the passage abounds with moral caves, or things which reveal many of the mystic facts about events which take place in this universe. This is exemplified in the story of Moses and the good slave (al-Kahf 18:65) (a man whom Allah favoured with unlimited knowledge). The true meaning of this is that we should not judge things according to their external features. The scuttling of the boat (18:71) that was owned by poor people, which Moses judged as an evil act, was in actual fact a good deed, because it saved those who owned it from an unjust tyrant king who had planned to seize the boat. Likewise, the slaying of the young lad (18:74) appeared, on the surface, to be a wicked sin, but this deed had behind it the good motive of saving his virtuous parents and rewarding them with new offspring free from evil. So was the building of the wall (18:77) for the inhospitable villagers who refused to give them food or hospitality. Although it did not appeal to logic as a good deed, the truth behind it is that it was built to protect a treasure which was left to two orphaned children by their dead father. If the wall had been left to collapse, the villagers would have taken the treasure and deprived the children of receiving it when they reached adulthood.

These parables cannot be summed up in a few lines, but at least give an indication of just how significant the word 'cave' actually is. Allah wishes to impress on us in this Sūrah certain facts which are mostly implied and not easily accessible to human comprehension. This also serves to remind us not to take things at their face value or be deceived by superficiality, for what is sometimes interpreted as wicked and evil can in actual fact be a blessing in disguise.

The Meaning of the Cave:

The cave which Allah mentions in this Sūrah was an actual cave in which seven Christian youths, who firmly believed in Allah, once hid. They fell asleep and remained asleep for some generations. The cave is, in fact, the symbol of a sanctuary where faith is protected from the tyranny of disbelief and oppression.

Three parables may help to clarify some of the facts that at the time the Qur'ān was first revealed were mysteries to man.

The first of these parables is concerned with Dhū'l-Qarnayn or Alexander the Great.

The actual historical personage of Alexander – however, is not to be dwelled on here as it merely distracts from the main point of the Qur'ān's teaching. This applies throughout where individuals are mentioned primarily to serve as universal symbols. All that matters is the person to whom these characteristics apply, regardless of time or place. Thus Noah's wife and Lot's wife are types which stand for every woman who betrays a good and virtuous husband. Likewise, when Allah mentions Pharaoh's wife, He means every chaste woman who believes in Him and whose husband is a heretic. These incidents are not restricted in time or place. They recur throughout history. The only incident that has not been, and will not be, repeated is Mary's story. This is the reason why Allah has identified her as "Mary daughter of 'Imrān", her full name. It is evident, therefore that when we mention Alexander, we are in fact referring to a man whom Allah has enabled to possess all that he longed for and has given the means to do everything. We should not concern ourselves with Alexander's identity lest we be distracted from the moral point that Allah wants to stress.

Now let us turn our attention to the following important verse, where we are told:

> "Till, when he reached the rising-place of the sun, he found it rising on a people for whom We had appointed no shelter therefrom." (al-Kahf 18:90)

The story ends at that point, and the Sūrah shifts to another topic. In the above verse, Allah did not say more than that Alexander had reached a people whom He had not provided with protection from the sun's heat. What does Allah wish to say, and what does the sentence "for whom we had appointed no shelter therefrom" actually mean? Does it mean that this people's land was barren, without vegetation or trees to protect its dwellers from the burning sun?

Does it mean that they had no homes to live in, or perhaps wore no clothes? Any of these conjectures is possible. But the sun is always present irrespective of these shelters which, although they may not protect them from the sun, cannot completely hide it or eclipse it; what actually causes the sun to disappear is darkness or nightfall. It is only at night that the sun is veiled and cannot be seen.

In preceding verses it is revealed that Allah has established the duties that are binding upon anyone who is given the means to rule others. It also mentions how Alexander reached a tract between two mountains where he found people who did not understand a word he said to them, and how he taught them to defend themselves against the attacks of Gog and Magog.

The inquisitive reader of the Sūrah may wonder that although Allah has told us about the work that Alexander carried out on his arrival at "the setting-place of the sun" and the work he did when he arrived at the two mountains, He did not tell us about anything that he might have done when he arrived at the "rising-place of the sun". All we know is that when he arrived there he met a people for whom Allah had denied shelter from the sun.

Because every word in the Qur'ān is exact and every verse has a specific meaning and a definite purpose, it is obvious that there is some important hidden fact about the sun that Allah wants us to discover. He did not mention Alexander's work so that we would be distracted by it and miss the point. In fact, the important point which He wanted us to look at is that in his expeditions Alexander reached a land where the sun set for only a very short time and did not follow the same pattern as that of the rest of the world. It is now common knowledge in the polar regions the sun sets for nearly six months leaving the land in total darkness. Allah wanted to tell us that there are places on earth that do not follow the normal pattern of day and night experienced by the rest of the world.

As mentioned before, the actual cave referred to in Sūrah al-Kahf was that used by seven Christian youths who, fearing Roman persecution, sought refuge in it. The lesson that Allah wants to teach us is that faith in Him is always present, even when the whole world seems to be in the grip of heresy and oppression. It might be hidden from us, but in truth it is alive.

In addition to this spiritual lesson, the Sūrah relates other miracles, which Allah wants us to reflect upon.

The first miracle describes how He put the seven youths to sleep,

> "Then We sealed up their hearing in the Cave for a number of years." (al-Kahf 18:11)

In this verse, we are told that unlike all other sense organs the ear is the only sense organ that is always active and is never dormant. Our ears are constantly receptive whether we wish to hear or not, and we cannot stop them from functioning naturally. This is not the case with the eyes, over which we have control.

The important thing that Allah wants us to learn is that if we isolate the ear from the noise of the world, a person will go to sleep for a very long period of time. Thus when He wanted to put the dwellers of the cave to sleep for years, He did not shut off their sight, or slow their heartbeat, as is the case when we are in a state of normal sleep, but He simply sealed off their hearing, as the most effective way of isolating them from the world.

The verse continues to tell us more about these sleepers:

> "And you would have deemed them waking though they were asleep, and We caused them to turn over to the right and to the left . . ." (al-Kahf 18:18)

Here one should pause to reflect as to why they were made to turn over to the right and to the left, and what purpose Allah has in telling us this. Every word in the Qur'ān has its intrinsic meaning and purpose which is sometimes obvious and at other times remains veiled for generations.

Reading this Sūrah, we discover that Allah has made the resurrection of these seven youths a portent to mankind, by setting down the health rules to be observed in the case of sick persons who are forced to lie in bed for long periods of time. Such sick persons are advised nowadays to keep changing their sleeping position to avoid circulatory complications, ulceration of the skin and blood clotting in the lower region of their bodies and legs.

Allah's will

> "And say not of any thing: Lo! I shall do that tomorrow, except if Allah will. And remember your Lord when you forget . . ." (al-Kahf 18:23-24)

We should give deep thought to this verse because of its immense bearing on behaviour and attitudes. Not infrequently, people seem to be oblivious to their limitations and tend to take the future for granted, forgetting that they have no power over their destiny. Yet it is not uncommon to hear someone say "I'll do so and so tomorrow", thereby ascribing to himself power and knowledge that only Allah possesses. One who makes such an assertion should have total control over variables such as time, health, transport and myriad other circumstances. In other words, if one says that he will meet a certain person tomorrow, he must have the power to stay alive until that hour. But no mortal has the power to stop death for a few minutes, let alone hours and days. The statement is inevitably false because there is no certainty as to whether they will be alive then. Life is entirely in Allah's hands. The ability to go to the meeting is also beyond one's control. There are so many unexpected circumstances that could intervene and hinder one from fulfilling plans. Even if death does not catch up with one, there is no guarantee that a meeting will take place, simply because of the lack of control over the running of events. In addition to all these uncontrollable circumstances, there are also myriad hazards that can jeopardize one's plans.

The important thing to remember is that mortals are in no position to impose their wills on the future. It is only Allah Who has the power to say unto a thing "Be" and it is. He is Eternal and nothing distracts His attention or stands against His will and decrees. There is no other power that can obstruct, halt, adjourn, delay or advance what He commands or ordains. He alone has the power and freedom of action and fulfilment. It follows, therefore, that anything one plans must hinge on His will, and that actions achieve their end only if they are in line with His will.

The second part of the verse reminds one not to forget Allah. ". . . And remember your Lord when you forget" (18:24). Here Allah wants to stress the fact that He alone is the Efficient, and man, being created of dust, cannot do much. In other words, Allah wants man to realise his inferiority and not become deluded by vanity.

It is Allah Who has granted man the power to do things. He has created this universe and enabled man to harness its elements and tap its wealth. He has granted all this to a creature made of a handful of dust. In his own creation there are lessons for him to reflect upon. Furthermore, Allah cautions us that all we enjoy and possess in this world could not have materialized without His will, and that He can take it all back if He so desires.

It is a gentle reminder to those persons who show no compassion for the weak and the needy that it is He Who has given them their wealth and power and Who can easily take them back if they act as if they are lords over their destiny and fate.

The following verse sums up the whole issue:

> "If only, when you entered your garden, you had said: That which Allah willeth (will come to pass)! There is no strength save in Allah! Though you see me as less than you in wealth and children, yet it may be that my Lord will give me better than your garden . . ." (al-Kahf 18:39-40)

This verse corrects the proud man's confused ideas and puts things back in their right perspective. The poor man here reminds his companion of Allah's will, which he has forgotten, and draws his attention to the fact that Allah is the true Giver, and, were it not for His means, it would not be possible to acquire such a garden and authority. Here we should remember the moral cave mentioned earlier, for the giving here is hidden inside the cave of reality. The Giver is Allah. But this reality is hidden. This is the kind of reality that is expressed in the comment of the man with less money and offspring when he says,

> "Yet it may be that my Lord will give me better than thy garden, and will send on it a bolt from heaven, and some morning it will be a smooth hillside, or some morning the water thereof will be lost in the earth so that you cannot make search for it." (al-Kahf 18:40-41)

Why has Allah only emphasized these two penalties? Why did the man not say to him that Allah could strike him dead for his arrogance or inflict him with a sickness that would incapacitate him?

The answer is that these two main favours are more responsible than the other favours for the productivity of this garden and the prosperity of its owner. They also represent two divine acts and refer to powers that are totally beyond man's control. Therefore the arrogant man cannot claim that the flourishing of his crop and the productivity of the land were entirely due to his own labour and plans. Here Allah reminds us of His power which, though hidden from us, is responsible for all our prosperity. The water which irrigated this garden was not initially created by the ungrateful man, nor was it provided by him. It was Allah Who made it available to him. Indeed, after fourteen centuries and since the revelation of this verse, mankind has not been able to make one glass of water by using materials other than those which were originally created by Allah. One finds a good example in the vast deserts of the world. If man had been able to create water, he could have turned these deserts into fruitful green lands. Yet man, with all his knowledge, could not make one single river, but Allah's power has provided this earth with thousands of rivers, sufficient for the needs of man, animals and plants.

Allah's providence does not end there, for He also protects plants and crops from all natural hazards such as floods, gales and pests which could destroy them.

Water is, therefore, the main source of all productivity and the welfare of man, and only Allah can provide it in such abundance.

Then Allah tells us what the poor man said,

> "Or some morning the water thereof will be lost in the earth so that you cannot make search for it." (18:41)

Here we are informed that the availability of water is not in itself a guarantee that gardens or plants will grow and become fruitful, but that they also need protection from floods, gales and pests, over which man has no control.

But Allah can also withhold His favours from one person or another if He so desires, and man has no power to intervene or prevent His decision or alter its course once it has been made.

From the above discussion it is clear that Allah wants to emphasize two realities which are sometimes overlooked. The first is that it is He Who provides to this green land in which we live water, which is the main source of all human and plant life; and the second is that He protects it from destruction. Because both actions are beyond his power, man cannot pretend that his prosperity is entirely of his own making. Although man may sow the seeds and water the soil, it is Allah's will that causes the seed to germinate and grow into a plant and the soil to become fertile, and it is He who protects the crop from disaster.

The lesson continues in the next verse wherein we are told that:

> "And his fruit was beset (with destruction). Then began he to wring his hands for all that he had spent upon it, when (now) it was all ruined on its trellises, and to say: Would that I had ascribed no partner to my Lord!" (al-Kahf 18:42)

It is obvious that Allah had destroyed this man's crop to teach him how powerless and weak he was, and that his wealth and his men whom he thought provided him with all the safety and power he needed in this world could do him neither good nor harm, nor was there any human or material power capable of halting Allah's design once it had been ordained. He had been given his garden by the will of Allah; but when he became oblivious of this fact and put his trust in his wealth and his offspring Allah took back His favours, leaving him destitute, so that he would learn of his own arrogance.

Then suddenly he realized how foolish he was, and looked around for support, but found none,

> "And he had no troop of men to help him against Allah, nor could he save himself." (al-Kahf 18:43)

Even if he had found such support, it would have proved powerless against Allah's will.

Finally, at the moment of truth, he is overcome with feelings of remorse and guilt; saying:

> "Would that I had ascribed no partner to my Lord." (al-Kahf 18:43)

He is in no doubt about his dilemma. He knows that all he owned in this world was from Allah, and that the Giver has punished him by taking it back.

Chapter 4

Allah's Knowledge and Human Knowledge

When dealing with parables in the Qur'ān, one should not be too concerned with names, for names for their own sake have no significance and neither add nor detract from the moral lesson which the parables are intended to teach. The divine purpose of a parable is to enrich us with wisdom and insight. In fact the only two holy persons in the whole of the Qur'ān who are called by their complete family names are Mary and Jesus. Thus Mary is always referred to as 'Mary, daughter of 'Imrān', and Jesus as 'Jesus, son of Mary'. The reason for this identification is that their miracle was not to be repeated. All the other characters mentioned in the Qur'ān, such as the Pharaoh at the time of Moses, and Dhū'l-Qarnayn, were all left without complete identification or reference to their family mainly to spare us unnecessary and never-ending arguments about their identity while at the same time ensuring that one's attention is constantly focused on the lesson.

In the parable of Moses and the good slave mentioned in Sūrah al-Kahf, all one needs to know is that the latter was a man whom Allah endowed with great knowledge; while Pharaoh is a symbol of every unjust and oppressive man who worships mundane power, and Dhū'l-Qarnayn is a symbol of every man to whom Allah has given the means to rule justly.

Sūrah al-Kahf tells us how Moses met the good slave:

> "Then found they one of Our slaves, unto whom We had given mercy from Us, and had taught him knowledge from Our presence." (al-Kahf 18:65)

The good slave referred to in the above verse was a man freed from the ordinary happenings of daily life who was entitled to interpret the inner meaning events. He knew the secrets of the paradoxes of life which ordinary people either do not understand or misinterpret.

The above verse refers to a symbolic cave concealing a divine truth; for as Moses was Allah's Messenger, it should follow that all knowledge would be transmitted to mankind through him. But Allah wants to inform us of His unrestricted will and His freedom to choose from among His worshippers someone upon whom He would bestow greater wisdom than He would otherwise bestow upon His apostles and prophets.

The parable of the good slave reflects a series of incidents (or symbolic caves) whose true meaning is not immediately apparent. Moses was no exception, for while he witnessed the external apparent acts he was unable to understand their underlying purpose: hence his impatience and misunderstanding of the peculiar behaviour of the good slave and the strange acts he performed. But the good slave was fully aware of Moses' limited aptitude in higher knowledge and of his impatience, and seemed reluctant when Moses requested to accompany him on his travels in order to be taught.

> ". . . Lo! you cannot bear with me." (al-Kahf 18:67)

then added,

> "How can you bear with that whereof you cannot compass any knowledge?" (al-Kahf 18:68)

Throughout his quest for this higher knowledge, Moses judged events in terms of his imperfect knowledge. The good slave's actions however were always motivated by that special knowledge with which Allah had favoured him. Because of this special knowledge, the good slave's actions, although appearing to be wicked, were actually aimed at preventing evil results. Moses' limitations caused him to judge the good slave's actions only by their appearance while their underlying, intrinsic wisdom was beyond his perception.

Like all mortals, he could see only the apparent motives of an act or deed, because he was not gifted with an insight capable of understanding the divine acts.

Only Allah knows the inner motives and sincerity of human acts. A hypocrite, for example, may perform the five daily prayers in order to give the impression that he is a virtuous believer, while he disobeys Allah's injunctions in his other affairs. To the casual observer he is as virtuous as the believer who prays in search of Allah's pleasure and mercy. But Allah knows which one is sincere and which one is using prayer as a disguise for his lack of virtue. He can also distinguish between men who give charity for the purpose of gaining fame or material rewards, and those who give it in the hope of gaining Allah's pleasure and His eternal rewards.

There are many examples of such symbolic caves in our worldly affairs. Actually, life is but a world of caves inside which are concealed many truths. We often try to delude ourselves and others by veiling our unlawful deeds in good intentions, or inflicting harm on others under the guise of mercy and concern for their welfare.

The Conflict of the Two Judgements

When the good slave's and Moses' judgements clashed and the latter became incapable of understanding the paradoxes of the good slave's actions, he acknowledged his limitations and hasty judgement and said:

> "Allah willing, you shall find me patient and I shall not in aught gainsay thee." (al-Kahf 18:69)

No man from whom the secrets of such divine acts were concealed could have stifled his curiosity in the face of such paradoxes. Only a person commissioned by Allah, who knew of their intended outcome, could have exercised such patience and self-restraint. Moses, lacking such foresight, could not hold back his desire for an explanation. Finally, the good slave asked Moses to promise not to ask any more questions until he was ready to explain his actions to him.

This verse illustrates how man, in the absence of immediate explanations for divine acts, is prone to become impatient. This lack of patience and faith in Allah's wisdom is one of man's most common weaknesses. We are always impatient to seek rapid explanations of all divine acts, and to question Allah's wisdom. If we were endowed with the divine gift to see beyond the immediate situation, our judgement would possibly be different.

Because of this limitation in one's capacity to foresee an ultimate purpose in divine acts, one is often hasty in judging them according to their apparent outcome, or in being deceived by what one sees. We should not take for granted that what at present seems to be good for us will inevitably be beneficial for us in the long run, or that what appears to be bad for us is necessarily so. For evil sometimes comes to us in the guise of goodness, and vice versa. It is not uncommon for us to feel elated when we achieve some success or satisfy a long wished-for desire, only to discover later that it was a curse in disguise. One might long to possess a car, working hard to make this wish come true, and then a few days later one could be involved in a crash. Likewise, a man may feel upset because he has missed his flight, but a few hours later he may consider himself the luckiest man on earth when he learns that the plane has exploded in mid-air.

Examples of such curses and blessings in disguise are numerous. They form an integral part of our daily life and activities. Millions of us have experienced or been witnesses to such paradoxes. How often has one grieved over the loss of an opportunity to obtain a certain job, only to be grateful that it never materialized when you later discover that the job you obtained a few months later was a more rewarding one? How often have you thanked Allah for having denied you something that you had desired intensely, because you later discovered that getting it would have brought with it misfortune of one sort or another?

Despite our knowledge of Allah's wisdom and judgement

in concealing from us the real good or evil of the opportunities that He provides for us as a test of our faith in His wisdom, we are never able to check our impatience. Patience can be nurtured only through faith in His wisdom and purpose. A true believer should know that there is good in whatever Allah chooses for him and unhappiness in whatever He withholds from him.

Returning to the parable of Moses and the good slave, we see how theory is put into practice. To theorize about something is one thing and to put thoughts into action is another. When real action, not mere words, is in progress, man seems to be overcome and governed by external impressions that the action impinges upon him. This is a common reaction for everyone. The psychological effects of the spoken word and the actual action are immensely different, for while man can have some control on his reactions to spoken words, or narrated action, he is prone to lose this control in the face of emotional excitement once the words are put into action.

According to the story, Moses and the good slave boarded a boat which was crowded with people who had been reduced to great poverty and deserved great commiseration, the more so because they preferred earning an honest living to begging for charity. They did not know that the boat would be seized by an unjust king. Had the boat been taken from these self-respecting people, they would have been reduced to utter destitution and forced to beg. By the simple act of making it unseaworthy, the boat was saved from being seized. Because the damage was not serious, the boat could be repaired once the risk of its being seized by the king had passed.

But Moses saw in the damaging of the boat a wicked act that violated Allah's laws and injunctions which dictated that they should assist these people and alleviate their misery, rather than add to it. He gave vent to his displeasure, lost his patience and reproached the good slave:

> ". . . Have you made a hole therein to drown the folk thereof? You verily have done a dreadful thing." (al-Kahf 18:71)

At this point the good slave reminded him of the pledge he had made earlier and said to him:

> ". . . Did I not tell you that you could not bear with me?" (al-Kahf 18:72)

Moses quickly realized his breach, saying to the good slave:

> ". . . Be not wroth with me that I forgot, and be not hard upon me for my fault." (al-Kahf 18:73)

If Allah had bestowed on Moses the same knowledge that He had bestowed on the good slave, he would undoubtedly have done exactly the same thing as the good slave did. But his lack of awareness rendered him prey to impatience and susceptible to judging events on the basis of their outward appearances.

Continuing their journey they then encountered a young lad whom the good slave put to death. Moses saw this as a more wicked and sinful act than the scuttling of the boat. He forgot his earlier pledge, asking the good slave:

> ". . . Have you slain an innocent soul who has slain no man? Verily you have done a horrid thing."
> (al-Kahf 18:74)

Here lies the distinction between a person who knows the hidden truth and a person from whom it has been concealed. But this unprovoked slaying of an innocent person seemed so inhumane and cruel that Moses could no longer restrain himself from seeking an explanation.

Once more the good slave reminded him of his pledge not to ask further questions, to which Moses replied apologetically:

> ". . . If I ask you after this concerning aught, keep not company with me. You have received an excuse from me." (al-Kahf 18:76)

In other words, Moses would not feel offended if the good slave declined his company after once again breaking his promise.

They then travelled together until they came to a village. They were tired and hungry and expected some hospitality. But the villagers, contrary to tradition, refused them such hospitality, even when they had asked for it. Yet, instead of showing any sign of indignation or disappointment, the good slave responded with generosity and kindness and started to rebuild for them a wall which had fallen, while Moses watched in bewilderment and said to him for the third time forgetting his pledge:

> ". . . If thou hadst wished, thou couldst have taken payment for it." (al-Kahf 18:77)

In view of his limitations in higher knowledge, Moses seemed quite justified in making this remark. In his own judgement he felt that these spiteful people ought to be reprimanded for their conduct, rather than be rewarded with generosity and kind deeds. But with this third breach the good slave brought their companionship to an end, telling Moses:

> ". . . This is the parting between you and me! I will announce unto you the interpretation of that you could not bear with patience." (al-Khaf 18:78)

Then the good slave revealed to Moses the underlying wisdom in his deeds which had caused him such consternation.

The good slave then explained that he had damaged the boat so that it would not fall into the hands of the cruel king who had planned to seize it, thereby depossessing its poor owners of their only means of making a living and that it was better for those people to spend time repairing it than to lose it altogether. Indeed, if they had been given the freedom to choose between the two misfortunes they would have given full approval to his act. Thus, although damaging the boat may have seemed a wicked deed to the casual observer, its long-term result was good.

As for the young lad, he was a deviant and a menace to his parents, whom we are told were people of faith who had brought him up with love, but he had strayed from Allah's way and sold his soul to the devil, thus becoming a source of constant sorrow and humiliation to his virtuous parents. Such a deviant lad would stop at nothing and was likely to go as far as forcing them to denounce their faith. The pronoun 'We' (18:81) implies that the good slave was not acting on his own, but was divinely inspired. It is not uncommon for parents in such cases to wish that Allah had replaced such a corrupt son with a more obedient and Godfearing one, for corrupt and deviant children may indirectly induce their parents to commit unlawful acts.

Virtuous people do not see this temporal life in isolation from the next one. They are constantly aware of the fact that they will have to account for all their unlawful deeds on the Day of Judgement and are, therefore, never happy with material gains secured through unrighteous means.

Surely if a virtuous parent knew that having a son would cause him to violate Allah's laws or to stray from his right path, he would choose to have none. The slaying of the corrupt lad was in fact a blessing in disguise and a mercy from Allah, for it saved his parents from the dire consequences of a sinful life that he would have led had he reached manhood. Nevertheless, Allah, in His divine mercy, promised to comfort their hearts and repay them for the loss of this wicked son with the birth of a more caring and virtuous son:

> "And we intended that their Lord should change him for one better in purity and nearer to mercy."
> (al-Kahf 18:81)

The emphasis in the above verse is that the parents were people of faith who should not be misled, for it was a significant factor underlying Allah's plan to take away the lad's life and deliver his parents from his evil. The good slave knew that with such deeply-rooted faith in Allah's wisdom and justice, the parents would be ready to forsake their deviant son in favour of their faith.

This act, judged by man's limited standards, may have seemed inhuman and sinful. Allah had, however, safeguarded the righteous parents' faith, replaced their deviant son with another kinder and more virtuous one, and at the same time saved the first son from the evil life that he was bound to have indulged in. Allah deemed it more merciful not to let his evil disposition grow and take possession of his soul, thereby provoking his wrath and causing his own damnation.

Parents afflicted with evil offspring may sometimes wish that they were dead. This wish does not emanate from hatred but rather from a desire to spare them damnation and the punishment they must suffer on the Day of Judgement.

Concerning the parable of the villagers who refused to give hospitality to Moses and his companion, and how, despite their meanness and offensive conduct, the good slave volunteered to rebuild the wall which had fallen to the astonishment and disbelief of Moses: here again, the good slave's act was not intended to appease the villagers, but rather to prevent a hidden treasure buried by a righteous father for his children, to be discovered. Had the wall not been rebuilt, the villagers would have discovered the treasure and used it to satisfy their lusts. But because the father was righteous, and his treasure had not been collected by unlawful means, Allah safeguarded it for his children, whom He knew would also grow to be righteous and would use it in lawful trade and in advancing righteousness among an otherwise wicked community.

The wisdom in this last parable differs clearly from the others. Whereas in the first two incidents the apparent action seemed to be motivated by wickedness and lack of compassion, it appeared in the third incident to be motivated by good will and the repaying of meanness with kindness. In fact, what appeared to be repaying wickedness with kindness was but a divine plan aimed at preventing the ungracious folk from getting a reward they did not deserve.

Indeed Allah has included many lessons in this Sūrah to contemplate. He is telling us not to assess or judge His acts in terms of their outward or immediate outcome, or according to our own mundane standards, for He alone knows the ultimate implications of His acts. He draws our attention to our impatience and asks us not to wonder at some of the things that seem to conflict with the believer's expectations and faith in divine justice. Not infrequently, we see that the unrighteous are rewarded with wealth and power and the righteous are afflicted with privation and hardship. But good fortune and misfortune should not be judged in terms of their immediate or worldly profits and losses. Misfortune might be but the crust under which is found comfort and blessings. In contrast, power and wealth might hide within their fold misery and sufferings in this world and the next.

We should not, therefore, be fooled by what we see or be distressed by the dramatic fluctuation of fortune; nor question Allah's wisdom and purpose.

The Caves of Life:

All the above examples and moral lessons have been given to illustrate the diverse "caves" of life which conceal more than they reveal to the uninformed. There are hidden truths which are veiled from human knowledge. We have no control over Allah's acts and cannot evade them or alter their course; in every divine act there is a concealed divine purpose and end. We should not, therefore, try to interpret them in terms of their apparent or immediate outcome or within the framework of our limited knowledge. Only in this way can we bear the upheavals of this life: armed with unwavering faith in Allah's wisdom and cherishing care for all of us, we can show this faith through an acceptance, with humility and resignation, of all that may befall us, knowing that His ultimate purpose is our welfare.

As for the parable of Alexander Dhū'l-Qarnayn, we find it begins with the verse in which Allah says,

> "They will ask thee of Dh'ul-Qarnayn. Say: I shall recite unto you a remembrance of him." (al-Kahf 18:83)

The Qur'ān here does not give us material on which we can give a positive answer as to who Dhū'l-Qarnayn actually was, or when and where he lived. All it tells us is that he was a most powerful king and that Allah, in His universal plan, gave him his power, and provided him with the ways and means for conducting his great work. His rule extended over East and West, and over people of diverse civilizations. He was just and righteous, not selfish or covetous. He protected the weak and punished the unlawful. Three of his expeditions are portrayed in Sūrah al-Kahf, each embodying the ethics of kingship or power. For Alexander recognized that his power was given to him as a trust by Allah, in Whom he had sincere faith and Whom he never forgot. But Alexander did not stop at the means given to him by Allah, but he also devised his own means. This is one of the lessons that Allah wants us to learn. We should not be content with the means readily available to us, but we should try to add to them if by doing so we are helped in our just cause. Thus, if Allah grants to someone a plot of land he should try to use it to the fullest, expanding it and using it to produce food rather than leaving it barren. Similarly, money is not to be hoarded in safes. It should be invested justly and righteously in projects that are aimed at multiplying it, and at the same time promoting the welfare of the community.

Then the verses tell us how Alexander used this power,

> "Till when he reached the setting place of the sun, he found it setting in a muddy spring, and found a people thereabout. We said: O Dhū'l-Qarnayn! Either punish them or show them kindness." (al-Kahf 18:86)

This was indeed a test for Alexander, for Allah had given him the freedom of action. He had to choose between punishment or kindness. To this, Alexander says:

> "As for him who does wrong, we shall punish him." (al-Kahf 18:87)

Why did he not say: "O my Lord, he who does wrong will be left to face his punishment in the hereafter"? The answer is that in order to avoid chaos, order for any community must entail swift punishment for outlawed acts. In any community there are those who believe in Allah's ways and those who do not. There are the malicious people and there are law-abiding ones. Moreover, in any community, judgement comes before reward or punishment. Allah has established the rules governing man's conduct in this universe. An unrighteous man who steals must be punished on earth. Anyone who violates these rules should be asked to account for his conduct and pay the due penalty. No society can afford to postpone punishment for offences in this life to be carried out in the Hereafter.

It may also be noticed, in the above verse, that Allah mentioned the guilty first, then those who do right:

> "But as for him who believes and does right, good will be his reward, and We shall speak unto him a mild command." (al-Kahf 18:88)

The distinction is due to the fact that judging the merits of a deed or effort must precede any reward. If we, in our human affairs, fail to reward the honest and industrious and instead give the reward to the idle and the indifferent, we shall only be encouraging laziness.

Another point worthy of consideration is the fact that the guilty will have to face two trials and face punishment twice for wrongdoing, once in this world and again in the Hereafter. The words translated as 'unjust' or 'wrongdoer' often mentioned in the Qur'ān refers both to those who do injustice to themselves and those who do injustice to others. Those who wrong themselves cause their own damnation in the Hereafter. They are the people who do worship, resent Allah and His favours, and inflict harm on others for no reason other than to see people suffer, with no material or personal gain to themselves. Such persons differ from those who do injustice to others in that they do not seek the material gains coveted by others who, in fact, do injustice to themselves in this life and the next. They are the people who have bartered the Hereafter for the glitter of this transient world and who have forsaken all that is eternal.

There are two kinds of punishment. The first kind involves overt acts such as stealing and fraud. In such cases the guilty party is promptly punished. The second kind involves acts committed secretly in defiance of Allah's commands and the duties He has imposed on man. The punishment of such deviations rests with Allah.

This is the reason why Allah has determined and defined the role of each of His creatures upon whom He bestows the power to maintain justice on earth. This role commits them to ensuring a harmonious order in society. This balance cannot be maintained unless the guilty are punished for their crimes. It is neither wise nor reasonable to postpone punishment for the Hereafter. There must be some sort of prompt punishment for those who have forgotten Allah and His commandments to mankind.

The following verse deserves deeper thought; it reads:

> "But as for him who believes and does right, good will be his reward, and We shall speak unto him a mild command." (al-Kahf 18:88)

Why does this verse stop short of stating that good men will be rewarded with eternal blessings in Paradise? The answer is that faith represents a bond between Allah and His worshipper and it is Allah alone who knows whether the worshipper is applying himself sincerely to the terms of this bond. It follows, therefore, that no matter how efficient are our standards for judging moral actions, they cannot distinguish between the true believer and the hypocrite. Judgement in these matters must necessarily rest with Allah, for He alone knows what is hidden in man's inner heart and mind. He knows those persons whose acts arise from a sense of sincere faith and a desire to seek His pleasure, and those persons whose acts, although superficially they may give that impression, are in fact aimed at securing some personal worldly gain. Only Allah is capable of judging these acts and to Him these pretenders have to be turned for either reward or punishment.

The verses continue to tell us that Alexander continued his expedition until:

> ". . . When he reached the rising-place of the sun, he found it rising on a people for whom We had appointed no shelter therefrom." (al-Kahf 18:90)

Here, Allah informs us that there are parts of this world that do not follow the normal pattern of sunrise and sunset, or day and night.

Wealth and power

In the second episode of Alexander's expedition we are told that he followed another way until he reached a tract between two mountains, on the other side of which he found a people who scarcely understood a word of what he said to them. He learned from them that they were constantly raided by the marauding tribes of Gog and Magog who pillaged their land.

What we should mainly be concerned with in this parable is its spiritual interpretation. Apparently the people he met were a peaceable and industrious race constantly subject to incursions by the wild tribes of Gog and Magog. They were willing to purchase protection by paying Alexander a tribute. In return they asked him to close the mountain gap through which the marauding tribes came.

But Alexander was not possessed by greed and found the tribute to be an unfair burden for such an industrious and peace-loving people, so he said to them:

> ". . . That wherein my Lord has established me is better (than your tribute). Do but help me with strength (of men). I will set between you and them a rampart." (al-Kahf 18:95)

By this reply Alexander teaches us a worthy lesson. He is well aware of the power which Allah has given him, as well as his responsibility and duty of protecting his subjects without imposing too heavy a taxation upon them.

Furthermore, the verse establishes two divine axioms which Allah wants us to recognise. The first axiom is embedded in Alexander's recognition that gaining Allah's satisfaction and pleasure through the fair and just exercise of the power which He had bestowed upon him would be better than the gathering of wealth. It teaches us that a godly and faithful person does not regard money as an end in itself, nor does he strive to amass it and store it as a source of power. In contrast, he is always aware that spending his money or investing it in worthy and honest enterprises is the surest way to make it grow. Alexander is shown to us as the good and virtuous man whose example we ought to follow. In other words, Allah is saying to us that we should show greater interest and enjoyment in the opportunities He may provide for us to do good in this world, rather than in the wealth that He may put before us, and that the rewards for the first are richer and more lasting than in the latter case.

The second axiom is reflected in Alexander's wise plan, viz.: "Do but help me with strength 'of men'". The underlying meaning in this verse is that to fight injustice we must work together; we should be united in our purpose and in our efforts to purge the community of those who are bent on defiling it, to make use of the knowledge that Allah has bestowed upon us to promote the welfare of the community, rather than to waste it in futile debates about unseen realities far beyond our comprehension.

Allah has given us the gift of reason so that we can use it to explore the resources of this earth and to enhance mankind's welfare and prosperity, for when Allah gave us intellect, He also created the domains where it ought to be exercised. Some people however try to use their intellect in realms which do more harm than good. They use it to cast doubt about unseen truths, to alienate people from Allah and to sow corruption in the hearts of men. Allah has not intended that the Unseen be one of the fields of activity of the mind, for the range and scope of the human mind is limited, and Allah has no limit or restriction. Indeed, the realm of the human mind should be confined to the universe and all that Allah has put in it for man to harness for his own welfare and to establish harmony with his Creator.

Giving protection to the weak:

A good deed whose ultimate purpose is to gain Allah's pleasure and satisfaction makes its executor eligible for the following divine favours and rewards:

> "We are your protecting friends in the life of the world and in the Hereafter. There ye will have (all) that your souls desire, and there ye will have (all) for which you pray." (Fuṣṣilat 41:31)

> "Lo! Allah defends those who are true . . ." (al-Ḥajj 22:38)

> ". . . And whosoever keeps his duty to Allah, Allah will appoint a way out for him, and will provide for him (from a *quarter*) whence he has no expectation . . ." (al-Ṭalāq 65:2-3)

All these verses point to one fact: that the righteous and the virtuous in this world will be rewarded with endless gifts, both material and spiritual, their prayers will always be answered, and they are assured of Allah's protection from all intrigues, malice and harm that are aimed at them. A man who enjoys such favours is likely to find a safe exit from any difficulty and a solution to all his problems even when all hope has deserted him. He will never suffer poverty or hardship, because Allah will always plan new channels for him to secure ample sustenance in ways of which he had never thought. In addition to all these worldly gains he will be rewarded in the Hereafter with everlasting blessings.

These were the rewards which prompted Alexander to decline the tribute that the oppressed people had offered him. Indeed, his statement "That wherein my Lord has established me is better (than your tribute)" (18:95) leaves no room for any doubt about his values and inborn virtues. He had wisely chosen the option which every other believer, looking for the everlasting spiritual rewards, would have made.

But how did he build the barrier? Did he simply take their protection upon himself – which would naturally have ended when he left their land – or did he, rather, teach them to be self-reliant and to fend for themselves after he had gone?

His words "Do but help me with strength (of men)" answers all these questions. He made them participate in building the barrier, thereby teaching them to rely on their own resources to defend themselves. Indeed, there is wisdom in all this, for a good leader who has been given the right means can help the weak and the oppressed to stand on their own feet, gain strength, and overcome their backwardness and decadence, by uniting their efforts and by encouraging them to learn from others with greater knowledge.

Within Sūrah al-Kahf there is much wisdom to be gained concerning our life in this universe. The first and most important lesson is that Allah is the principal executor of all acts, and that nothing can be achieved outside His Will. The second is that all our gains in this world are gifts from Allah, and that there is always a hidden purpose in all that befalls us. We should not therefore, lose hope in the face of hardship, nor question His acts and His favours to His slaves whether they appear to be righteous or not. The third lesson is that we should not judge happenings by their outward appearance or short-term end, for misfortune could be a blessing in disguise and vice versa. We should accept misfortune with resignation and humility. The next lesson is that there are happenings beyond our control. They are acts of Allah, and He alone knows their final outcome and their hidden purpose. Man does not make his own destiny; it is held in the hands of Allah and no one can predict what the future holds for him until it is revealed to him by the Will of Allah.

And finally, we can always learn from others upon whom Allah has bestowed greater knowledge and power, and add to it from our own resources.

Chapter 5

Allah's Reproof of Muḥammad (SAW)

Some Orientalists try to defame Islam by ascribing to some verses in the Qur'ān, particularly to those verses in which Allah seems to reprove Muḥammad (SAW), meanings other than those which they truly denote. They then use these new meanings as evidence against Muḥammad's (SAW) integrity and the way in which he delivered Allah's message to mankind. The following are examples of these controversial verses:

> ". . . And ask forgiveness for thy sin . . ." (Muḥammad 47:19)

> ". . . And if We had not made you wholly firm you might have inclined to them a little. Then had We made you taste a double (punishment) of living and a double (punishment) of dying, then had you found no helper against Us." (al-Isrā' 17:74-75)

The same kind of reproof was made to him following the Battle of Badr and his willingness to free his captives if they agreed to teach Muslims how to read and write, which resulted in Allah's saying:

> "It is not for any prophet to have captives until he has made slaughter in the land (or: thoroughly subdued the land). You desire the lure of this world and Allah desires (for you) the Hereafter . . ." (al-Anfāl 8:67)

It was said that Muḥammad (SAW) could not hold back his tears when this revelation was made to him.

The above verses are only a few examples of such reproving remarks.

Sceptics who make use of these verses to inveigh against Islam are, in fact, giving indisputable evidence that the Qur'ān is indeed the original words of Allah as they were revealed to Muḥammad (SAW). The mere fact that none of these reproving verses were omitted or misquoted proves the originality of the Qur'ān and confirms Allah's promise to preserve it intact and guard it from corruption, as is stated in the verse.

> "Lo! We, even We, reveal the Reminder, and lo! We verily are its Guardian." (al-Ḥijr 15:9)

The whole of the Qur'ān, including these reproving verses, was revealed to Muḥammad (SAW) in person. It follows, therefore, that if he had been in any way dishonest or had any doubt about the divine message, he would have concealed these verses without anyone knowing about them or suspecting him. If the Qur'ān had been made up by Muḥammad (SAW), he would not have left any such verses in it. After all, he was but a man, and men by nature resent being criticised and are inclined to believe that they are immune from error. There is no human doctrine whose author is self-critical or does not try to convince us of its wholesomeness.

Hence, the mere fact that these reproving verses had been revealed and were transmitted intact to Muḥammad's (SAW) followers confirms the fact that the Qur'ān is truly Allah's original speech and provides us with evidence as to Muḥammad's (SAW) integrity and honesty in delivering the message.

Regarding the Sūrah al-Tawbah (9) some Orientalists have remarked that this chapter, unlike all the other passages of the Qur'ān, does not open with the basmallah i.e., "In the name of Allah, Most Gracious, Most Merciful". They considered this omission to be clear evidence that the Qur'ān was not of divine origin, and that Muḥammad's (SAW) memory – whom they alleged was its true author – had betrayed him.

It should be noted that in this Sūrah Allah is speaking about the heretics who have been deprived of His mercy, and, therefore, the passage could not have opened with the words of mercy which Allah withheld from them, as is stated in the following verse:

> "Freedom from obligation (is proclaimed) from Allah and His messenger toward those of the idolators with whom you made a treaty." (al-Tawbah 9:1)

The same withholding of mercy is stressed in other verses, of which the following are only a few examples,

> ". . . Allah is free from obligation to the idolators, and (so is) His messenger" (9:3)

> "Give tidings (O Muḥammad) of a painful doom to those who disbelieve" (9:3)

Then Allah tells Muḥammad (SAW) how to deal with these idolators and non-believers:

> "Then, when the sacred months have passed, slay the idolators wherever you find them, and take them (captive), and besiege them, and prepare for them each ambush . . ." (9:5)

> "How can there be a treaty with Allah and with His messenger . . ?" (9:7)

> "How (can there be any treaty for the others) when, if they have the upper hand of you, they regard not pact nor honour in respect of you? They satisfy you with their mouths the while their hearts refuse. And most of them are wrong-doers. They have purchased with the revelations of Allah a little gain, so they debar (men) from His

> way. Lo! evil is that which they are wont to do. And they observe toward a believer neither pact nor honour. These are they who are transgressors." (9:8-10)
>
> ". . . then fight the heads of disbelief – lo! they have no binding oaths – in order that they may desist. Will you not fight a folk who broke their solemn pledges, and purposed to drive out the messenger and did attack you first? What! Fear ye them? Now Allah has more right that you should fear Him, if you are believers. Fight them! Allah will chastise them at your hands, and He will lay them low and give you victory over them, and He will heal the breasts of folk who are believers." (9:12-14)
>
> "It is not for the idolators to tend Allah's sanctuaries, bearing witness against themselves of disbelief. As for such, their works are vain and in the Fire they will abide." (9:17)

The verses go on to say that Allah gives no guidance to wrong-doers:

> "O ye who believe! Choose not your fathers nor your brethren for friends if they take pleasure in disbelief rather than faith. Whoso of you taketh them for friends, such are wrong-doers." (9:23)
>
> "Fain would they put out the light of Allah with their mouths, but Allah disdains (aught) save that He shall perfect His light, however much the disbelievers are averse." (9:32)

If the people referred to in the above verses are those pagans who have been denied Allah's mercy and forgiveness, how, then, could the Sūrah have begun with words of mercy when there was no room for its granting? Muḥammad (SAW) had not forgotten anything! It was, rather, Allah's plan that this Sūrah should not open with the usual statement of His mercy, in order to show His wrath and the punishment that those heretics were doomed to suffer.

Returning to those verses in which Allah reproves Muḥammad, it is seen that in the Sūrah 'Muḥammad' Allah says to His Prophet

> "And ask forgiveness for your sin . . ." (Muḥammad 47:19)

Yet in the Sūrah al-Fatḥ (48) He says to him,

> "Lo! We have given you (O Muḥammad) a signal victory, that Allah may forgive you of your sin that is past and that which is to come . . ." (al-Fatḥ 48:1-2)

How can this paradox be explained? How can Allah ask Muḥammad to beg forgiveness for his sin and also tell him that He had granted him forgiveness for his past and future sins? Furthermore, what is this sin which caused this reproof?

If we examine thoughtfully all these reproaching verses we find that the reproach was aimed at Muḥammad's (SAW) excessive zeal in carrying out the message and his taking on himself more than he could endure, as is stated in the following verse from the Sūrah 'Ṭā' Hā'

> "We have not revealed unto you (Muḥammad) this Qur'ān that you should be distressed." (Ṭā' Hā 20:2)

Then Allah says to him,

> "Yet it may be, if they believe not in this statement, that you (Muḥammad) will torment your soul with grief over their footsteps." (al-Kahf 18:6)

> "O Prophet! Why do you ban that which Allah has made lawful for you . . ?" (al-Taḥrīm 66:1)

> "We know well how their talk grieves you . . ." (al-An'ām 6:33)

> "A likely thing, that you would forsake aught of that which has been revealed unto thee. . . " (Hūd 11:12)

> ". . . So not let your soul expire in sighings for them . . ." (al-Malā'ikah 35:8)

> "He frowned and turned away because the blind man came unto him . . . " ('Abasa 80:1-2)

> "Had it not been an ordinance of Allah which had gone before, an awful doom had come upon you on account of what you took." (al-Anfāl 8:68)

> "You are not at all a warder over them." (al-Ghāshiyah 88:22)

> ". . . Say: I am not put in charge of you." (al-An'ām 6:66)

All these verses contain some sort of reproof of Muḥammad, (SAW) but the reproof is made because of his being overzealous in carrying out the message and in taking on himself more responsibility than he could endure. This is remarked in the first of the above verses when Allah says to him:

> "We have not revealed unto thee this Qur'ān that you should be distressed." (Ṭā' Hā' 20:2)

That is, because Muḥammad's (SAW) task was to deliver the message and explain its truth, leaving to the listener the responsibility of accepting it or not. This fact is emphasized in the following verse:

> "Say: (It is) the truth from the Lord of you (all). Then whosoever will, let him believe, and whosoever will, let him disbelieve . . ." (al-Kahf 18:29)

Again in the Sūrah of Yūnus (10), Allah (still) reminds Muḥammad (SAW) of the goal of his commission when he says to him:

> ". . . Would you compel men until they are believers?" (Yūnus 10:99)

In the above verses, Allah has excluded coercion as a means of spreading the message of the faith. For faith which is imposed, or which does not come from within the soul, has no merit. Furthermore, Allah has shown man the right way and the rewards of following it. He has also cautioned him against wrongdoing and informed him of the penalties that wrongdoers must pay. But because He has given man freedom of will the option to follow one way or another has been left entirely up to him.

Muḥammad's (SAW) awareness of the consequences of resisting Allah's faith, as well as his concern and pity for those who rejected it, caused him to do all he could to persuade them to come to their senses and accept the truth. But Allah saw that Muḥammad (SAW) had taken upon himself an unnecessary and wearisome task which he was not required to perform, and He had to draw his attention to it.

One should here bear in mind two noteworthy points. The first is that all those who use the reproaching verses to cast doubt over Islam are intrinsically motivated by malice. They single out only the reproaching verses and leave untouched the numerous verses in which Allah pays tribute to Muḥammad's (SAW) worthy conduct and integrity, as is stated in the following revelations.

> "And lo! you are of a tremendous nature." (al-Qalam 68:4)

> "We sent thee not save as a mercy for the peoples." (al-Anbiyā' 22:107)

> ". . . Obey Allah and His messenger if you are (true) believers" (al-Anfāl 8:1)

The above verses are only a few examples. Indeed, only a dishonest critic who knew that he was defending a lost cause would, in his attempts to establish the relationship between

Allah and His messenger, resort to such deceit by obscuring a true meaning, accentuating certain verses and overlooking others.

The second point concerns the nature of the reproof, for there is indeed a marked distinction between a reproof used to chastise for wrong-doing and inflicting harm on others, and a reproof whose underlying motive is to sympathize with the reproved. For one who is excessively keen to do a good deed might unconsciously involve himself in tasks that are beyond human endurance. Reproof is a sort of blame for a mistake that the reproved must have made, and can only take place when there is some kind of sympathy and understanding between the reprover and the one reproached. It is uncommon for reproof to take place between strangers. A non-believer, therefore, cannot be reproached for his deeds, the reason being that there is no sin greater than not believing. Likewise, one does not reproach an enemy, expecting his antagonism.

On the contrary, reproof is something natural and necessary between people bound together by kindness and fellowship. Its magnitude depends on the strength or weakness of the relationship between the reprover and the reproved. If the relationship and the concern are very strong, then the reproof could be voiced, even for the slightest error or misdeed. If the relationship is weak then the reproof can be made only when the error is very serious. For instance, one does not reprove a distant acquaintance for a trivial error. But if he were a close relative the whole situation would be different and one's reproof would be frequent and concerned in relation to the strength of your feeling for him. You would most likely reprove your brother for things for which you would never reprove a friend, and reprove a friend for things over which you would not reprove a distant acquaintance. The extent of and the reasons for the reproof depend on the closeness of the relationship between the two parties.

The relationship between Allah and Muḥammad (SAW) was a very close one indeed. It is this divine love and concern for Muḥammad (SAW) that made Allah address him in sympathetic and concerned words; not to chastise him for some misdeed or because he had violated His decrees, but rather because He cared about him and wanted to caution him about overburdening himself.

One might have two sons, one of whom is neglectful and pays no heed to his school work, and the other of whom is so engrossed in his studies that he skips his meals and never gives himself enough time to rest or sleep. A common reaction in a situation of this nature is to rebuke the first son for his negligence and to reprove the second for his zeal and for endangering his health. This reproof stems from anxiety about his health. Thus, in asking him to leave his studies for a while or to do them in moderation and give more thought for his food and sleep, one reproaches him for something to be done. While one may have instructed him to study well and achieve success in the past, one reproves him for overexerting himself – but the reproof is for his own good and not a chastisement.

All the verses which carry reproof of Muḥammad (SAW) are of this nature. The reproof was made for something which he was not obliged to do. Yet he regarded it as compulsory, regardless of the additional burden it added to his already heavy task, thereby overlooking what was easy and possible and focusing his attention on tasks that were too difficult and energy-consuming, as expressed in the following verse:

> "He frowned and turned away because the blind man came unto him." ('Abasa 80:1-2)

Certainly it was easier for Muḥammad (SAW) to sow guidance in the soul of a blind man whose heart was full of faith, than to exhaust his brain trying to convince the resentful pagans of Quraysh of the truth of Allah's message and religion. But Muḥammad (SAW) chose the more difficult task. He wanted to support Islam by gaining the hearts of the influential men of Quraysh, thus forsaking an easy gain for a more difficult one. Here the Divine Will intervened, advising him not to seek something too painstaking, to obtain and to be content. He was told not to waste his time and energy over non-believers who reject guidance outright, but to give his attention to those persons who long to be close to Allah and His way. Indeed, all the reproving verses are of this nature.

Although Muḥammad (SAW) knew that Allah had forgiven him all his past and future sins, he continued to spend most of his nights in prayer even when his legs began to swell. When his wife 'Ā'ishah noticed this and asked, "Hasn't Allah forgiven you all your past and future sins?", he replied "Shall I not be a thankful slave?", showing that forgiveness should not be a reason for us to relax in our full duty of worship, or to be ungrateful.

There is much to be learnt from Muḥammad's (SAW) answer. If we consider man's position in his relationship with Allah, and compared all the favours that He bestows upon us with the divine injunctions we are ordered to obey and perform we find that whereas the former are inexhaustible the latter are only a few simple duties. The believer is aware of Allah's favours and knows that if he wanted to establish a balance between his duties and Allah's favours neither day nor night would be long enough for him to show his gratitude. Indeed, the believer's heart knows that Allah's favours outweigh by far any gratitude he might offer in the form of worship. Although he might be very keen to exert a supplementary effort in obedience, gratitude, and all other worship-related duties, he nevertheless feels that he is wanting in the expression of his devotion and humility. Likewise, Muḥammad (SAW) had made himself responsible for those who adamantly refused to believe. He felt that he had not done enough, and his lack of progress was beginning to distress him. But nothing escapes Allah's attention, and He intervened and told Muḥammad (SAW) to exercise moderation in his efforts and not to blame himself for the non-believers' rejection of the message. Surely, this is not the kind of reproach whose aim is to chastise. On the contrary, it reveals Allah's tremendous concern for His Prophet, which is clearly stated in the verse.

> "We have not revealed unto you this Qur'ān that you should be distressed . . ." (Ṭā' Hā' 20:2)

> "Why do you ban that which Allah has made lawful for you?" (al-Taḥrīm 66:1)

> "So not let thy soul expire in sighings for them." (al-Malā'ikah 35:8)

It is obvious that these verses speak of Muḥammad's (SAW) self-denial and his anxiety over the non-believers' resentment of Allah's message. He is told not to grieve or consider himself accountable for their defiance or for his inability to reach their hearts and souls.

There are, however, two verses which have been widely misinterpreted by sceptics and used to inveigh against the message of Islam. The first is the verse in which Allah says to Muḥammad (SAW) "Ask forgiveness for your sin" (47:19), the true meaning of which is clarified in the following Sūrah:

> "When Allah's succour and the triumph comes. And you see mankind entering the religion of Allah in troops. Then hymn the praise of thy Lord, and seek forgiveness of Him. Lo! He is ever ready to relent." (al-Naṣr 110:1-3)

Here Allah is apparently telling Muḥammad (SAW) to seek forgiveness. But what does this forgiveness involve? This question is answered by the following verse from Sūrah 'al-Mu'min' (40), wherein Allah says to him

> "Then have patience (O Muḥammad). Lo! The promise of Allah is true. And ask forgiveness for thy sin, and hymn the praise of thy Lord at fall of night and in the early hours." (al-Mu'min 40:55)

It is evident that the forgiveness in question has to do with the praise of Allah. The same thing is repeated in the Sūrah 'Muḥammad' wherein Allah says

> "So know (O Muḥammad) that there is no God save Allah, and ask forgiveness for your sin and for believing men and believing women . . ." (Muḥammad 47:19)

It appears, therefore, that the intrinsic meaning is concerned

cerned with matters of worship, and has nothing to do with any guilt that warrants punishment. The purpose of the verse is to direct rather than to chastise, for both the seeking of forgiveness and praising Allah are integral facets of the duties of correct worship, obedience and drawing nearer to Allah. There is actually no case for blame or chastisement in this situation. The same thing applies to all believers, both men and women. According to a Ḥadīth, good deeds alone do not guarantee an entry into paradise, unless they gain Allah's mercy.

Asking Allah's forgiveness and mercy are desirable acts from every believer irrespective of the depth of his faith. They are both integral aspects of good deeds and essential conditions for their acceptance by Allah.

What does it mean to 'ask forgiveness'?

Asking forgiveness is a kind of faith in which man expresses his submissiveness to Allah. Whereas the believer may find a great deal of satisfaction in his relationship with others he likewise obtains the same satisfaction in his submissiveness to Allah. In contrast, you seldom find a non-believer seeking Allah's forgiveness. A person of this nature might be ready to show submissiveness to his fellow man, and is ready to commit, in his attempts to gain his pleasure, all sorts of unlawful acts that are condemned by Allah. Yet this same person might be too arrogant and too proud to ask Allah's forgiveness or show submissiveness to Him. Only persons with firm faith who find pleasure in their feeling of submissiveness are always ready to acknowledge Allah's greatness and might and constantly ask His forgiveness. In this respect Allah says,

> "But Allah would not punish them while you were with them, nor will He punish them while they seek forgiveness." (al-Anfāl 8:33)

This verse clarifies what it means to ask forgiveness, and

tells us that it does not happen unless faith is deeply rooted in the heart of the person who seeks it. The verse shows that Allah would not punish those defiant non-believers while Muḥammad (SAW) still lived among them, because He had sent him as a mercy for all mankind, and because His mercy precedes His punishment. The verse explains what would happen when Muḥammad (SAW) died. It says,

> ". . . Nor will He punish them while they seek forgiveness." al-Anfāl 8:33)

Here we are informed that forgiveness could be granted to the non-believers after Muḥammad's (SAW) death, and that they would be spared punishment if they sought forgiveness and pledged submissiveness to Allah, for in doing so they would show that faith had entered their hearts, and once faith has been established, then Allah's mercy would be assured. With these words Allah shows how greatly He values the asking of forgiveness and how it prevents punishment and obliterates sins.

Allah stresses the virtues of seeking forgiveness when He says,

> ". . . And if, when they had wronged themselves, they had but come unto you and asked forgiveness of Allah, and asked forgiveness of the messenger, they would have found Allah Forgiving, Merciful." (al-Nisā' 4:64)

The first and most important stage of redemption is to seek forgiveness; humility and submission to Allah are its most significant signs. We should not, therefore, expect a non-believer to be eager to seek Allah's forgiveness.

Because Allah cherishes those who ask His forgiveness, Muḥammad (SAW) always urged his followers to make it an integral part of their daily life, and said that he asked forgiveness no less than one hundred times each day.

Asking forgiveness is an integral part of faith that is deeply entrenched in the heart of the believer and cannot be exercised sincerely except by a person who fears Allah. Furthermore, the asking of forgiveness that is not sincere is worthless and misses one of the main rewards of faith. Thus, when Allah commanded Muḥammad (SAW), who was the best example to be followed by all mankind, to ask forgiveness, He was in fact ordering all believers to follow his example.

By repeatedly asking forgiveness the believer, apart from being in close touch with Allah, is also constantly aware of his own weakness and his need for Allah's mercy. It works as a safeguard against his becoming oblivious of the Day of Reckoning or becoming engrossed in his own worldly desires, and deters him from sin and doing injustice to his fellow men or to himself.

But to understand fully the meaning of the verse "and ask forgiveness for your sin" (47:19), we have to consider it in the light of two facts. The first is that Muḥammad (SAW) was sent as a mercy to mankind, and the second is that Allah is Almighty and All-Capable, and His justice, while it may not be instant, is nevertheless certain.

Muḥammad (SAW), in taking upon himself more than he could endure, and in his endeavour to gain the hearts of the adamant non-believers, suffered a great deal of distress and disappointment. Allah noticed this and showed His concern by telling him that He had not revealed the Qur'ān to him to cause him distress (20:2). On another occasion the hypocrites came to him and made excuses in order to avoid joining him in the expedition of Tabūk. Apparently Muḥammad exempted them from taking part in this campaign, a decision which was considered to be too liberal from the point of view of Jihād. Allah made this point clear when He said to him:

> "Allah forgive thee (O Muḥammad)! Wherefore did you grant them leave ere those who told the truth were manifest to you and you did know the liars?"
> (al-Tawbah 9:43)

Surely there is no question of fault or rebuke in this verse. Both remarks involve Muḥammad's (SAW) excessive kindness. But Muḥammad (SAW) nevertheless continued to ask forgiveness for those dead non-believers who had in the past tormented him and fought his message. Here again Allah tells him "And never pray for one of them who dies, nor stand by his grave . . ." (al-Tawbah 9:84). Praying for the dead is no sin, but an act of excessive pleading for mercy for those who have rejected guidance. Muḥammad (SAW) not only pleaded for Allah's mercy, but also asked Him for forgiveness, to which Allah replied,

> ". . . though you ask forgiveness for them seventy times Allah will not forgive them . . ." (al-Tawbah 9:80)

It is obvious that Muḥammad's (SAW) concern for those who had fought him and tried to discredit him is in no way less than his concern for those who accepted his message and supported him. But Allah told him that those heretics did not deserve his unwarranted concern, and that their doom had been decided, reminding him of his precise role:

> "You are not at all a warder over them."
> (al-Ghāshiyah 88:22)

> "And never pray for any of them when he dies . . ."
> (al-Tawbah 9:84)

Some sceptics say that Muḥammad's (SAW) excessive zeal and over-anxiety about the fate of those misguided heretics and opponents contradicts with the verse in which Allah says,

> "Nor does he speak of (his own) desire." (al-Najm 53:3)

The Orientalists' interpretation of the above verse is that in taking upon himself more than that with which he was charged by Allah, Muḥammad (SAW) followed his own intuition and the dictates of his own mind.

This is far from true. The correct interpretation is that as long as Allah revealed the truth to Muḥammad (SAW) and showed him the right way, then Muḥammad (SAW) had no choice but to adhere to it, irrespective of what he would have liked to do. Thus after the revelation of the verse "And never pray for one of them" (9:84) he refrained from doing so, following the revelation of the verse, "He frowned and turned away because the blind man came (80:1-2), he did not give priority to gaining the heart of any of the eminent leaders of Quraysh over any one of the humble folk, no matter how much he believed that gaining the former would support the cause of Islam.

An example of his complying with this rule was illustrated when his uncle's doom was foretold:

> "The power of Abū Lahab will perish . . ."
> (al-Masad 111:1)

a man for whose guidance Muḥammad (SAW) had always been praying.

Despite the doom the Revelation predicted for his uncle, Muḥammad (SAW) could not conceal its content, and had to make it public to his people even though he might have wished otherwise. In fact Muḥammad (SAW) never attempted to bypass the ordinances of the religion and Allah's commands, no matter how much they conflicted with his own feelings.

Let us now turn our attention to the verse referred to at the beginning of this chapter which begins with the words, "And had We not made you wholly firm . . ." (al-Isrā' 17:74-75)

Orientalists interpret the above verse to mean that Muḥammad was about to accept a compromise with the non-believers, according to which they would alternately worship Allah for one year and their own idols for one year, and so on.

This interpretation is very misleading, and there is nothing in the verse that justifies it. In fact, linguistically, the phrase translated 'had We not' denotes firmness, as well as immunity from digression from the ordinances of the religion and Allah's commands. Similarly, the phrase translated 'thou mightest' indicates that the action, though approached, was not done. In fact, the action is absolutely negated by the phrase "had We not". In other words, Allah is saying to Muḥammad (SAW) that even if he were not supported by His divine guidance and His making him wholly firm, his natural piety would have guarded him against any such evil compromise.

The verse goes on to say, "Then had We made thee taste a double (punishment) of living and a double (punishment) of dying". (17:75) For whom is this "double punishment of living and a double punishment of dying" intended? Was it Muḥammad (SAW)? Obviously not, for he was safeguarded by divine support, as well as by his virtuous nature, from committing any such sin. It follows, therefore, that the verse did not apply to him but rather to those who might attempt such a compromise, involving Allah's religion, with the non-believers.

There is wisdom in the above verse which should not be overlooked, for in it Allah stresses the fact that the closer we are to Him and the higher we are ranked in His esteem, the more severely we will be judged by Him for our faults. This is repeated emphatically in Sūrah al-Mā'idah (5).

> "When the disciples said, O Jesus, son of Mary! Is your Lord able to send down for us a table spread with food from heaven? He said: Observe your duty to Allah, if you are true believers. (They said): We wish to eat thereof, that we may satisfy our hearts and know that you have spoken truth to us, and that thereof we may be witnesses. Jesus, son of Mary, said: O Allah, Lord of us! Send down for us a table spread with food from heaven, that it may be a feast for us, for the first of us and for the last of us, and a sign from Thee. Give us sustenance, for You are the Best of Sustainers."
> (al-Mā'idah 5:112-114)

The disciples believed in Allah and accompanied Jesus and helped to propagate submission to Allah. One day they asked him for a sign from Allah in the form of a table spread with food, which God fulfilled but cautioned them:

> ". . . And whoso disbelieveth of you afterward, him surely will I punish with a punishment wherewith I have not punished any of (My) creatures." (al-Mā'idah 5:115)

In this verse, Allah leaves no doubt in our minds that the closer we are to Him and the higher our position in His service, the more severe will His judgement be on us. The same thing is stressed in the Sūrah al-Aḥzāb (33) wherein Allah says to the Prophet's (SAW) wives:

> "O ye wives of the Prophet! You are not like any other women . . ." (al-Aḥzāb 33:32)

What is meant here is that, being close to Muḥammad (SAW), and hence to Allah, his wives would be judged differently from other women.

As for the meaning of the controversial verse "Had We not made you wholly firm . . ." (17:74), it is obvious. It involves the severe punishment of those persons ranked highly in Allah's esteem, or those who have been shown His portents, should they break Allah's law or be weakened in their faith. But they did not include Muḥammad (SAW), whom Allah had made wholly firm and immune against error in matters of religion. The verse was not referring to him personally, but rather establishes a basic rule regarding the punishment of all believers who are highly esteemed by Allah.

Chapter 6

The Miracle of the Prophet's 'Night Journey' (Laylah al-Isrā' wa 'l-Mī'rāj)

The miracle of al-Isrā' differs from the other miracles in both definition and meaning, as well as in many other aspects. In fact, no other miracle has aroused as much controversy as the miracle of al-Isrā'. All the other miracles involved natural observable phenomena and universal laws, which the miracles disrupted, as previously discussed.

Allah as the Creator of this universe has the power to intervene in the laws of the universe for the sake of any one of His worshippers or Messengers, which thereby gives rise to miracles. The observable miracle was usually ordained to consolidate faith in the hearts of believers in particular cases where the believers seemed to be overcome by distress, or when they were faced with difficult and desperate circumstances.

The purpose of this kind of miracle was to restore confidence in the Messenger, as well as in the power of Allah. But all of them were observable and tangible miracles which were usually performed before an audience, as was the case of the miracles of Abraham and Jesus.

The difference between those miracles and the miracle of al-Isrā' for whereas in the former miracles Allah disrupted the physical laws which controlled the forces of nature on this planet, in the presence of an audience, the miracle of al-Isrā', involved the disruption of cosmic and heavenly laws away from witnesses. Furthermore, Muḥammad (SAW) was the only human to be carried by night upon a heavenly horse, from the Sacred Mosque in Makkah to the Farthest Mosque in Jerusalem, to be shown some of the greatest portents of Allah. Ḥadīth includes details of that physical Journey in which Muḥammad (SAW) was first transported to the site of earlier revelations (Jerusalem), and from there taken through the Seven Heavens to the Sublime Throne.

Some commentators take the physical Journey literally, but admit that there were other occasions on which spiritual journeys or visions occurred. In Muḥammad's (SAW) case, they are more inclined to say that his body was transformed into a spiritual form. The sceptics, on the other hand, cast doubt on the whole event and deny the possibility of its occurrence. A third group find it too difficult for the human mind to conceive, and prefer not to become deeply involved in such mystical phenomena, but, however, lean toward the view that the Journey could have been a spiritual one, and that this does not detract anything from its significance.

To all these groups, it should be said that the physical journey is fundamental to the miracle. For we cannot possibly apply our own reason and logic to Allah's power and capability and it is beyond our mental ability to fathom such divine powers. If we therefore try to put restrictions on the miracle of al-Isrā' by postulating that it is more logical to understand it as a spiritual journey than as a physical one, we are putting restrictions on Allah's power and freedom to do as He will. This is where we go wrong, because we are thinking and assessing Allah's power in terms of our own limited capacities and knowledge.

It is inconceivable that mortals should set limits on the power of their Creator, Who is also the Creator of this universe and all its laws. Indeed there is an enormous gap between His power and ours which was initially bestowed upon us by Him. It is He Who gave us the power and knowledge that enabled us to discover these laws and make use of them for our benefit.

Observed miracles were aimed at strengthening the faith of those who watched them being performed, at a time when the supporters of the Messengers seemed to be confounded and in distress. But they were temporal miracles that could never be repeated, and whose effect was limited to those who watched them.

Their acceptance or rejection by those who did not see them being performed depended on those people's faith, and on many other factors. If these miracles had not been recorded in the Qur'ān, many of us would have doubted that they had happened.

But the miracle of al-Isrā' was unlike all these other miracles in that no one except Muḥammad (SAW) saw it being performed, and it was not aimed at strengthening the believers' faith. In fact many of them did not believe Muḥammad (SAW) when he told them of it. But if the miracle was not intended to consolidate the believers' faith, what was its purpose? The answer is that because Allah regarded prayer as the principal pillar of the five pillars of faith and a compulsory duty on all Muslims, He deemed it more worthy to convey these rules directly to Muḥammad (SAW). Unlike other duties such as Ḥajj (pilgrimage), Ṣawm (fasting) and Zakāh (the payment of alms), wherein Allah had made some allowance with regards to their observance, no such allowance or compromise was made regarding prayer. Prayer must be conducted in all circumstances. Neither sickness, war nor any other impediment exempts Muslims from fulfilling this compulsory obligation. Besides, as it forms a link between Allah and His worshippers, it should not be interrupted or neglected for any reason or pretext. In view of the strictness of this commitment Allah made minor allowances in the rules of practice in the cases of sickness, travelling, purification (ablution) and the Qiblah. Thus, for instance, a sick person can perform his prayers while lying in bed or sitting in a chair. Likewise, a traveller is exempted from adhering to the correct position of the Qiblah.

The miracle itself required this two-stage journey, for Muḥammad (SAW) had to inform his followers of the rules of prayer which Allah had imparted to him personally in the absence of any other witness. This privacy and the fact that he was acting as vice-regent whose task was to carry the worthiest of Allah's commands to His worshippers required a great deal of honesty on the part of Muḥammad (SAW).

In fact, the Isrā' was a twofold necessary prelude to the

Mi'rāj, for in addition to providing him with terrestrial evidence to confirm his story on his return it also consolidated his faith and prepared him for the second stage of his journey.

The Isrā' was a terrestrial portent involving the journey from Makkah to Jerusalem. The journey between the two places, at that time, was not something which was impossible, as caravans in those days could travel the distance in three or four weeks, or perhaps longer, according to the travellers' means. The miracle, therefore, nullified the laws of time as we know them on earth. Thus, Muḥammad (SAW) was carried from Makkah to Jerusalem, then to the heavens and back in one single night. At first, people were doubtful of what Muḥammad (SAW) described. They soon became convinced that the miracle had happened, however, when he gave them a detailed account of the caravans he had seen travelling between the two cities, and an accurate description of Jerusalem.

This preliminary convincing of His followers and their acceptance of the first part of the miracle prepared them to accept the second part of the journey, and removed from their minds all doubt that Allah had truly disrupted the cosmic laws, thus making it possible for Muḥammad (SAW) to ascend to heaven. The terrestrial portents were, therefore, a necessary prelude aimed at convincing the Muslims of the truth of the second, less readily credible, miracle which culminated with his arrival at the Heavenly Throne of Allah.

The Isrā' was, then, a miracle aimed at providing evidence that Allah had violated the terrestrial physical laws to enable Muḥammad (SAW) to travel between Makkah and Jerusalem in a very short time, or perhaps in no time at all, and that if He was able to violate the terrestrial laws, He was likewise able to violate the cosmic laws. It could also be said that the Isrā' was a miracle of consolidation and affirmation aimed at bringing closer to the human mind the truth of the events that took place afterwards.

There are some sceptics who argue that it is now possible for man to fly from Makkah to Jerusalem in half an hour or so, but this does not detract from the miracle in any way. Allah's miracles will remain intact and unmatched till the end of time. Jesus, for instance, cured leprosy and blindness with a mere touch of his hand. Nowadays, medicine can cure these illnesses, but never in the same way as Jesus did. Likewise, it may be possible for man to fly from Makkah to Jerusalem in a few minutes, but never will he be able to fly bodily as did Muḥammad (SAW). For this flight was a divine miracle and will remain as such, challenging man, until the end of time, never to be reproduced or matched by him.

But if Allah had spoken to Moses while he stood on earth, why did He raise Muḥammad (SAW) to the heavens to instruct him on the rules of the prayer? Why did He not speak to him on earth as He spoke to Moses?

To answer these questions one must take into account Allah's mercy, the limitations set on the human mind and the fact that when Allah wants to impart to man some spiritual phenomena which He deems to be beyond his limited intellectual capacity, He always relates it to another event that is less mysterious and easier for him to perceive. In this way, He affirms his faith and at the same time protects him from all beguiling attempts by those who plot against religion or try to cast doubt on the miracle's occurrence. For Allah knew that one day some people would become fascinated with the discoveries of science, and would forget about Allah's power, as is clearly stated in the following verse:

> ". . . Lo! those on whom you call beside Allah will never create a fly though they combine together for the purpose . . . So weak are both the seeker and the sought!" (al-Ḥajj 22:72)

Indeed, though science has made it possible for man to land on the moon and probe beyond our planetary system it has not been able to create a single-cell organism. There are many other verses about life and death and resurrection which bring these phenomena closer to man's intellect, all of which accentuate man's impotence in matters related to creation.

So why did Allah raise Muḥammad (SAW) to His Throne

to instruct him about the duties of prayers, and not simply speak to him on earth as He did in the case of Moses? One must bear in mind that the Planner and Designer of this act is Allah, Whose power is not limited in time or space. We should not try to assess this power in terms of our own limited human powers.

When we talk about divine acts we should not look at them in the light of our definitions of time and space, for both of these have been created by Allah for the purpose of organizing life in the universe. But these laws have no bearing on Allah's unrestricted Will which is not limited to time or space. It is therefore futile to assess the validity of the miracle of al-Isrā' or even to try to conceive of it in terms of our own definitions of time, space and potential. We should, rather, try to understand it in terms of Allah's unlimited divine attributes and powers. For instance, the meaning and action implied by the word translated 'raised' in Allah's terms is entirely different from the meaning we usually ascribe to it. For 'to raise', in man's terms, means 'ascension' in Allah's terms. The act here is relative to the power, and it is by this same divine power and will that Muḥammad (SAW) was given a higher rank than that of the angels. We should bear in mind that it is Allah Who made the laws governing the earth and the heavens, and being the Maker and Maintainer He has the power to operate them as He will. Certainly, no one in his human form can reach the heavens or go beyond the immediate world unharmed as Muḥammad (SAW) did.

We all know that the stars and the planets are controlled by strict, integrated laws and must function in total harmony according to these laws. Any disruption in the functioning of any of the planets in our solar system would certainly upset this harmony and bring about the disintegration of the whole system. Indeed, this solar system was carefully planned and created to serve man and ensure his survival on earth. To make this survival possible all elements of nature have been subdued and harnessed. We also know that there are millions of other solar systems like ours, all of which have their own laws and whose secrets are known only to Allah.

Allah suspended all these laws to enable Muḥammad (SAW) to travel unharmed from this solar system to the highest and farthest heaven, and to allow him to witness what no other human had ever seen. This does not mean that the Journey was accomplished according to the laws of time and space as we know them. Witnessing indicates that he was raised from this solar system to a higher heaven, and that such a journey must have involved some kind of transmutation (or change) of bodily form and state.

Allah, being aware of the limitations of the ḥuman mind to readily conceive such overwhelming mysteries as those demonstrated in the miracle of al-Isrā', has endowed us with the capacity of dreaming in order to show us glimpses of these mysteries and the ways in which it might operate. For example when we are awake, we live our normal worldly life which is governed by the material world and its laws. Yet all these laws seem to vanish once we are asleep and we seem to be governed by new laws that are entirely different from the customary physical laws that govern our actions and movements when we are awake. Thus we see strange places to which we have never been before, meet persons who have long been dead, fly unaided and remain suspended in midair, travel from one country to another instantaneously and so forth. All these things vanish once we are awake and begin to resume our daily activity.

What does all this mean? It is obvious that the laws which apply to our movements and actions when we are asleep are entirely different from the laws of conscious activity. During sleep, a person sees with his eyelids closed, speaks while his tongue is motionless and hears voices and sounds that are never uttered or vocalized. All this happens during sleep because the human nature has changed, and with this change the laws which govern conscious vision, speech and all other sensations are suspended. Now, if this can happen to us when we are asleep and our bodies are motionless, then surely Allah can subject the waking body to the same laws as when it is asleep, and allow it to perform greater and more incredible acts than those it can perform under the influence of sleep. With this visualization in the front of our minds it would be possible for us to assimilate all the events that took place during Muḥammad's (SAW) journey. The miracle should be accepted because nothing is too difficult for Allah to perform. The only difference between the miracles of Muḥammad (SAW) and Moses is that whereas Muḥammad (SAW) was shown some of Allah's signs in the heavens Moses was shown some of His signs on earth.

Allah spoke to Moses at the place where the miracle happened. All the divine portents which Allah revealed to all His other Messengers took place on earth. Muḥammad (SAW) was the only Messenger to be spoken to in the heavens and the only Prophet allowed to see some of Allah's heavenly signs.

The ascension to the heavens and Allah's conversation with him should not, however, prompt us to assume that Allah resides permanently in the heavens, for, indeed, as we have said before, He is not limited to time or place and is omnipresent. The fact that Allah spoke to Moses on earth and to Muḥammad (SAW) in the heavens gives indisputable evidence of His omnipresence, and invalidates the unfounded view that He raised Muḥammed (SAW) to Heaven because this is where He is to be found. Surely, Allah is present everywhere and can speak to anyone He chooses anywhere, on earth, in the heavens or in any other place in His endless universe.

The Isrā' and the Mi'rāj must, therefore, have been realised both bodily and spiritually. This is only one of the many miracles which Allah performed to support His Messengers, during which the laws of nature were disrupted. As in Abraham's miracle, He neutralized the burning property of fire, He likewise cancelled the laws that govern the horizontality of water to enable Moses to cross the sea, and gave Jesus the power to disrupt the laws of life and death and to cure the diseased and the sick.

Similarly, in Muḥammad's (SAW) miracle Allah broke His own terrestrial and cosmic laws. Muḥammad's (SAW) bodily 'Night Journey' from Makkah to Jerusalem in a matter of seconds or minutes was a terrestrial miracle in which all known physical laws were rendered inoperative. But, in addition to this, Allah also halted all the cosmic laws from operating while Muḥammad (SAW) travelled in space.

The verse in which Allah tells us that Muḥammad (SAW) "drew nigh and came down till he was (distant) two bows' length or even nearer" (al-Najm 53:8-9) has some bearing, for although the verse appears to be referring to measurable distance, the true meaning is different. This is due to the fact that we take time and space as a basis for the estimation of proximity and distance. But as both time and place are created by Allah, then in Allah's judgement there is no time or place, nor should we apply our own laws to Him.

Allah, in His continual mercy for mankind, gives us examples relative to life which bring that which is beyond human intellect closer to our understanding and perception.

If, for instance, one said that X is closer to Y's heart than M, would one not be talking about physical distance? For being physically close to someone does not necessarily imply emotional closeness or understanding.

The same thing could be said about two persons who, though they may be living under the same roof, live in entirely different worlds of thought, emotion and interests. Therefore being near a person does not at all imply closeness of heart, nor is nearness to or farness from a person essentially concerned with distance. Accordingly, we should not take the verse "Till he was (distant) two bows' length or even nearer" (53:9) to indicate shortness of distance, but rather nearness to the heart, and this can only be reached through Allah's uncovering to His favourite servants the secrets of His universe and of all His creatures.

Because Muḥammad (SAW) was granted this power he was able to hear the pebbles, which he carried in his hand, praise Allah. Of course all inanimate things in this universe never stop glorifying Allah, even though it is beyond our senses to hear or comprehend such glorification, because Allah has not granted us such power or knowledge.

Muḥammad (SAW) was able to hear the pebbles because Allah had bestowed this power on him, and revealed to him the secrets of this phenomenon. The bestowal of this gift upon him by Allah was a clear indication that he was highly ranked by Him, for only those who are so nigh unto Allah are allowed to know the secrets of this universe. This special favour is stated in the verse wherein Allah speaks about David:

> "Lo! We subdued the hills to hymn the praises of (their Lord) with him at nightfall and sunrise." (Ṣād 38:18)

> ". . . And there is not a thing but hymns His praise, but ye understand not their praise . . ." (al-Isrā' 17:44)

These verses indicate that the entire creation – animate and inanimate – praises Allah. But David was the only human whom Allah endowed with the power and knowledge to hear and understand the language of the inanimate creation. Some sceptics are quick to ask what language these inanimate things speak but communication need not necessarily be through words. For instance, wireless transmission is a special language which only those who use it can understand, as are cipher codes and other forms of signal transmission. Surely there are, besides verbal languages, many other forms of communication which only those who have their keys or codes can understand. Indeed there are many means of communication that are used on this planet and of which many of us have no knowledge.

If Allah, in His grace, revealed to Muḥammad (SAW) the secrets of the heavens and showed him some of His great portents, we should not attempt to evaluate them in terms of our physical definitions of time and place or try to subject the miracle to the same laws, nor should we attempt to calculate the distance that Muḥammad (SAW) travelled. For the same reason we should not ask how long he took to complete his journey, for to Allah there is no such thing as distance or time.

But we can say that all this truly happened, because He Who created time and place and everything else can easily change their laws or render them inoperative so that a miracle may take place.

All that which we have said about Muḥammad's (SAW)

ascension to the heavens can also be said about his closeness to Allah, for such closeness actually means a closeness of heart and soul, as in the case when the angelic messenger Gabriel appeared to Muḥammad (SAW) to inform him of his destined role. This, perhaps, is the reason why Muḥammad (SAW) fell into a trance-like state at the moment of revelation. These abnormal circumstances were clearly observable to others. The revelation was an ecstatic experience during which Muḥammad (SAW) gave every evidence of being in direct contact with the source of the message.

According to traditional accounts, Gabriel commanded Muḥammad (SAW) to 'recite' in the name of Allah. When Muḥammad (SAW) failed to respond, the angel embraced him as he repeated the command, until Muḥammad was compelled to repeat:

> "Read: In the name of thy Lord who creates, Creates man from a clot. Read: And thy Lord is the Most Bounteous, Who teaches by the pen, Teaches man that which he knew not." (al-'Alaq 96:1-5)

When Muḥammad recounted to his followers what he had witnessed in the Heavens, some of them, particularly his close companion Abū Bakr, believed him. He had complete faith in his integrity and needed no other evidence than Muḥammad's (SAW) own words.

Those who doubted his story became convinced of its truth when he told them of the caravans which he saw travelling between Makkah and Jerusalem, and gave them a detailed description of the latter city. Indeed Allah had planned things in such a way that the earthly portents became a convincing prelude to believing the greater portents revealed to Muḥammad (SAW) in the Heavens, for if his followers were convinced of the truth of the first stage of the journey of al-Isrā' then they would be more inclined to believe the second journey of al-Mi'rāj.

This was the miracle of the Isrā' and the Mi'rāj – a miracle in which Allah rendered inoperative the laws of this universe and of the heavens in order to show His Prophet some of His greatest portents, and to impose on him the rules of prayer, considered to be the worthiest and most holy part or pillar of faith, and the link between man and Allah. The aim of the miracle was to honour and affirm Muḥammad (SAW) himself, rather than to consolidate faith in the hearts of worshippers, and therefore, did not require witnessing.

But what can we learn from this miracle? In fact, it shows us signs of Allah's infinite power and His capacity to bestow immense favours and powers on whomever He chooses, as well as how nigh Muḥammad was to his God. It also provides us with evidence that Allah is present everywhere, both in the heavens and on earth.

PART III

Chapter 1

The Unity of the Universe and the Power of Allah

> "He it is Who created for you all that is in the earth . . ." (al-Baqarah 2:29)

Allah constantly reminds us of His Unity and the unity of this universe. His unqualified capacity is reflected in all aspects of creation, and particularly in the unrevealed secrets of life and death which have so far defied the best attempts of science to unfold them. Yet despite the clarity of the verse, some sceptics are always ready to dispute its validity. They consider the discovery by man of new species of food crops and the various new inventions in the fields of aviation, wireless transmission and the like to be a contribution and addition to the divine process of creation, and to be no less significant than it.

Everything on earth is classified as either inanimate, or mineral, vegetable, or human. What concerns us here are those things over which there is no control. In animals and man, for instance, respiration, heart-beat, blood circulation and similar phenomena are processes over which man has no control. He cannot order his heart to stop beating, his lungs to stop inhaling and exhaling air, or obstruct the functions of his digestive system. All these processes operate outside his volition and the limited freedom of choice which Allah has bestowed upon him.

In other words the physiological functional and growth processes of a living organism are not subject to human volition. They are all organised by a power other than that of man, and each is compelled to function in accordance with its restricted and exclusive role. The inanimate objects (or matter) are controlled to fulfil specific functions, as are plants. We sow the seed, which interacts with its surrounding elements. It germinates, grows a root and a stem and develops into a living plant without any aid from us. Thus plants grow freely in the forests, deserts and even under the sea unaided and unobserved by man. In fact, anyone can observe this process by simply watching a seed in a test-tube filled with water grow under its own power, and in harmony with the functions which Allah has ordained it to perform in this universe. It is this same power which makes different seeds sown in the same soil grow into different plants, each absorbing its own exclusive minerals and each yielding a different crop, regardless of the fact that they share the same soil and the same source of water.

This is the harmony which makes each plant grow to perform a specific function in the chain of life. This specialized function did not, however, happen accidentally or of its own accord, but was carefully planned and designed by Allah. The same can be said about both wild and domesticated animals. Each has a specific role in the ecological chain and helps to maintain the balance of nature and the harmony of this world.

Man and his Ability:

In man, all the parts of his body which function independently of his volition also operate in harmony with their specific roles and functions. Respiration, for example, happens freely and without difficulty, and each living organism receives its supply of air effortlessly; the same is true of the heart and all other bodily systems. They function, unnoticed by us, in perfect co-ordination and harmony whether we are asleep or awake. This perfect function is often disrupted by man through his excessive intake of food, tobacco, alcohol and all the other harmful habits which upset the natural functions of these organs. It is needless to say that most of mankind's sufferings are but the side effects of man's attempts to tamper with the natural gifts that Allah has granted him, or to try to change them to suit his own desires and fancies. This however upsets the balance and harmony which was initially planned by Allah. Our present ailments and difficulties cannot be remedied and overcome unless we revert to the divine laws and disciplines which are purified of all desire or ambition.

Man in his insistence upon satisfying his own desires and greed has tailored his own laws to fit these desires, thereby laying the foundation of his own misery. For if every man were content with what is considered to be enough for his daily living, there would be no poverty on earth. But, under the pretext of security, man is never satisfied with enough and justifies his expressed need for amassing wealth, forgetting that security is but a gift from Allah, which He can grant or withhold as He pleases. He can make us rich or poor in a matter of days or months. We should, therefore, seek security with Allah, rather than look for it in material possessions, for it is by His Will and power that security is granted or denied, maintained or withheld.

No one can deny that Allah is the Creator of this universe and all its celestial bodies and forms of life on earth, or dispute the fact that the process of creation was accomplished through His divine will. This fact reflects itself in all the things He has provided on earth, as well as in the laws He has decreed to maintain their proper functioning and man's survival. No mortal can claim to have anything to do with the process of creation, nor can he claim that the first palm tree or apple tree or corn was created by his prehistoric ancestors. They might have ploughed and irrigated the soil but the seed they sowed in it was the fruit of the first tree created by the will of Allah on this planet. Some people may say that man has been able, through crossbreeding of plants and scientific means, to create new species of seeds and crops. Nevertheless, the truth remains that all these improvements have happened to a seed which was originally created by Allah and the experiments themselves were but the work and plan of Allah Who constantly provides mankind with the means of achieving such improvements. Moreover, in conducting his experiments the experimenter does not invent his material, but rather uses already-created material.

Modern Science:

The same fact applies to all inventions and scientific discoveries, which could not have been achieved without already-existing natural elements and their universal laws. For example, the engineer who invented the aeroplane could not have succeeded without the help of the earth's atmosphere and the materials of which the plane was made, both of which are of Allah's creation. It is He Who has given man the knowledge and the laws which enabled him to invent and make this flying machine. The same rule applies to all other inventions. Surely, man has not created the matter of which all elements are made, nor has he established the laws that govern this universe; all he has done is to discover, by the will of Allah and according to His plan, a few of the secrets of this universe and some signs of His ingenuity and excellence. Obviously, the above verse applies to everything created by Allah, past, present and future. Any assumption that man has participated in creating anything is entirely unfounded. In many Sūraḥs of the Qur'ān Allah draws our attention to the fact that He created all the established systems and bodies of this universe and their systematic and harmonious laws in order to maintain life on earth. Once this life has ended and the Hour of Doom has come, the whole universe, including the earth, the planets and the stars, will disintegrate, and the life which depends on the existing means will be replaced by a new life where man is granted all his wishes effortlessly in response to his mere thoughts.

The unity of the universe is derived from the capacity and will of the Creator Who has put signs in it to remind us of His capability, and how He has subjected the course of events to His unqualified will, lest we forget and worship the means of sustenance. He also sẹnt us Messengers to remind us that He is the Creator of all life to Whom we must return.

One of the controversial issues frequently raised by Orientalists concerns the support which Allah gave to the Muslims during the battle of Badr. In this battle Allah commanded His angels to give support to the Believers in their fight with the pagans of Quraysh. The Orientalists argue that the outcome of that battle did not justify such support, because of the very small number of combatants and the losses of both sides on the one hand, and the immense devastating powers of the angels on the other.

These sceptics have failed to grasp the wisdom behind this divine plan and the support of the angels. There is no doubt that the angels' participation helped to consolidate the Believers' confidence and dispel their fears of the superior power of Quraysh and their dominance over the other tribes. Surely the angels' participation played a decisive psychological role in gaining victory. But the outcome of the incursion and the low rate of human loss was wisely devised by Allah, Who knew that some of the strongest men of those pagans who came to fight the Muslims would eventually embrace Islam and become some of the most zealous defenders and supporters of the religion.

The ultimate goal of the battle was to destroy only those non-believers whose doom had already been sealed and decided by Allah and who He knew would never stop waging war against Muḥammad (SAW), nor desist from urging other tribes to join them in their war against His religion, as long as they lived. It was, therefore, a necessity that they perish.

In fact, the angels' participation had a twofold purpose. In addition to enhancing the believers' resolve and dispelling their fear, they helped to identify those pagan leaders who had escaped the swords of the believers, and to slay them. Even if the size and scale of the battle did not justify the angels' support, the wisdom behind it did indeed justify it. For had Allah wished to destroy all of the non-believers He could have done so in an instant. His plan however was to destroy only those few pagans whom He knew would never mend their ways nor embrace Islam. As for the rest of the pagan fighters, He likewise knew that they, in due time, would embrace Islam and become some of its most eminent supporters and defenders.

If the above deduction is true, why did Allah not destroy these pagan leaders without resorting to war? The answer to this is that Allah wanted the support for His cause and religion to come freely and voluntarily from those who believed in Him. He did not want people to believe that His absolute power was the decisive factor in the struggle between believers and non-believers. He wanted every man to come to Him willingly and without compulsion. Surely, if the belief that Allah's unqualified will was responsible for the victory had been entrenched in people's minds, the whole cause would have suffered a serious blow. It would have undoubtedly given reason for the sceptics to question the true resolve and dedication of Muḥammad's (SAW) supporters and Allah's wisdom in sending Messengers to guide mankind and convince it of His true cause.

In this battle, Allah wanted to strengthen the confidence and faith of the believers, in readiness for the many battles which were to come. He emphasized this battle in the Qur'ān to tell those who were not present at that time that His angels would take part in any holy war that was fought for His own sake and in defence of His true cause, thereby dispelling fear of their enemy's strength.

When Allah explains something to mankind, He always provides the theory and its application together. The theory was embedded in the norms and decrees established in the Qur'ān. The application was demonstrated in the battle of Badr. For the consolidation and affirmation of faith through the support of the angels had an everlasting faith-instilling purpose. The losses among the pagan combatants were restricted to their leading instigators who stirred antagonism among the tribes and encouraged them to wage war against Muḥammad's (SAW) followers and the new religion. There is therefore no inconsistency between the verse, its underlying purpose, and Allah's support for those who fought for His cause. The actual goal and its application are illustrated in the outcome of the battle. The unseen and long-term end was that some of those who fought against Muḥammad (SAW) later declared their Islam and joined his camp.

Indeed when Allah reminds man of His powers (and

capability) He is doing so as a mercy to him, and to spare him the dire consequences of forgetting or disregarding them.

In the Sūrah al-Ṭāriq (86), we are repeatedly reminded of Allah's capability. This Sūrah begins with the words "By the heaven and the Morning Star" (86:1), which actually refer to everything that is found above the earth. Early scholars and scientists thought of the heaven as the immediate sky, but this definition or perception changed with the first discovery of seven of the nine planets in orbit round the sun; hence the assumption of the existence of seven heavens and not just one. But this idea was corrected when the remaining two planets were discovered.

But Allah tells us precisely how the heavens were built. He says:

> "We have built the heaven with might, and We it is Who make the vast extent (thereof)."
> (al-Dhāriyat 51:47)

It is obvious that the heavens have no boundary or limit.

It was stressed in the previous chapters that Allah's power is limitless, and it is beyond our ability to define any of His attributes. For nothing can bring us any closer to His true attributes. Therefore, when He says "And We it is Who make the vast extent (thereof)" (51:47) we should immediately understand that the heavens are endless and infinite and that the imagination of this expanse is something which is beyond our mental capacity. Moreover, to say that the stars we see are the limits of the heavens is, likewise, an untrue assumption, for in Allah's own words they are only the lower floor of the infinite heavens, as is stated by Him:

> "Lo! We have adorned the lowest heaven with an ornament, the planets" (al-Ṣāffāt 37:6)

Accordingly, all the planets and the stars which we are able to see are found in the lower heaven and act as a protective shield for the higher heavens from evil intrusion. When Allah avows "By the heaven and the Morning Star

(86:1)" we should know that He is stressing their enormity and imperceptibility by the human mind, and that their structure and functions are one of His many miracles.

What is the 'morning star' (al-Ṭāriq)?

What does the word "al-Ṭāriq" actually signify and what is Allah's purpose in His solemn use of the word? The answer is given in the following verse:

> "Ah, what will tell thee what the Morning Star is?" (al-Ṭāriq 86:2)

The implication here is that it may be too difficult for us to infer the connotations embedded in that name, and that He would give us their meaning.

In grammatical terms the word 'Ṭāriq' is the active participle of the verb ṭaraqa 'to knock in order to attract or arouse attention'. The word also means 'nocturnal visitor' whose footsteps, because of the stillness of night, can be heard, but could not be heard during the day because of daily sounds. It could also mean the ideas and thoughts that impinge on our minds. All these meanings seem to focus on one thing: that there is something – sensual, material or psychological – which arouses our attention to something of which we are unaware or inattentive. Although it is an external stimulus it does influence our inner self. But Allah explains that 'al-Ṭāriq' is the Morning Star which shines in the dark sky to guide us on our way and illuminate our path. Thus, during the night we are guided by these luminous bodies, and during day we are guided by the light of the sun.

The Sūrah goes on to tell us that:

> "No human soul but has a guardian over it." (al-Ṭāriq 86:4)

But what is the relationship between the heaven, the morning star and the guarding of every soul? Though on the surface there seems to be no relationship at all, in fact they are closely related, in that they remind us of Allah's capability and might which manifest themselves in the enormity of the heaven and in His swearing by it.

But knowledge of the seven heavens belongs to the Unseen which Allah has veiled from us, and although we can recognize the immense divine power behind them, it is beyond our ability to conceive of them or to form a clear image of their nature and secrets.

We can see glimpses of this divine power in the immense variety of things that Allah has created on earth. We can see it in the colourful flowers and fruitful plants, in the mountains, in the seas and oceans and in everything that lives and thrives together with man. Indeed, there are portents in each of them that illustrate this divine power, and draw our attention to it. Thus when Allah mentions the piercing star which penetrates the dark night with its luminous light, He wants to draw our attentions to the fact that His power is always there with us wherever we may be. He is always watching us and no one can hide from His vigilance no matter how he might try. Like the piercing star that penetrates the dark night, Allah's light can penetrate our inner souls and uncover our hidden motives, exactly as the morning star illuminates the darkness of the night. By the same token, the man of faith and truth has nothing to fear for Allah is always there to protect him from the perils of this darkness. The morning star, or Allah's light, is there to guide him, illuminate his path and dispel his fears. For Allah's power is limitless and He can see us in daylight or in darkness. He knows all our overt and covert thoughts and deeds, whether we are alone or among others.

We are also told that Allah not only has knowledge of all our deeds but that they are also registered and filed in His records, to be brought out again on the Day of Judgement when the wrongdoers will say:

> ". . . What kind of Book is this that leaves not one small thing nor great thing uncounted? And they find all that they did confronting them, and your Lord wrongs no one." (al-Kahf 18:49)

Divine power is, therefore, present by day and by night, and is able to penetrate our souls and minds and register all our good and bad deeds alike, for with each word we say or deed we do, we are in fact dealing with Allah. Where there is punishment, it will have been earned by the wrongdoer's own deeds, not imposed on him unjustly. Likewise, all good deeds will receive their due rewards. In no way can anyone deceive Allah or escape His justice, but Allah will always stand on the side of the weak and the aggrieved against the malicious and the tyrant, in order to create a balance in human interaction. If Allah were to stand on the side of the latter group, all life would be corrupted; oppression would become a way of life and the whole of mankind would be divided into masters and slaves.

There are many examples of how this divine power operates and governs our lives, as can be seen in the tragic downfall of men who once reigned supreme and thought that they had mastery over their destiny and the destiny of others, and then are suddenly reduced to nothing, and forced to seek mercy by their former slaves. This sudden change of fortune is but one of Allah's signs to mankind to remind them of His constant watchfulness and prompt justice.

Allah loves no one except for his good deeds, and dislikes no one except for his wrongdoing. In this way His justice is well-balanced and complete. The mere remembrance of these facts gives us immunity from evil-doing and makes us recognize that it is Allah Who is the giver of all things; that all human ability vanishes in the face of His will and power; and that He Who gives sustenance to billions of people on this earth is capable of granting the Believer all that his heart desires and of protecting him from the many dangers that threaten his life.

The important lesson in all this is that we must not forget, even for a moment, that all our deeds are carefully observed and recorded, and that one day we will be faced with them. By recalling that it is safer for us to judge our own selves before we are judged by Allah in the Hereafter, we may be able to exercise control over our desires and prevent them from leading us away from Allah's right way.

In addition to recording man's deeds, the worthy guardians (i.e. the angels) also protect the believers from all sorts of evil which no human power can avoid or repulse. For example, we sometimes escape certain peril and misfortune in some mysterious and unexpected ways that defy all explanation, and which we usually attribute to Allah's providence. This belief in Allah's protection arises from our conviction that no human power could have diverted the course of those events that threaten our lives. Indeed no one can deny the existence of this mysterious divine protecting power or dispute its source. Thus, Allah does not only defend those who believe in Him, but He also protects them from many evils of which they are entirely unaware.

The Sūrah continues:

> "So let man consider from what he is created. He is created from a gushing fluid that issued from between the loins and ribs." (al-Ṭāriq 86:5-7)

Here again, man is cautioned against becoming possessed by his own vanity and belief that he can beguile Allah or that he can escape His justice. He is advised to consider how he was created and to contrast his inferiority with Allah's might and supreme power; to contemplate thoughtfully how he grew, by the will of Allah, from a tiny cell into a living being, and how from this tiny cell all his bodily parts and organs have developed into an integrated and infinitely complex organism that works together in total balance and harmony. In other words, Allah is telling man not to strut like a peacock or become rapt in his own power and rebel against the powers of Him Who made him and gave him the faculties which have elevated him above all other creatures.

Some critics contend that this is not the way in which Adam was created, and ask whether the verse refers to him. There is a difference between the two acts of creation, for in Adam's case the process of creation was observable, and he knew how he was created, and saw Allah. He, therefore, was in no need of being reminded of it. But all creation that came after him belongs to the Unseen, for none of us has ever been aware of how he was created or has seen the process itself; we tend to take it as a natural phenomenon, forgetting the divine power behind its occurrence.

It is obvious, therefore, that Allah wants us to be constantly aware of His power, because such remembrance and our knowledge that we are constantly watched by His worthy guardians who record every deed we do, act as a deterrent if ever we become lured by our own power or become oblivious of the ultimate divine power that created us and made us supreme over all other creatures.

Some may ask about the relationship between the piercing star and the creation of man. Although they may seem to be independent and have unconnected themes, they are, in fact, closely related. For instance, the piercing star and the creation of man both remind us of Allah's capabilities: the morning star reminds us that nothing is hidden from Allah's knowledge, and creation reminds us of His infinite ingenuity and capacity.

With regard to death and resurrection we are told:

> "Lo! He verily is Able to return him" (al-Ṭāriq 86:8)

The Creator Who has been able to create from a single cell the co-ordinated human body with all its complex functions can surely give it life after physical death has occurred, and restore man's identity in the new world of the Hereafter.

An engineer who designs or builds a new machine can easily destroy it and rebuild it. In fact, the experience he has gained makes it easier for him to reassemble it or to build many other machines like it. If man, with his limited powers can accomplish such work, could Allah not, with all His limitless powers and knowledge, recreate the creature He had previously made? Man after all, is but a human mechanism. But if Allah created man from nothing – that is, from something so infinitely minute as to be unobservable by the naked eye, and, unlike the maker of the machine, using no readily available material – would He not be able to resurrect him or remake him? Of course He could!

This analogy only serves to highlight the issue, for to Allah there is no such thing as 'difficult' or 'easy'. Every thing is subject to His will and can be promptly materialized with the mere utterance of the word "Be".

When Allah reminds us of His ability to recreate us or make us anew, He does not do so because He is in need of us or needs to compel us to believe in His supreme Being, for such belief does not add nor detract from His power and supremacy, but He reminds us of it out of mercy towards us; to inculcate in us a sense of humility and an awareness of our insignificance and weakness. He wants us to be constantly aware that it is He alone Who has the upper hand in this world. No man can challenge His authority or escape His justice in this world and the next, or doubt that in the process of our creation are found the best portents of His magnificence and absolute power, as well as marked evidence of our insignificance and inferiority where power is concerned.

The Sūrah goes on to tell us:

> "On the day when all hidden thoughts will be searched out." (86:9)

On the Day of Judgement (or in the next world) all our actions, motives and thoughts, however secret, will be disclosed and tested, not by the standards of worldly norms, customs or partiality, but by the standards of divine justice and truth. In other words, nothing will be concealed from Allah, and that intention will be the scale by which Allah's judgement will be made and His justice applied. The seat of intention is the heart and it represents the free will of man. Where it is possible for men to compel others to lie, perform unlawful and unjust acts, to persecute them or to put restraints on their freedom of action, no one can exercise his will on another person's heart or force it to feel or believe in something it rejects. Allah has kept this domain entirely free from compulsion because it is the domain where man will be judged. For the judgement to be just and fair, coercion had to be eliminated. This area has been left entirely to man's free will. Accordingly, Allah has excluded from punishment all acts that have been forced upon a person whose heart rejected and disapproved of them, even when they involved matters of belief or disbelief which form the core of faith and religion. On this Allah says:

> "Whoso disbelieves in Allah after his belief – save him who is forced thereto and whose heart is still content with the Faith – but whoso finds ease in disbelief: on them is wrath from Allah. Theirs will be an awful doom." (al-Naḥl 16:106)

This exception extends to adultery that is committed under compulsion. Hence, man will be judged for only those deeds that are done by his free will – whose seat is the heart – for his true intentions develop willingly and independently from any external compulsion. Nevertheless, Allah cautions us not to attempt to beguile Him through self-deception or pretending that we were coerced into wrongdoing, for He surely knows our innermost intentions. No matter how cunning and scheming we are, we can never conceal anything from His knowledge.

Then we are told that on the Day of Judgement wrongdoers will have no might or helpers, for in that test, no privileges or advantages in this life will have any influence or force. But why has Allah mentioned might? The answer is that might encourages and lures men into doing injustice and oppressing the weak who cannot retaliate or claim their rights. The oppressors in all cases are always supported by collaborators who are always ready to serve their purposes. Hence came Allah's emphasis that there would be no helpers of any sort to support the wrongdoer when he is confronted with his wicked deeds. In short, Allah is reminding us not to let our own ambitions and desires blur our minds and hide the truth from us, nor to have any illusions about His constant observation of our deeds and acts. We should not let our vanity and self-deceit lure us away from His right way, and we should know that salvation and redemption can be secured only through humility and the full acknowledgement of His power.

Allah constantly reminds us of the Hereafter because He knows that sinners are always hopeful, or try to convince themselves, that there will be no judgement after death. In fact such foolish persons are trying to stifle their terror of what awaits them on that Day by denying its truth.
The Sūrah continues:

> "By the heaven which gives the returning rain." (86:11)

In this verse, Allah reveals a significant fact which remained unknown to man until many centuries after the revelation of the Qur'ān. We all know that surface and ocean water, through the heat of the sun, evaporates, turns to clouds, condenses and falls back as rain, and that, in an ever-recurring cycle, the heaven returns to the earth the water that rises to it. We should not miss the accuracy of the expression 'the raining heaven', for it clarifies this scientific process to anyone who has no knowledge of how rain is formed. For those who know this scientific fact, the meaning and accuracy of the verse becomes more vivid and comprehensible.

> "And the earth which splits (with the growth of trees and plants)." (86:12)

Here again the cyclic regeneration of plants and the splitting of the soil points to Allah's power and laws. Every thing comes and goes in an everlasting cycle. If Allah is capable of ordaining this continual process of regeneration (or rebirth), then surely He can subject man to the same laws. In all these cycles Allah gives us simple examples of what will happen to man after death. It is as simple as all the natural phenomena which are acted out before us on the stage of life day after day and year after year.

Then the Sūrah tells us that the Qur'ān, the ultimate truth and "conclusive word" (86:13) "is no pleasantry" (86:14). In this verse is expressed the depth and seriousness of the whole issue. We should not take all that has previously been said lightly, for once we have left this life, our chances to repent will have passed. Hence came Allah's cautioning to take His words seriously, because there will be no second chance. The whole issue will be settled once and for all and Allah's verdict will be final and irrevocable. Nor will it help anyone to pretend that he was not fully aware of this.

Those who say "The Fire (of punishment) will not touch us save for a certain number of days" (al-Baqarah 2:80), and those who believe that Allah will be lenient, and those who speak lightly of hell and its torture, are greatly mistaken and foolish. Indeed the Day of Judgement will be an awesome day, and Allah's reminding us of it is done out of mercy toward us. His cautioning should be taken solemnly and be understood in terms of His unlimited power and what He can do on that Day.

In the concluding Āyāt, Allah gives Muḥammad (SAW) advice on how to deal with such wrong-doers:

> "Lo! they plot a plot (against you, O Muḥammad), and I plot a plot (against them), so give a respite to the disbelievers. Deal gently with them for a while." (al-Ṭāriq 86:15-17)

In this verse Allah draws our attention to those evil and unregenerate men who plot and scheme against the beneficent purpose of Allah. But their plotting will be of no avail, and Allah's purpose will always prevail. There is, however, a point in the quotation "I plot a plot (against them)" which requires some deeper thought and elucidation, for sometimes we come across words which ought not to be attributed to Allah in their normal sense, e.g. 'Allah plots'. The word 'plot' (kayd, from kāda) has come in conjunction with other words in order to simplify the meaning. For instance, when Allah says, "The reward of an ill-deed is an ill the like thereof" (al-Shūrā 42:40), He does not do harm for the sake of harm: His underlying purpose is to reform the wrong-doer. The subsequent word derives its meaning from the preceding word and from the context. The meaning is that if you do a wrong deed, you will be repaid with a counter-act which is equally distressing to you. But the underlying purpose of this punishment is good because it stops you from repeating the wrong deed. The verse addresses those persons who cannot curb their thirst for revenge. It reminds offenders who plot against Allah's purpose and religion that they will be dealt with in exactly the same way, i.e. that Allah will plan to foil their intrigues and ill-intended schemes.

The same warning is applied to that group of scientists and Orientalists who use their discoveries and studies to sow the seeds of doubt in the hearts of believers through the postulation of unfounded hypotheses and false assumptions.

In spite of this determined invective against the Qur'ān and Islam, the faith, nevertheless, has expanded and flourished all over the world. For in addition to uniting the Muslims against such malicious attacks, it has brought its truth home to millions of people who until recently had little knowledge of Islam.

Some zealous Muslims seem to be apprehensive of these heretical attempts, perhaps because they fear the long term influence of such invectives against religion and faith. But there is no reason for this apprehension, for all attempts to dislodge the Muslims' faith, by trying to show that the Qur'ān contradicts many of today's scientific facts – proved to be false and futile – have, rather, added to the credibility of the faith and have not blemished it in any way.

Allah, in stating that many plotters would eventually emerge and plot against both His faith and the believers, has not only informed us about them, but also wants to assure us that He is able to encounter their plotting and foil their schemes, and at the same time ease our anxiety and apprehension, as is clearly reflected in the following verse:

> "And when those who disbelieve plot against you (O Muḥammad) . . .
> . . . but Allah (also) plots; and Allah is the best of plotters" (al-Anfāl 8:30)

Allah's knowledge, which encompasses all things, hidden or visible, gives Him the upper hand where plotting is concerned. The plight of these plotters is that they overlook

Allah's power. In their attempt to hit at the religion in secret they forget that their innerselves are an open book to Allah.

They seem to be oblivious of the only true power in this universe and are inclined to put their faith in the means, forgetting that it is Allah Who has given them the means and can always divert their effects, annul them at will, obstruct them from serving the purpose for which they were established, or moreover, reverse their outcome. Man therefore cannot live and prosper on this earth without Allah's help. It is equally true that no man who plans anything against Allah's will or attempts to defy Him ever succeeds, and all such attempts end with the opposite results and bitter disappointment.

Allah wants to instil peace and security in the hearts and minds of believers, as has been clarified in the above Sūrah. He is asking them to remember His power at all times and in all situations where they become subject to persecution and oppression or when their faith becomes a target for attack from those heretics who are bent on smearing it. They should always have faith in Allah's overwhelming power and His ability to turn the tables on those plotters and repay them in the same coin many times over. Once they put their trust in this divine power and might, their anxiety will be dispelled, and they will be able to confront the world, fearing no one but Allah.

The Sūrah ends with the verse:

> "So give a respite to the disbelievers . . ."
> (al-Ṭāriq 86:17)

Here Allah is asking Muḥammad to give the disbelievers a little more time and be patient until His command regarding their punishment has been pronounced. This is a reminder to those impatient persons who are always eager to see Allah's justice applied promptly; they are always disappointed when they see the wicked and the unjust commit their evil deeds with impunity. We say to these people that Allah's justice may be delayed, but it is never-failing. We must not imagine that if some evil seems to go unpunished it is not known to Allah or has escaped his attention. Indeed Allah's justice is ever present and His power is also present, and no one can escape from it. In fact, the wisdom of creation would be abolished if every ill-deed was punished instantaneously, for Allah wants His believing worshippers to come to Him voluntarily with no compulsion exerted on them. If He wanted to coerce people to obey His commands, He could have done so with ease. But instead He gave man freedom of choice and showed him the way to gain His pleasure. He wanted man's love for Him to come from within man himself and for that love to grow until it overcomes all worldly temptations and the temporary glitter of the world.

If punishment, or reward, were applied instantaneously, no one would have rejected faith or strayed from Allah's right way. If man suffered prompt punishment for his ill-deeds, or even knew that his due punishment would not be delayed, he would steer clear of all wrongdoing. But what encourages man to violate Allah's laws is that punishment is unseen, so he is hopeful that there will be no such penalty, or that he may dodge it in one way or another, helped in his perilous way by the temptation that is readily offered to him by Satan. In fact the invisibility of future punishment represents the true test for the human self. Temptation is the test, which man may pass or fail, and the purpose of the test is to make him a witness against himself, lest he pretend on the Day of Judgement that he did not know. The result of this test is recorded and will be made known to him on that Day.

When Allah tells Muḥammad (SAW) to give the non-believers more time, He means that He does not apply punishment immediately following the ill-deed, but that He gives the deviant enough time; and that this should not fill him with despair or disappointment or make him feel that Allah has abandoned the believers, for punishment, though delayed, will surely come. The delay is but a test of the strength of our faith and trust in Allah's plan which can never be frustrated.

But some people believe that punishment is only applied

in the Hereafter. I say to these people that punishment is applied in this life and the next, for Allah does not leave the unjust wrongdoer and the rebellious to go unpunished for ever, but rather makes the punishment a lesson for those who may be tempted to embark on the same perilous path of vanity and conceit. But when Allah's retribution is brought into force it is never applied through a faithful and righteous man. It is always carried out by another, more unjust, rebel, as is stated in the following verse.

> ". . . He is able to . . . make you taste the tyranny one of another . . ." (al-An'ām 6:65)

But this delay in applying punishment is in itself an act of mercy which Allah has undertaken to grant to all mankind, including the rebels among His worshippers, for if He punished everyone promptly for every sin, he would not have left a single being on this earth unpunished. The delay of punishment is intended as a test of faith for believers, and as an opportunity for the misguided to mend their ways and seek forgiveness.

Chapter 2

Hidden Forces in the Universe

When Allah created this universe, He also established specific laws for everything in it and subjected these laws to the powers of those creatures for whom they were decreed. Thus man has his human laws which are compatible with his clay-created nature. The Jinn have their own laws which are compatible with their being created of fire. The laws of the jinn, for instance, make it possible for them to penetrate, unobstructed, any material barrier or change their form. The angels, too, who have been created from light, have their own laws and can rise to the heaven or come down to the earth in obedience to Allah's commands.

Where science is concerned, there should be no restriction on its activities and explorations as long as they are confined to the physical aspects of the material world and all its constituent elements and phenomena that can be subjected to empirical research and laboratory tests. This domain is wide open for the human mind to seek further knowledge and add to what it already possesses of it. Indeed, it is both beneficial as well as desirable for man to explore the universe and see glimpses of Allah's portents which He has promised to show him:

> "We shall show them Our portents on the horizon and in themselves until it will be manifest unto them that it is the truth . . ." (Fuṣṣilat 41:53)

Here, Allah is referring to the disbelievers who denied His truth, for, if they had believed in Him, the emphatic phrase "until it will be manifest unto them that it is the truth" would have not been introduced. This is because the believer has no need to be reminded of the truth about Allah and His holy book, the Qur'ān, or His messenger, Muḥammad (SAW). But Allah wanted the disbelievers to discover these portents and dispute their validity so that He could use their own argument as supporting evidence for His existence, for He knew that these disbelievers would try to confuse His worshippers and throw doubt upon the facts recorded in the Qur'ān using their own defective knowledge and understanding of the true meaning of its verses and their misleading scientific hypotheses about the realities of His universe.

But since the Qur'ān was first revealed, Allah has always used such beguilers to confirm faith among believers. Thus, in the first days of Islam, came the revelation condemning Abū Lahab:

> "The power of Abū Lahab will perish, and he will perish. His wealth and gains will not exempt him. He will be plunged in flaming Fire. And his wife, the wood-carrier, will have upon her neck a halter of palm-fibre." (al-Masad 111:1-5)

This verse represented the first act of faith-confirmation among Muḥammad's (SAW) followers, using one of Islam's cardinal enemies. For Abū Lahab could have challenged Muḥammad (SAW) and the message by simply confessing his Islam in public, thereby demolishing the whole religion. Even in this situation where he had the freedom of decision, he could not choose other than the choice which Allah had predicted and planned. The same thing happened when the position of the Qiblah was changed and Allah predicted that

> "The foolish of the people will say: 'What has turned them from the qiblah which they formerly observed?' . . ." (al-Baqarah 2:142)

The use of the future tense (sayaqūl) in the above quotation indicates that the remark took place after the revelation of the verse. The sceptics could have abstained from making that remark, and then accused Muḥammad (SAW) of making a false statement by ascribing to them something they had not said. But they did say it and fulfilled Allah's prediction, thereby confirming the truth of every word that Muḥammad (SAW) said.

About the challengers of Allah's truth in modern times, He tells us:

> "I made them not to witness the creation of the heavens and the earth, nor their own creation; nor choose I misleaders for (My) helpers." (al-Kahf 18:51)

This means that in the course of time there would emerge some heretics who would try to mislead others. This refers to all the modern theories about the origin of man and the assumption that he belonged to the ape species; the origin of our solar system; and all the scientific theories which are taught these days. The fact that such theorists have come and postulated their hypotheses which deny the role of the divine power in the process of creation dispels all doubt about the truth of the Qur'ān and its predictive power.

Indeed, because of the constant challenge launched by the Qur'ān and its inexhaustible fund of knowledge which it reveals to successive generations, we should expect more of these attacks and the emergence of new theories and new heretics who would try to cast doubt about Allah's existence and His being the creator of everything in this universe. Yet all these unfounded hypotheses and attacks have, conversely, helped to consolidate faith and affirm Allah's revelations to mankind rather than to detract from them.

The above is a necessary introduction, showing Allah's power and how He can turn to the advantage of His religion the disbelievers' malicious attempts to cast doubt about His existence.

The Laws of the Jinn and the Angels.

We often meet people who try to delve into such unseen

areas as the world of the jinn, the nature of the Hereafter and the world of the devils which, in addition to their being beyond the scope and capacity of the human mind to visualize, do not lend themselves to any empirical study. Those who volunteer to formulate new theories or voice any opinion which contradicts what Allah has conveyed to us should support their theories with corresponding material and testable evidence which could lend itself readily to logical discussion and verification. Allah has informed us – in general rather than specific terms – about the laws of all other creatures.

Thus, when someone tries to refute the Prophet's (SAW) saying that "the devil flows in the human body like the blood," we should ask him if his refutation is based on scientific knowledge about the molecular structure of the devil's organism, and whether germs, for instance, are not able to invade the human body and circulate in the blood. Surely, as long as we are ignorant of the nature of the devil, we are in no position to deny what has been conveyed to us by Allah's Messengers and Prophets as long as we know that everything in this universe has its own exclusive and governing laws. The sun and the earth, for instance, are not governed by the same laws, nor are man and the jinn. The angels, too, have their laws. There are also a few chosen worshippers whom Allah favours with immense knowledge, and has established for them special laws that provide them with suprasensory powers in their interaction with the universe.

In this respect we ought to pay attention to two 'Sūrahs' which Muslims recite frequently at night, namely the Sūrahs of al-Falaq (113) and of al-Nās (114).

In the first, we seek refuge in the divine guidance from the forces (and matters) which are beyond our control and knowledge. In the second, we seek Allah's help in matters over which we have some control but fear that we may weaken in our resolve and succumb to temptation.

> "Say, I seek refuge in the Lord of the Daybreak; from the evil of that which He created; from the evil of the darkness when it is intense, and from the evil of malignant witchcraft, and from the evil of the envier when he envies." (al-Falaq 113:1-5)

These evils from which we seek Allah's refuge and guidance are physical dangers from without us; that is, we are not accountable for their outcome, they form no part of Allah's injunctions, "This you must do, and this you must not do". Thus when Allah tells us to seek refuge in Him He knows that there are evil forces which threaten man's life and security, and that He alone can ward off the evil of these forces.

Allah asks us to put our trust in Him, because He is the ultimate and true source of security and light; if we take refuge in His divine guidance and goodness, we are guaranteed freedom from ignorance, superstition and every other kind of evil. The Sūrah also refers to the dispelling of darkness and the spread of light, or life and existence. This could be taken literally to mean the light which Allah has created to dispel the darkness of the universe and ensure life. It also represents the divine light which penetrates our hearts and souls to give us enlightenment and eradicate our fears.

We should, however, give some thought to the phrase "from the evil of that which He created" (113:2) for it leaves no doubt in our mind but that evil does exist and threaten man's life. But all that Allah has created is good. It is man himself who has marred his life by fostering evil and nourishing corruption in this world, through his lust for power and material ambition.

Earthquakes and Floods

But if all that Allah has created is good, then what is the evil to which the Sūrah refers? There are two views which we must consider when answering this question. The first is concerned with the wisdom of the Creator, and the second with creation itself. With regard to the wisdom of the Creator, Allah has created enormous forces in the universe and subdued them to man's service. Thus the sun, the moon, the earth, the stars and all domesticated animals have been ordained by His will to serve man. But man, in his vanity, pretends that it was he who subdued them to his will and power. He takes all these divine gifts and the means which Allah has provided for his survival as natural phenomena, brought about by the interaction of physical and chemical processes, over which no power, divine or otherwise, has any control.

Allah, in order to bring man to his senses, shows him signs of His presence and His domination over all these forces. Thus He turns the gentle wind into devastating storms, the rain into floods and reduces whole cities to rubble through earthquakes, to remind him of His presence. This serves only as a light punishment for his ingratitude and arrogance, rather than to bring about his destruction, and to show him that if he had been allowed to enjoy the benefits of these natural forces, he was able to do so only by His will, since He alone has domination over this universe.

In addition to these reminders which occur from time to time on a limited scale, there are other permanent and continuous signs, many of which can be seen in man's relationship with his environment and with other species and in his ability to subdue them to his will and service. A young boy, for instance, can train a horse to serve him and obey his commands despite the enormous difference in their strength; because the horse was created to serve man, it was subdued by the will of Allah and made to obey man's commands. On the other hand, although Allah has not subdued venomous reptiles to man's will, they do not represent an absolute evil, for their venom is now used in a variety of antidotes which save thousands of lives. Even germs are not an absolute evil, for from them we are now able to produce serum.

But the fact remains that there are things in this universe which are a threat to man, and he can only protect himself from their evil by seeking refuge in Allah. As for creatures unknown to us such as devils and jinns, they too are not subdued to the will of man. They have the power to make evil suggestions and influence man's thoughts and actions, thereby causing his own peril, while they remain invisible to him and beyond his power to confront or evade. Here, too, we have no alternative but to seek refuge in Allah and ask for His divine protection, for His power alone can build a barrier between their evil suggestions and perilous influence and our minds and souls. This is, perhaps, one of the main reasons why we are always careful to seek Allah's help even when we are under the most skilful medical care and taking the most effective medicines.

Indeed, there are things in the form of natural forces, beasts, man himself, and the invisible evil forces that inhabit the universe besides man, which Allah has not subjected to man's will. It is a common practice among men to seek Allah's help when they are sick, because they are hopeful that with His help the medicine they take will produce its healing effect. It is not uncommon for someone suffering from a disease and taking medicine to be cured, while another in the same situation continues to sicken and perhaps to die. How many times have we heard doctors say, after having done all they could to save a patient's life, that any additional help must come from Allah? It is the same when a patient for whom there was no hope suddenly recovers after all medical skill failed to save him. This is what is meant in the following verse from the Sūrah al-Shu'arā':

> "And when I sicken, then He heals me."
> (al-Shu'arā' 26:80)

This is because although the worldly means available to man are a basic factor in fighting the disease the final outcome of healing rests with Allah. Doctors who witness, almost daily, this divine miracle of healing are in constant touch with this divine power and are always hopeful that it will show itself when all their professional skills fail to produce results.

The wisdom of the Creator in creating these evils which threaten man's peace and life is to draw his attention to the true and ultimate power which has subjected the universe to his service. Indeed the influence of germs, venomous reptiles and other harmful creatures of man's life is far less important than the influence of the other forces in the universe.

All these forces have been subdued and made to serve man by the will of Allah. Man had no part in their creation, nor can he exercise any power over even the minutest organisms, let alone the formidable natural forces. No matter how powerful he may think he is, he cannot disengage himself from the will of Allah and His guidance. He will always be in need of His protecting power and His mercy. In fact, man's fear of these unpredictable and invisible forces binds him to Allah and reveals to him his own vulnerability in the absence of His care, and that he can gain strength and confront these invisible and uncontrollable forces by seeking refuge in Him.

Man can see the wisdom in the creation of such forces by comparing between the forces which are subject to his control and use and those which are not. In this is a reminder for those who are inclined to become oblivious of Allah's might, trusting in nothing but their vanity and self-idolization. Such persons are often selected by Allah as models for contrasting His divine power with the incompetence and inferiority of men, when He suddenly afflicts them with disease, infirmity and misery.

We are also advised to seek refuge in Allah from "The evil of the darkness when it is intense" (113:3). Here Allah is saying to us that He has created day and night and lit the day so that life could go on, and to enable mankind to persue its daily business and activity. In contrast He has made the night dark so that all activity is stopped, and to allow man to rest. But darkness is the cloak under which evildoers, human and non-human, can safely hide and practice their plots. It deprives the unwary prey of the safety and security of daylight. Yet this security is assured if we seek refuge in Him and put our trust in His ever-present care and protection.

The verse continues to enumerate the invisible dangers, and mentions "the evil of malignant witchcraft" (113:4). Scholars have long pondered over this passage. Literally, it refers to the evil of "blowers (feminine plural) upon knots", which was a common form of witchcraft in Arabia, where women used to tie knots in a cord and blow upon them with an imprecation. But Pharaoh, too, had his own male sorcerers. This made scholars apply the name to both men and women, on the grounds that the whole practice represented an unseen issue, rather than a topic that can be tested logically and empirically. Because of this difficulty and the abstracted definition of the term, witchcraft became a controversial issue rejected by many. But to such persons we ask: were our ancestors able to see minute germs and viruses? Of course not; yet they existed. We are able to see them today only with the help of the microscope. The microscope did not create these germs; all it did was to remove one of the barriers of the Unseen and enable us to discover things the existence of which, until recently, was unknown. There is great divine wisdom in this, for Allah reveals to us every day new things about this universe to show us that all the unseen things He has told us about do exist and that we should believe in them even though they may seem invisible to us.

Therefore, if Allah has mentioned sorcerers and witchcraft in the Qur'an, then we should not doubt their existence but have faith in His word, for one day, by His will, the secrets of witchcraft may be unfolded to mankind; but until then we should accept His word that it does exist and that it is harmful to man.

Witchcraft and the Human Perception

Allah says in the Sūrah al-A'rāf:

> ". . . And when they threw they cast a spell upon the people's eyes, and overawed them . . ." (al-A'rāf 7:116)

There are two kinds of witchcraft. The first is practised through man's own powers, and in the second he is assisted by non-human powers. In the first kind, man is able to impose his powers on the perception of his audience, influencing it to visualize things in a different and untrue form. In other words, he bewitches (or deceives) their eyes and minds. The object of witchcraft does not undergo any true physical change, as is confirmed in the above verse. In fact, if we analyse all the kinds of magic that are performed by ordinary magicians we will find that they all rely on the skill of the performer in deceiving the audience's visual perception. The science of perception abounds with such phenomena and shows how configuration and background can distort the true image. The mirage, for instance, is one example, as are the colours of the spectrum which in certain conditions may give rise to images of flying saucers and so on. Similarly, the eye is not equipped to identify or follow the rapid movement of the blades of a spinning electric fan or the propeller of an aeroplane, which, when spinning, appear to be a turning disc or wheel. The deception of the eye is, therefore, a natural and a common phenomenon experienced by all humans. It is a kind of magic the existence of which no one can deny.

But evil witchcraft involves both deception and terror. In this, the performer begins by instilling fear in the heart of his victim before subduing him entirely to his will. Sometimes, they use such objects as bones, and resort to terrifying rituals and incantations to create a certain atmosphere. These persons usually practice their evil craft in the secrecy of darkness. Yet although the warlock, or witch, cannot change the state of the object of the spell, his swift movement and skill make the beholder see it otherwise and imagine that he is faced with a supernatural power and readily submit himself to it. This kind of witchcraft was demonstrated when Moses faced Pharaoh's magicians, as is told in the verse

> ". . . Their cords and their staves, by their magic, appeared to him as though they ran." (Ṭā' Hā' 20:66)

The use of the phrase 'appeared to him', (yukhayyalu ilayhi) should not pass unnoticed, for it means that the wizards did not change the state of their rods, but only made them appear to their audience to be living snakes, and that this result was helped to a great extent by the wizards' skill, as well as by the awesome atmosphere that surrounded them. In contrast, when Moses threw his staff it turned to a writhing serpent which "swallowed straight away all the falsehood which they faked". On seeing this miracle, the magicians fell down prostrate in adoration, for they knew that what they witnessed was no illusion, but was rather a sign of Allah's overwhelming power bestowed upon His Messenger.

The Preparation of Moses

Moses had to be prepared by Allah for such an experience. He had to be taught how to distinguish between a mere spell and a divine miracle on the one hand, and be shielded against the fear and influence of sorcery on the other. Thus in order to immunize him from being bewitched, Allah had earlier taken him through a similar faith-instilling experiment:

> "And what is that in thy right hand, O Moses?" (Ṭā' Hā' 20:17)

to which he replied

> "This is my staff whereon I lean, and wherewith I beat down branches for my sheep, and wherein I find other uses." (20:18)

Allah then said to him, "Cast it down, O Moses". He did so, and instantly it changed into a live serpent. Moses was overcome with fear when he saw this happen. But Allah reassured him and said to him:

> "Grasp it and fear not. We shall return it to its former state." (20:21)

With these divine words, Moses watched the snake change back into a rod.

Why did Allah subject Moses to such an experiment? To answer this question, we begin by saying that in all divine actions there is an underlying purpose and wisdom. Nothing happens haphazardly or by chance. The changing of the rod into a serpent was not only a miracle, but also an unsurpassable act. For Allah knew that Pharaoh's sorcerers would use their sorcery to put a spell on all those, including Moses, who watched the challenge. He found it necessary to teach him about the art of witchcraft and how to differentiate between mere illusionary magic and a true miracle, and at the same time to immunize him against the fear which He knew would seize him on seeing the sorcerers' rods turn into serpents.

If Moses had shown the slightest sign of fear, he would have raised serious doubt in the hearts of his followers who believed in him as a Messenger from Allah, as such fear would have given them the impression that the sorcerers' power was greater than that of Allah Who had sent him and stood behind him. His prior training was, therefore, a necessary preparation for this situation. But even after all this preparation, Moses could not prevent fear from creeping into his heart and "conceived a fear in his mind" (20:67). But again Allah reassured him and said to him:

> "Fear not! Lo! you are the higher. Throw that which is in your right hand! It will eat up that which they have made. Lo! that which they have made is but a wizard's artifice, and a wizard shall not be successful, to whatever point (of skill) he may attain." (20:68-69)

Thus Allah reassured Moses twice, once when He turned his rod into a serpent and again when fear crept into his heart. The sorcerers' belief in Moses and his God, hours before they were put to death by Pharaoh, gained Allah's mercy and forgiveness, even though they had spent all their previous years fighting Him, making use of their witchcraft. Indeed there is a worthy lesson in this parable for the whole of mankind, namely that we should never despair of Allah's mercy and forgiveness, no matter how long we have rebelled against Him or strayed from His right way.

It is obvious from the above that ordinary sorcery which relies on man's own resources rather than on non-human or supernatural powers depends entirely on perceptual deception and illusion and the skill of the sorcerer in inducing fear and awe in the heart of his victim. This kind of sorcery cannot change the state or form of the object of the experiment.

Furthermore, we are told by Allah not to be scared of this kind of sorcery, and always to seek refuge in Him from the evils of such invisible danger.

But there is another kind of sorcery which makes use of non-human, or supernatural, powers. A good example of this kind is illustrated in the Sūrah of 'The Ants', where Solomon requested that the throne of Bilqis, queen of Sheba, be brought to him in Jerusalem from Yemen:

> ". . . O chiefs! Which of you will bring me her throne before they come unto me surrendering?"
> (al-Naml 27:38)

Solomon, who had total mastery over the jinn and the devils, did not determine which of his subjects had to carry out his master's request. All that the request indicated was that Bilqīs had left Yemen, together with her companions, on her way to meet Solomon who wanted to have her throne transported to his court. A giant powerful jinn volunteered to fulfil his master's wish and said

> "I will bring it to you before you can rise from your place" (al-Naml 27:39)

Here we should notice that the volunteer was a most powerful jinn, and not just any ordinary jinn, who estimated that the time needed for the task would last no longer than the duration of the meeting, according to his own laws. But when the one "with whom was Knowledge of the Scriptures" heard this he volunteered to do the job in a much shorter time and said:

> "I will bring it to you before you can rise from your place" (al-Naml 27:39)

Here we should notice that the volunteer was a most powerful jinn, and not just any ordinary jinn, who estimated that the time needed for the task would last no longer than the duration of the meeting, according to his own laws. But when the one "with whom was Knowledge of the Scriptures" heard this he volunteered to do the job in a much shorter time and said:

> ". . . I will bring it to you before your gaze returns unto you . . ." (27:40)

Apparently, the one who had knowledge of the Scripture was acting according to more powerful and higher laws. One would infer that each one of those who attended the court of Solomon spoke in terms of the laws established by Allah for his own kind. There were no human volunteers because their laws were inferior for such a task. None of the common jinn volunteered, despite their formidable capabilities, powers and enormous speed, because they knew that these powers fell short of the required conditions for transforming the throne into some transportable form so quickly. Only one who had the knowledge of the Scripture and the arts of magic knew that the task could be accomplished only according to his laws. In establishing these laws, Allah had made some of His creatures more powerful than others. Man was created of clay and his laws had to be compatible with his nature and limited powers; the jinn were created of fire and had laws entirely different to those laws pertaining to man. As for those creatures who had knowledge of the Scripture, they were endowed with the power to violate natural laws. In this gradation Allah has given us the evidence that He alone has the power to change the nature of things from one state or form into another.

Hārūt and Mārūt

Before discussing the parable of the two angels Hārūt and Mārūt, we should understand that the whole of creation is based on equal opportunity and that every person has the same opportunity as others. This equality is jeopardized when people seek the assistance of non-human powers whose laws exceed by far the powers available to man through his own laws. The goal of such persons is to deceive others by pretending that they use these non-human forces for the benefit of man, whereas they intend to use them to promote their own evil ends and ambitions. But in the end, through Allah's planning, these evil forces often turn against them, and afflict them with all sorts of calamities, and even insanity. About these people Allah says to His Messenger

> "And indeed (O Muḥammad) individuals of humankind used to invoke the protection of individuals of the Jinn, so that they increased them in revolt (against Allah)." (al-Jinn 72:6)

About the story of Hārūt and Mārūt, Allah tells us that the above persons

> ". . . followed that which the devils falsely related against the kingdom of Solomon. Solomon disbelieved not, but the devils disbelieved, teaching mankind magic . . ." (al-Baqarah 2:102)

According to the narrative, Allah had given Solomon mastery over all other creatures, and one day Solomon discovered that the devils had been using magic to spread corruption on earth, so he collected all their charms and buried them in a secure place. When he died, the devils alleged that he had obtained his kingdom and his mastery over them through the power of magic, and revealed the place where Solomon had hidden the talismans. But Allah corrected this accusation and absolved Solomon from any guilt, and confirmed that all his knowledge and powers had been bestowed by Him.

The phrase "teaching mankind magic" indicates that there is another kind of magic apart from that which is practised by men skilled in beguiling others with illusion and perceptual deception. This type is often practised by non-believing ministers of evil or wicked spirits which can assume the forms of animals or humans or any other form. But in doing so they are subject to the laws of shape and form. Allah, in His mercy to man, has planned things this way, for if these spirits were allowed to assume this change of form without any kind of controlling law, life would have been exceedingly difficult on earth, and these evil ones would have reigned supreme on it. But their being governed by the laws of the form they assume and their inability to stay as such for long made them vulnerable to man's power and his ability to destroy them or get rid of them. Sometimes these evil ones assume the form of ugly creatures and stand between man and his wife, giving the latter a very ugly image, and so sowing discord and hate between the two of them.

The verse continues to tell us that these evil ones exploited what they learnt from Hārūt and Mārūt:

> "But the devils disbelieved, teaching mankind magic, and that which was revealed to the two angels in Babel, Hārūt and Mārūt. Nor did they (the two angels) teach it to anyone till they had said: 'We are only a temptation, therefore disbelieve not (in the guidance of Allah)'. And from these two (angels) people learn that by which they cause division between man and wife, but they injure thereby no-one save by Allah's leave. And they learn that which harms them and profits them not. And surely they do know that he who trafficks therein will have no (happy) portion in the Hereafter; and surely evil is the price for which they sell their souls, if they but knew." (al-Baqarah 2:102)

The Opportunity and the Reckoning

Indeed there are many principles which we should learn from

the above verse. The first is that the ability to change form with the intent to hide the truth or distort reality can only be accomplished by evil ones or devils. All other forms of magic are but illusions and perceptual deception in which no change of form or shape can materialize. The second is that the former kind of magic was introduced initially by the two angels, Hārūt and Mārūt, who never failed, when teaching their secrets to anyone, to inform him that they were but a temptation and that learning this kind of magic would lead the learner to rebellion and disbelief. That is because obtaining such powers gives the possessor an advantage over his fellow men, and hence the means to oppress the weak and subdue mankind to his ambitions and desires.

The question that forces itself upon us is: why did Allah introduce man to such temptation? The answer is that all sorts of temptation are but a test of faith. Wealth is temptation; family power through the multiplicity of offspring, authority and thrift have all been introduced by Allah as a test of man's faith and devotion to His right way, as is stated in the verse:

> "O deemed you that you would enter paradise while yet Allah knows not those of you who really strive, nor knows those (of you) who are steadfast?"
> (Āl 'Imrān 3:142)

There are, therefore, many sorts of temptation in the universe. A man may ask Allah for wealth upon the pretext of helping others or to use it in a worthy cause, but once his wish is answered he is suddenly possessed by greed and selfishness. Another may ask for offspring to help him, and when his wish is granted he uses them to terrorise peaceful folk and enforce his own laws of extortion upon the helpless and the needy. All these acts come under the meaning of trust: all Allah's grants to man are given to him as a trust, and one day he will have to account for it and how he managed it.

In previous chapters, we explained the meaning of 'the trust' and how Allah offered man a limited freedom of choice. But man, instead of using this freedom in promoting his welfare and the welfare of mankind, has used it to corrupt his own life and the world. In fact all divine favours granted to man, whether they involve supernatural powers or material gains, are intended to test his faith and honouring of Allah's covenant and trust; not because Allah is ignorant of the strength or weakness of everyone's faith, but rather because he wants everyone to stand as a witness for or against himself.

It is obvious that magic which uses supernatural powers can cause immense harm. It breeds discord between the sexes, cultivates hatred among members of a single family and encourages theft and the breakdown of social ties. Yet although it is invariably used to inflict harm on innocent persons, its harmful effects seem to spill over both the user of magic and the victim, as is vividly stressed by Allah:

> ". . . And they learn that which harms them and profits them not . . ." (al-Baqarah 2:102)

The underlying meaning in the above verse is that those who use this sort of magic are prone to lose faith in all divine powers, as the use of magic gives the users immense advantages over other men. They tend to transgress against others, foster corruption, and finally lose their faith in Allah's power and mastery over the whole universe.

Magic, therefore, whether practised according to human laws or supernatural laws, does not alter the nature or the material state of things. According to human laws it is but an illusion, or perceptual deception, and it is according to supernatural laws a fear-arousing phenomenon; it involves phenomena performed according to the laws of non-human creatures and gives us the false impression – in view of our inferior laws – that a change of state has taken place, whereas in actual fact no such transformation has occured. In both cases the two kinds of magic rely on perceptual deception and trickery with the aim of inducing fear and awe in the heart of the beholder with the concurrent goal of forcing him into submissiveness to the will of the person who has been able to master such skills and harness such forces for his own ends.

Faith in Allah builds a barrier between this sort of magic and the man who puts his trust in Him and seeks His protection. Faith arms a man with the conviction that there is no one in this universe, except Allah, who can transform the state of matter into something other than that which it appears to be and that in seeking Allah's protection he is securely shielded from such evil. For Allah protects and defends all believers who seek refuge in Him, and reflects any evil aimed at believers back at its instigators, as is here confirmed:

> ". . . and the evil plot encloses but the men who make it . . ." (al-Malā'ikah 35:42)

Similarly, Allah decided the doom of those people who try to terrorize or deceive mankind through the use of magic when He said:

> ". . . and surely they do know that he who trafficks therein [i.e. in magic] will have no (happy) portion in the Hereafter . . ." (al-Baqarah 2:102)

In the Sūrah al-Falaq (113), we are asked to seek refuge in Allah from "the evil of an envier". But what is envy? To envy someone is to wish the removal or abrogation of some gain or favour bestowed upon that person, or even to try to bring about this end. But is there any concrete relation between envy and vision or the eye, and if the answer is yes, would it mean that a blind man cannot envy someone else? This is not the case. In fact, both the blind and the healthy can envy others, for envy is concerned with the volition and will of the envier and not with his sight. A person who envies does so willingly and not by compulsion; that is because the seat of envy is located in the heart and not in the eyes.

Yet he who envies does not understand the meaning of divine favour, for it only comes from Allah, and no man can grant it to another outside His will. It is He who provides opportunities and opens the way for men to avail themselves of His bounty, or make it difficult for others to have access to it. But in order to ensure the permanence of Allah's favours, we should always be conscious of the predominance of His will:

> ". . . that which Allah wills (will come to pass)! There is no strength save in Allah . . ." (al-Kahf 18:39)

By reciting this verse, we should be able to shield ourselves against envy, for in this way we acknowledge Allah as the true benefactor and bestower of all favours.

Moreover, we should always remember that Allah has made equality of opportunity one of the main pillars of human interaction on this earth. This means that wealth and mundane powers do not always guarantee a contented and happy life. For no wealth can buy health or peace of mind; these are gifts from Allah and can only be sought through the acknowledgment of His supreme will. But, amazingly, we are always inclined to overlook this divine equality of opportunity in our striving for wealth and influence, and we seem to forget Allah's justice in distributing His favours among His worshippers. Whereas he may favour one person with wealth, He may favour the poorer with health and His blessings. He always compensates for the loss of one thing with a gain in another; a certain handicap is balanced with a substitute faculty or skill. Thus infirmity may be substituted with high intelligence, blindness with high hearing sensitivity, and so on.

Envy, as we have defined it, implies the wish by the one who envies to see the envied deprived of the favour bestowed upon him by Allah. This wish is frequently followed up with some action aimed at achieving this. Envy has many forms, as does magic. But Allah has informed us of them and of their existence, even though they are abstract and cannot be subjected to empirical testing. As we have already said, things which are beyond matter do exist in this universe and the mere fact that they are invisible does not warrant their denial. Surely, many facts which were once unseen and inconceivable are now common knowledge to all of us.

Both magic and envy are rebellious acts against Allah's

will and ways, and both lead to perilous ends and damnation, with no profit or gain from either one of them. The envier, for example, gains nothing from the removal of favour or good from the favoured or the envied. Both the user of magic and the envier are but sinners who wrong themselves in this world and the next, and both ought to know that all favours are granted by Allah from His inexhaustible bounty. They would secure greater and worthier spiritual and material rewards if they besought Allah to be generous with them rather than resorting to magic or envy. In fact, to envy someone is like objecting to Allah's will and His wisdom in bestowing His favours on whomever He chooses from among His worshippers, as well as ascribing the favour to man's own will and not to Allah. Both acts amount to disbelief.

In actual fact, envy harms no one but the envier, as long as the favoured person seeks refuge in Allah and is always conscious that the favour is ascribable to Him. But this protection is withheld once he forgets the true benefactor and becomes rapt in vanity and in the false belief that his prosperity is of his own making, forgetting that it was Allah who showed him the way and provided him with the means to reach it. Indeed, without Allah's blessings nothing would flourish. Health would deteriorate, wealth would disintegrate, and the means would cease to operate no matter how hard one strived or worked.

There are people who depend on Allah's will and attribute all their success and prosperity to Him. They enjoy the lasting favour of Allah and are always shielded by Him from envy. Then there are those who are vain and ungrateful, deny Allah's will, and falsely attribute their material success in life to their own skill and intellectual powers, thereby making themselves susceptible to losing the favours bestowed upon them.

If Allah has asked us to seek refuge in Him from the evils found in this universe, it is because of His knowledge of their constant threat to us and of our inability to confront them or repel their malice, mainly because of our ignorance of the laws that govern such evil forces. For instance, the evil spirits can see us, but we cannot see them, and the same is true of the jinn.

The same can be said about magic and witchcraft. Here, again, we are asked to seek refuge in Allah from such evil forces because of our inferior worldly laws which do not provide us with the means to identify them or avoid their malice. These unseen forces are beyond man's knowledge and power and no one is safe from their malice. Only Allah has the power to protect us from them, and particularly from the whispering of the devil.

Surely Allah has not informed us of these evil things to install fear in our hearts, but rather to assure us of His protection and of His mercy once we put our trust in Him.

But some people are always willing to consider nothing but outward means and believe that Allah has left this universe to be run according to its own laws, uncontrolled and unobserved by Him. This is not true, for Allah never ceases to watch over all His kingdom and nothing escapes His notice.

Chapter 3

The Unqualified Will of Allah

Allah created all things on earth, as well the means necessary for their interaction and their governing laws. The creation was instantaneous and materialized with the mere utterance of the command 'Be'.

It took six days to complete the creation of the earth and the heavens as we have been told in the Qur'ān. Because the Qur'ān came to address man, it was necessary that all the things it spoke about should be within the scope of his mental ability, whether the things it spoke about involved present events or future events deemed to be too difficult for the human mind to perceive.

But these laws do not put any restrictions on Allah's unqualified will and capacity, because if Allah had left things on the earth to be run mechanically men would have worshipped them and the whole world would have become devoted to the material rather than the spiritual. Thus, to save man from the perils of his vanity and remind him that nothing in this world is allowed to operate outside His absolute will, Allah maintained that absolute will and gave it precedence over the laws of cause and effect. Signs of this absolute divine will at work can be seen in the unjustified hardship suffered by some hardworking honest men when contrasted with the success and prosperity of some apathetic and dishonest individuals, or, likewise, when we see a weak and helpless man suddenly rise to fame and become the master of his oppressor. According to the laws of nature the opposite should be the case: the hard worker should be better rewarded for his effort than the apathetic, and the strong should have the upper hand over the weak. But once Allah's absolute power intervenes such laws cease to operate.

This line of thought does not always please many of those people who regard material gain as the most valuable goal in life. They describe Islam as a religion which is conducive to backwardness through the inculcation of a firm belief in the dominance of this absolute divine will over man's activity, sustenance and destiny.

They argue that the Qur'ānic assurance that "Allah gives without stint to whom He will" (al-Baqarah 2:212) gives man cause not to strive hard to earn his living or improve his lot, for if Allah promises to give without measure, why should anyone exhaust himself to obtain sustenance?

Those people who deny the dominance of Allah's universal will and its role in the determination of man's sustenance and rewards are but materialists who believe only in outward power. Their concept is that the reward is always equal to the effort: if you work less you gain less and if you work longer and harder you gain more.

I say to those people that their concept, though generally correct, does not exclude Allah's freedom to give without measure to whom He will. It should also be noticed in the above verse that Allah does not give indiscriminately to all, but that He only gives to "whom He will". Truly each man's sustenance is determined according to his effort and the time he spends in his work, but above all these factors stands Allah's absolute will.

If we, for instance, contrast the recent enormous economic growth of the oil-producing countries with that of the more developed countries, we will find that it exceeds it beyond measure in spite of the latter's industriousness, superior technology and production output. In fact, many European countries, and even America, have become reliant on the wealth of these less-developed and less-productive oil countries in order to save their economy and stabilize their living standards and the sustenance of their people.

Thus, despite their lack of modern technology and their unproductivity, these oil-producing countries have become, through Allah's absolute will, the most prosperous nations on earth.

Logically speaking these oil-producing nations could not have arrived at such wealth and prosperity without hard work and industrial development. Yet it is common knowledge that the greater part of the work which produced this wealth was accomplished by foreign companies, foreign labour, foreign material and foreign expertise.

If we tried to explain this paradox in terms of man's concept which says that gain is always equal to the effort, and then in terms of Allah's absolute and unrestricted will, it will soon become obvious that the former concept did not apply in the above case, nor could it have operated in isolation from the latter.

But why has Allah maintained His absolute power and not left the ordering of the universe to the mechanisms of nature? To answer this question we should take into consideration the fact that external efforts and their material ends represent the apparent or superficial aspects of life, and at the same time organize its normal course. But to put our trust in this alone keeps us away from Allah. Truly Allah has given some of His creatures some power over the means on earth to ensure the organization of human interaction and relationships. Thus some are given influence and authority, others wealth and so on, and He made these rewards appear as though they were the natural outcome, in order to ensure a smooth progression of life and harmony in the universe. But what happened was that some materialists tried to mislead others by giving precedence to wealth and authority over Allah's Will. Soon men began to drift from Allah's path and put their trust in their fellow men and in external efforts. They became willing to surrender themselves and their souls to the will and purpose of the rich and the high in office in return for some worthless reward in the guise of position or wealth or any other worldly profit, no matter how costly the spiritual loss in this world and the next would be. Indeed a person who is ready to barter his soul so cheaply does not hesitate to lie, steal, transgress against others and commit all sorts of ungodly acts with which we are quite familiar. When men become worshippers of outward means and those who have them, and when fulfilment of ambition becomes the most important thing in life, corruption festers and endangers the moral religious fabric of the nation. In a society of this nature, life cannot run according to Allah's decrees which aim at protecting the weak from the unjust and the oppressed from the oppressor.

This is a fact which has marred man's life since Pharaoh's time. Tyrants, like Pharaoh, and their followers have been denied Allah's mercy and are promised instant severe punishment on their death until they are resurrected again on the Day of Judgement to face their trial:

> "The Fire: they are exposed to it morning and evening and on the day when the Hour uprises (it is said): 'Cause Pharaoh's folk to enter the most awful doom'."
> (al-Mu'min 40:46)

The severity emphasized in the above verse accentuates the gravity of idolizing the ruler, and the dire consequences it brings, for the idolization of man lets loose human lust and fosters corruption and injustice.

It is obvious, therefore, that trusting in outward means alone leads to the idolization of the individual and man's readiness to surrender his will and destiny to the will of a ruler or anyone else who holds the means in his hands.

Balance must be achieved to remind man that it is Allah who has provided the means, and is capable of withholding them or reversing their course and outcome. All allegiance should be made to Him only.

In fact, the history of man abounds with examples of divine will, illustrated in the dethroning of kings, the rise and fall of rulers, in the rich becoming poor and the poor becoming rich, the oppressor becoming the oppressed, or a jailer becoming the jailed. These are but signs of Allah's absolute power at work. All these things happen in order to remind us of this absolute divine will; that all the means through which man can satisfy his ambition cannot operate outside it; and it is Allah who can reverse their outcome. Indeed, if the power to alter nature were of man's own design he would have things under his control forever.

Furthermore, the work of this divine power is neither

selective nor biased. It deals with all people on equal terms. It is felt and acknowledged by all people in their daily life. They express their faith in it and the hold it has on their life and activities with such expressions as "Allah is watchful" or "Allah's justice may be delayed but never fails" or "Allah is mighty" and so on. All these expressions reflect our innate belief in this divine absolute power and its ability to right all wrongs and correct the imbalance caused by the abuse of the means.

The fundamental divine wisdom behind the predominance of this absolute will is to remind man that he has no authority over the means. He can neither give nor take from any of his fellow men without this divine will. It is therefore futile for him to surrender his will and sell his soul to those who seem to have some power over the means, thereby bringing Allah's wrath upon himself. For Allah is the giver of all means and can give the steadfast believers who put all their trust in His predominant will a great deal more than those who hold the means in their hands can give.

Allah has not made His absolute capacity an unseen phenomenon. On the contrary, He has made it common knowledge and drawn our attention to it in many surahs and āyahs of the Qur'ān. Thus He says:

> "He selects for His mercy whom He will"
> (Āl 'Imrān 3:74)
>
> ". . . He forgives whom He will and punishes whom He will . . ." (Āl 'Imrān 3:129)
>
> ". . . He guides whom He will . . ." (al-Baqarah 2:142)
>
> ". . . He sends whom He will astray . . ." (al-Ra'd 13:27)
>
> "Allah gives without stint to whom He will"
> (Āl 'Imrān 3:37)

"He gives sovereignty to whom He will and He withdraws sovereignty from whom He will."
(Āl 'Imrān 3:26)

"Allah is able to do all things" (al-Baqarah 2:20)

These are but a few examples of the absolute divine power which stands guard over this universe and counterbalances man's abuse of the means with which Allah has provided him. What is significant is that it has never been kept secret from man's conscious awareness. It is expressed vividly throughout the whole of the Qur'ān, and most emphatically in the verse in which Allah says

> "But His Command, when He intends a thing, is only that He says unto it: Be! and it is." (Yā Sīn 36:82)

This indeed shows how surpassing and unrestricted by means this divine will is, or else Allah would not have said so or discarded the role of the means where His commands and decrees were concerned. But the word "Be" indicates that there is no place for the means in His will, and that things materialize and become reality with the simple pronouncement of the command "Be".

This is how the universe and man came into being. It is this same divine will which determines conception and the sex of what is in the womb.

> ". . . He bestows female (offspring) upon whom He will, and bestows male (offspring) upon whom He will . . . And He makes barren whom He will . . ." (al-Shūrā 42:49-50)

The wisdom here is that although Allah has made the union of a male and a female the means leading to pregnancy, He still holds in His hands the power to nullify the outcome of the means through barrenness.

When we come to the application of this absolute divine power in human affairs we find it to be most prominent in the miracles performed by the Apostles and Prophets, wherein the means were ordained to stand still and inoperative. Thus when Noah appealed to Allah to destroy the disbelievers, Allah sent down torrential rain, inundating the

the earth and causing the great flood. This rain did not come according to the normal laws of causation but rather in obedience to Allah's will. The same power was exhibited when Abraham was thrown into the fire, which instantly became "cool and peace for Abraham" (al-Anbiyā' 21:69). Throughout the whole of his life Moses lived with this divine power which manifested itself most gloriously in his crossing of the Red Sea with his people after their Exodus from Egypt. Here, all natural laws came to a halt until he and his people had crossed it safely, but resumed their natural pattern when Pharaoh tried to follow suit, drowning him and his men. The same divine will was demonstrated when Moses struck the rock with his staff, and water came gushing from twelve springs that flowed in the direction of his gathered people to quench their thirst and save them from death. According to the law of the means, Moses ought to have dug a well in order to obtain water.

All these miraculous acts materialized in the absence of the means, or without resorting to them. They actually reflect and exemplify the absoluteness of Allah's will and power at work.

Another example of this absolute will was demonstrated when Zachariah prayed to his God to bless his wife with a boy, and

> "the angels called to him as he stood praying in the sanctuary: Allah giveth thee glad tidings of (a son whose name is) Yaḥyā" (Āl 'Imrān 3:39)

At this point, Zachariah remembered his old age and the barrenness of his wife and that the conditions necessary for conception were unlikely in a man of his age, and he sought some divine assurance, to which Allah replied through his angels:

> ". . . So (it will be). Your Lord says: It is easy for Me, even as I created you before, when you were naught." (Maryam 19:9)

It is obvious that Allah was reminding Zachariah of His

absolute power and that nothing was difficult for Him, irrespective of its prerequisite means, and that if he had any doubt about Allah's ability to render his wife fertile, he had but to contemplate how he himself had been created from nothing.

The same absolute power is reflected in Mary's answer to Zachariah when he visited her in the sanctuary and noticed that she was well provided with food, and asked her where it came from, to which she replied:

> ". . . It is from Allah. Allah gives without stint to whom He will" (Āl 'Imrān 3:39)

It is again overwhelmingly demonstrated in such miracles as the creation of Adam and Eve, in the conception of Mary and the birth of Jesus and in al-Isrā' and al-Mi'rāj of Muḥammad (SAW), wherein the means were completely bypassed.

All of these miracles give us examples of the application of this absolute power and its ability to work outside the laws of means, or cause and effect.

This absolute power was not only provided to Allah's Apostles and Messengers, but it actually encompasses all our daily activities and life as is reflected in the following verse:

> "Lo! Allah disdains not to coin the similitude even of a gnat. Those who believe know it is the truth from their Lord; but those who disbelieve say: What does Allah wish (to teach) by such a similitude? He misleads many thereby, and He guides many thereby; and He misleads thereby only miscreants." (al-Baqarah 2:26)

If we examine this verse thoughtfully, we will find that Allah has used the gnat as an example. This example, like all other examples in the Qur'ān, is not made aimlessly or without a worthy purpose. In fact, when the disbelievers heard it they did not understand its underlying motive and treated it with indifference. But Allah wanted to draw our attention to His infinite capacity, for to create such a minute organism and provide it with all the physiological functions necessary for its survival can only be the work of a capable God.

There is great wisdom in the above example, for it tells us not to underestimate the smallest creatures on earth or to judge their power by their size, for the massiveness or minuteness of a creature or organism does not necessarily correspond with its impact and effect on man's life. Moreover, some of the smallest organisms are more powerful and more adaptable to environmental changes. For instance, whereas all the enormous species of dinosaurs became extinct by the end of the Mesozoic age, smaller insects such as ants, mosquitoes and fleas have been able to adapt to climatic changes and survive all the geological and climatic disturbances that have taken place on the earth. In explaining this phenomenon, scientists say that the brains of these huge animals were greatly inferior to those of the smaller species and therefore could not adjust to the changes that were taking place on earth.

But Allah explains the whole matter in different terms. He wants to tell us that survival is not subject to power or strength but rather to His divine will, and that this divine will is greater than any other power and can destroy it at will.

In contrast, viruses and germs have survived all these geological conditions, are still living with us, and have the power to destroy all life on earth if they were allowed by the will of Allah to do so. In these minute organisms and their devastating power, Allah manifests His absolute power, and at the same time reminds us of our weakness and vanity. It is a reminder to those transgressors who believe that their mundane power has made them invulnerable and kept them out of Allah's reach. The similitude is, in fact, aimed at purging us from vanity and conceit, and convincing us that without Allah's care and support we are feeble and vulnerable to all sorts of hazards and misfortunes.

Allah has given us these theoretical and practical examples so that the progress of faith may continue unhampered by fear, or intervention.

The most significant fact about this absolute divine power lies in the believers' conviction and faith in its support and favourable intervention when the means fail to respond to their will. It is this faith which puts the believers' mind at peace – even when the means do not respond – because they know that Allah will never abandon them.

The denial of this divine absolute will and the worship by some capitalist and communist nations of outward possessions has thrown these nations into a state of moral apathy, anxiety, insecurity and a loss of purpose. This loss of bearings is noticeable among the young generation; reaction to it is the recent revival of religious heritage and the call for a return to Allah's path.

When a materialist is suddenly in financial difficulty or becomes seriously ill he never thinks of his plight as a divine test. In contrast, he succumbs to despair and the whole world turns black before him. This is because he believes that his destiny is in the hands of man who has the means to make him happy or miserable. On the other hand, a non-materialistic person who puts his trust in Allah's absolute will is always hopeful of His assistance and that He will never abandon him in his moments of despair when the means seem to stand impotent and unresponsive. Thus he is always hopeful of cure when he is sick and of new means of sustenance when all the doors are shut in his face or when he is hit by poverty or hardship.

But Allah has undertaken to spare believers the misery of this material life, for He has promised them a good life wherein His mercy and blessings prevail: the same mercy as that which inspired the baby Ishmael to kick the earth with his foot causing the water to gush, after his mother, Hagar, had lost all hope of finding any.

This is the formidable miracle which Allah wants us to be aware of. In it we are shown signs of how this divine power can work outside normal means, and what it can do for us if we seek its support when the means fail to help us get what we need, as is reflected in the verse:

> "Is not He (best) Who answereth the wronged one when he cries unto Him . . . ?" (al-Naml 27:63)

"The wronged" refers to the person who is let down and stands alone, forsaken by all, unable to go anywhere. In a situation like this, man should not succumb to despair, for Allah is there waiting to offer him His help if he seeks it.

We are all quite familiar with this divine help. If each one of us looked back into his life experiences, he would soon recognize the many instances where this invisible power had manifested itself, releasing him from the grip of despair and distress, perhaps by providing a sudden unexpected solution to a conflict which had seemed insoluble, or by rescuing him from a perilous situation, and so on.

Indeed many of us have witnessed this divine power at work on a much larger scale, as in the sudden fall from power of an unjust ruler or a whole regime, at a moment when everyone believed that it would last forever.

Allah wants the believer to face the world trusting in His overwhelming power and support, his heart kindled with an ever-burning flame of faith, and for this faith to be his hope and link with Him. With this invigorating hope man will confront all the hazards which he is likely to meet in his daily life, knowing that nothing can endanger his security and peace of mind. Confident that Allah is there to lend him a hand and in his awareness of His overwhelming capacity, the believer should feel quite secure and peaceful.

The high suicide rate in the materialistic nations – in contrast with its very low rate in nations where faith in Allah's absolute power is predominant and unshaken – is undoubtedly the best example that one can give of the good life which Allah has promised His sincere worshippers.

The absoluteness of divine power elucidates the various phenomena which take place in the universe in isolation. We live in a world governed by both means to obtain sustenance and the absoluteness of divine power. Thus we see men in the highest seat of power ousted by men of less authority. Contemporary history is full of such events. According to the rules of nature, this could never happen. In fact, the opposite is theoretically the rule.

If, for instance, we consider a non-believing nation such as Russia, we will be able to see signs of the working of this absolute divine power. The Soviet Union was once the largest producer of wheat grain in the world, but because Allah's blessing has been withheld from it, it now relies on the United States for its loaf of bread.

The absoluteness of divine power gives Allah His unique and eternal attributes while all other things in the universe are transient and subject to decadence and decay. Thus we have seen nations and empires which once reigned supreme go into decline and oblivion, in spite of the fact that their people have remained the same, with the same intellect and capacities. But Allah has decreed the change, and so it has come to pass.

Everything in the universe, by virtue of this absolute divine power, has a preordained date. It is only through this absolute power that discoveries and new facts about life in this universe are systematically being revealed to successive generations. It is needless to say that Allah has always given something new to each new generation. To explain this point, we may refer to the verse where Abraham says, "And when I sicken, then He heals me" (al-Shu'arā' 26:80). This verse is wrongly understood by many persons who refrain from going to the doctor in accordance with their understanding of this verse. Others go to the doctor in the belief that the cure rests with him. But in fact there is a preordained time for any cure, and when this time is due, Allah reveals the cause of sickness to the doctor who diagnoses it and prescribes the appropriate healing medicine.

In many instances we consult the most renowned specialist without success, and yet, sometimes, we amazingly find the cure in the clinic of an ordinary practitioner. If we tried to account for this phenomenon in terms of normal means we would expect the chances of finding a cure with the specialist to be far greater than with the ordinary practitioner, mainly because of the specialist's wider knowledge and longer experience. But the latter was able to diagnose the disease because the time of its discovery had come. This discovery sometimes happens by chance, as when a sick person accidentally meets a doctor, while visiting friends, and mentions his case to him, who immediately recognizes the symptoms and prescribes the cure.

The same thing could be said about the varied scientific phenomena which Allah plans to reveal to mankind. For every new discovery has a predetermined date, and when this day is due, the phenomenon is ordained to reveal itself to the scientist working on it, but in the absence of any research the phenomenon reveals itself, perhaps to a scientist working on some other research. In fact the history of science abounds with discoveries of this sort.

But because Allah does not reveal to us the date of these events we usually ascribe them to the means or to mere chance and luck.

The absoluteness of divine power forms the core of faith. We should not,therefore, expect a non-believer to acknowledge the existence of such divine power or to believe in the Unseen; he would rather put all his faith in the means, trusting only in what is substantial and apparent, rejecting all that is spiritual or mystical and ridiculing such truths as punishment and spiritual rewards. In contrast,a person who believes in this unqualified divine power will have faith in these spiritual rewards and all that Allah has promised to those who believe in His omnipotence, as well as the bleak doom that awaits those who rebel against Him; and that all these promised rewards and punishments are not subject to the laws of nature, but are bestowed freely in isolation from them.

In living with this unqualified divine capacity and observing it at work, our belief in the existence of the world of the spirit and the Unseen is enhanced, and we find no difficulty in accepting it and living in harmony with it.

Belief in the absoluteness of divine will has to be deeply entrenched in our hearts before we can perceive and accommodate all the facts of the unseen world which Allah has veiled from us, as well as everything else, generation after generation. For this regular imparting of new facts and the unfolding of old secrets increases our faith in Allah's domination over the universe and fills our hearts with humility and submissiveness to His Will.

Truly one would expect this generation, in view of all the discoveries about the universe which Allah has revealed to it in recent years, to show more acknowledgement of this absolute divine power and submit to it with humility and resignation.

About the predominance of this divine will over man's life and destiny Allah says:

> ". . . till, when the earth has taken on her ornaments and is embellished, and her people deem they are masters of her, Our commandment comes by night or by day and We make it as reaped corn as if it had not flourished yesterday. Thus do We expound the revelations for people who reflect." (Yūnus 10:24)

The meaning of this verse is that Allah will, in due time, reveal to mankind new secrets about the universe, which will show them signs of His ingenuity and the perfection of His creation, but that man, in his vanity, will not perceive their true meaning and will incorrectly attribute all these discoveries to his own intellectual endowments and efforts, and claim that with the knowledge which he has accumulated, he has become master of this universe, and of his destiny. This is when Allah's decree will come to wipe out all that man has accomplished on earth. We should pay special attention to the irony in the word translated as 'deem' (ẓanna) which is used to accentuate man's foolishness in believing that he was the maker of his own knowledge or that it was he who subdued everything in the universe to his service by his own will and knowledge.

But when man reaches the zenith of vanity and thinks that he can rival Allah and appoint himself lord and master over the universe, the bell of the Hour will be tolled.

The same cautioning is reflected in the following verse:

> "We shall show them Our portents on the horizons and within themselves until it will be manifest unto them that it is the Truth . . ." (Fuṣṣilat 41:53)

The Qur'ān, being Allah's speech, will remain unaltered and unchanged until the end of time. The future tense of the word translated as "show" implies that the showing is continuous and involves all future generations, and that the Qur'ān will reveal to every future generation something new, encompassing both the survival of man on earth and the secrets of our solar system. Accordingly, man will continue to find new solutions for his present problems and diseases, discover new technology and learn more about his solar system.

In fact, all man's recent accomplishments in these fields seem to conform with the foregoing predictions which only Allah, being the Creator of all past and future things, could make with certainty.

When man puts his trust outside of Allah he usually attributes to himself powers which he does not truly possess. Therefore, when Allah sees that one of His worshippers has gone away from Him and put all his faith in the means, He leaves him until he has reached his goal and become fully convinced of their power, then He suddenly reverses their course or nullifies their favourable ends.

If man had complete control over the means and if it were true that the means alone were the true giver, they would never cease to give nor prevent the loss of gains previously secured. An example of this could be inferred from the verse wherein (Korah) says:

> ". . . I have been given it only on account of knowledge I possess . . ." (al-Qaṣaṣ 28:78)

The same pretension was expressed by the landlord of the two gardens:

> ". . . I think not that all this will ever perish."
> (al-Kahf 18:35)

and also by the men who plotted to defraud the poor folk of the crop of their gardens:

> "No needy man shall enter it today against you". (It was a custom throughout the East to allow the poor a gleaning of all harvests. – Pickthall's footnote)
> (al-Qalam 68:24)

These arrogant men thought that all their material gain had been earned by their own knowledge and merits, thereby bringing about their own misfortune and the withholding of divine favour. The crop of the two gardens was destroyed, and Korah's dwelling-place and his family were swallowed by the earth. As for the rich owners of the orchard, referred to in the above verse (68:24), who wanted to cheat the poor of their rightful share, it so happened that when they went to gather the fruit, they found the orchard destroyed beyond recognition. Only then did they realise Allah's universal will over all affairs.

The absoluteness of power means that Allah is One and Unique in that His attributes can never be found in man or in any other creature or any number of them. His qualities and nature are unimaginable. He is Eternal, without beginning or end, and His power over this universe is absolute in that He can say to a thing 'Be; and it is'. He is the Omniscient, and His knowledge encompasses all things.

Thus, when we say "Allah is Unique" we mean that He should not be compared with anything.

It is possible for a single object to have a double or a like; it can also be the sum and total of all its constituent parts. For example, we may say that a number of individuals are speaking with the same tongue, meaning that each of them is repeating the same argument or speech. Similarly, although a chair is made up of wood, leather and nails, it is still one thing: a chair. But the uniqueness of Allah negates all such composition. He is not created of a number of composite parts, for if this had been so, then which one was created first? Or, likewise, which one created the other?

Allah is mighty and eternal. These two attributes give us no alternative but to turn to Him and seek His mercy in our moments of need or when we feel helpless and distressed. But because man has been given a limited freedom of choice he is not compelled to make his pleas to Allah. In contrast, some other creatures, such as the angels, are deprived of this freedom of choice and cannot disobey Allah's commands, as are all the celestial bodies such as the sun and moon which have been ordained to serve man. They have no will of their own and must follow the patterns and role for which they were made.

As for man, Allah has given him the freedom of choice. Thus he is free to seek Allah's help or not, and to obey or disobey His commands while he lives on this earth, but he must account for all his actions on the Day of Judgement.

In being eternal, absolute and unique, Allah has given us the true perspective of religion and faith. For being absolute implies that absolute existence can only be predicated of Him; all other existence is temporal or conditional; He is not dependent on any person or thing, but all persons or things are dependent on Him, thus negating the idea of the existence of any other God but Him.

These attributes make Him the only giver and the only God to whom we should make our pleas in moments of need or when we feel helpless and distressed. His power would not be diminished if the whole of mankind strayed from His right path or rebelled against Him. He is the only one who can grant favours or withdraw them, make the weak strong and the strong weak. This is the difference between Allah's giving and that of man. A second difference is that when man offers or grants something, he cannot retrieve what he had offered. If, for instance, you gave some money to a person, but discovered later that he had betrayed you, you could not retrieve it once it had become his. Likewise, a doctor who cures a patient of a disease cannot make him sick again if the latter refuses to pay his fee. But Allah can do so: He can make poor the ungrateful rich, make the healthy sick and enrich the grateful poor.

When Allah gives someone the means to rule on earth, but it so happens that he has become an unjust oppressor, He always sends him a more severe and unjust rival to give him a taste of his own tyranny and injustice. He never sends him a good merciful man. This is because forgiveness, mercy leniency, self-restraint and charitable conduct, all of which have been commended by Allah, stand between this righteous man and the deserved punishment of this unjust wrong-doer. But in afflicting him with a more unjust opponent Allah ensures that the punishment will be as severe as and equal to the guilt.

The absoluteness of divine power is in fact a blessing to mankind, for Allah is above all desire. We are all His slaves, regardless of race or creed. We stand high or low in His esteem only according to our obedience to His laws and commands. The exercise of this absolute power is needed to organise man's life in this universe and to create a balance in his interaction with his fellow man, for through it Allah gives support to the weak against his oppressor and to the incapable against the capable. If this interaction were left to be run by the laws of nature, corruption would have run wild and unchecked. That is because a man who takes no account except of such laws soon becomes rapt in his own lust and greed, stopping at nothing, thereby sowing misery and corruption into the fabric of the whole society. But Allah's absolute freedom and supremacy over the universe have come to correct any deviation in the progress of the good life which He has promised to mankind.

Thus Allah has created the universe and given of His bounty to both believers and non-believers alike. But all Allah's gifts to mankind, whether they are good or bad, are but a sort of test or trial of our faith in Him. For sometimes what we consider to be bad for us may in fact be a blessing in disguise and more beneficial than many of the things which we sometimes strive hard to acquire, only to discover afterward that they are but a curse.

When Allah gave us the means so that life would go on, He maintained His freedom of will in order to create a balance between the two. He wants to caution us not to forget Him and worship the means which can neither give outside His will nor restrict His power and sovereignty over all affairs and events. He wants us to put our trust in Him and not in those who might have some power or influence over secondary causes. He wants to tell us that such means are but the medium through which He bestows His favours upon whomever He chooses from among His slaves, or otherwise withholds them. Nor should we ever succumb to despair when the means fail or fall short of responding to our efforts and capacities, because this same free will is always there to correct unfavourable results of the means or even bypass them altogether.

The maintenance of the freedom of divine will and its superiority over secondary causes is necessary to ensure man's welfare. It gives him ample evidence of Allah's unity and sovereignty over all things, and His capacity to act freely unhindered by time or place. It can satisfy all his needs without diminishing any part of Allah's inexhaustible bounty, either materially or spiritually; it is there to give courage to the helpless and to support them in their struggle against oppression and the bias of the means.

Finally, belief in the absoluteness of divine will is the essence of faith, because it convinces us (with firm certainty) of all the divine rewards that Allah is capable of granting to the believer and the righteous in the Hereafter, the eternal blessings which He has promised him. It is a constant reminder that Allah alone is All-Capable and the truest giver and executor of all things.

Chapter 4

Meditations on the Sūrah of Mary

The Sūrah of Mary reflects the unqualified divine will discussed in the previous chapter.

This unqualified divine will was manifested in Allah's choice of Mary to become the mother of Jesus; in His preferring her above all other women; in her purification; in her conception and the birth of Jesus; and in the way in which he carried out his holy message and in his ascension to heaven. All these divine acts came to demolish the materialistic world of the ungrateful Israelites, who were possessed and driven by their lust for material gains, and gave no heed to Allah's right way. Even after they had been shown signs of Allah's absolute power when He rescued them from Pharaoh's men and carried them safely across the turbulent sea, they still worshipped the calf which they made from their gold ornaments. They showed this same love for what is material when they showed their discontent with the divine sustenance of manna and quails – mainly because they were miraculous daily foods which they could not store, sell or use in profitable trade – and asked Moses for earthly crops. They showed it again when they resented Tālūt – whom Allah had sent to them – on the grounds that he was poor, thus revealing again their trust in the power of the material and their denial of all divine will and spiritual rewards. They went as far as doing away with those Prophets who came to guide them, ask them to give up their worship of the material and to follow Allah's discipline, and lead them back to his right way.

It may be relevant at this stage of our discussion to explain the difference between a Messenger and a Prophet: A Messenger (*Rasūl*) is sent with a discipline from Allah and is fully supported and protected by Him against plot and intrigue. On the other hand a Prophet (*Nabī*) does not come with a specific discipline, but rather to teach an exemplary code of conduct. He comes to pursue the correct application of the messages of his predecessors. When Allah sends a Messenger, He always selects him from among the human race. This choice is made on the premise that in the message and the injunctions it contains lie the discipline which He has chosen to ensure a good and peaceful way of life on earth for the whole of mankind. But when Allah decreed a discipline He always sent a Messenger to teach people how it should be applied. Thus, choosing a Messenger from among the people to whom he was sent removed any excuse or pretext that the discipline was too difficult for the human race to understand and apply, when they saw the Messenger apply it easily to himself, without adding any additional burden to his normal daily life or disrupting it in any way.

Choosing a Messenger from among the human race was, therefore, a wise plan where all divine messages were concerned, for choosing a messenger from a superior race would have given people valid reason to turn away from the messenger on the premise that they could not follow or accommodate a discipline which only a superior being could put into practice. By contrast, choosing a messenger from among ordinary people, with the same human capacity and limitations as all men, would make them better prepared to follow his example, rather than following a superior being with powers and capabilities far above those of ordinary men.

The story of Mary begins with 'Imrān's wife offering her unborn child to the service of Allah:

> ". . . My Lord! I have vowed unto You that which is in my belly as a consecrated (offering) . . ."
> (Āl 'Imrān 3:35)

Obviously 'Imrān's wife dedicated her unborn child to the service of Allah in the hope that He would bless her with a baby boy. This dedication and firm hope showed how deeply rooted was her faith in the will of Allah. She was, disappointed, however, when the child was born and she discovered that it was a girl:

> "My Lord! Lo! I am delivered of a female – Allah knew best of what she was delivered – the male is not as the female; and Lo! I crave your protection for her and for her offspring from Satan the outcast." (3:36)

'Imrān's wife was astounded when she was delivered of a girl, for having offered the unborn infant to the service of Allah she expected Him to give her a boy, whom she believed would be better suited to this holy task and more effective than a girl. But Allah comforted her and told her that He knew best of what she was delivered. In other words, it was His plan that the infant should be a girl, and He would have given her a boy if He had so desired. Thus Allah showed His absolute power and free will from the start by determining the sex of the unborn child.

At this point one might well ask how 'Imrān's wife could predict that Mary would have a child. Had Allah informed her of any such future offspring, or was it a customary prayer which every mother usually made? Because there is nothing in the Qur'ān which points to such a prayer, it would be more convenient to presume that the prayer was a wish that was made by all mothers.

Mary's first step in her encounter with Allah's universal will took place when He accepted that she would serve Him in the temple. This acceptance is not the same thing as choosing – which we will speak of later – and represents the first step along the road of the absoluteness of divine power and the miracles it was about to perform.

Allah then vouchsaved her goodly growth and purity, and she retired to her chamber in the sanctuary to practise worship. Then pious men and priests volunteered to become her guardians, and threw their pens to determine which one of them would be elected, but Allah had favoured Zachariah and caused him to be chosen. Finally, Mary entered the sanctuary and devoted herself to the worship of Allah.

Every time Zachariah entered the sanctuary to see to her food and needs, he always found her well provided with a variety of different kinds of fruit and food. But what attracted his attention most was that the fruit she was provided with was out of season.

This was Mary's second encounter with Allah's absolute will. She could see it vividly and clearly in the ample variety of food which the angels brought her and in Allah's ability to bypass all worldly means. In fact, she was being prepared for the unique miracle of her conception and her giving birth to Jesus without having been touched by a male. This preparation was aimed at affirming her faith in Allah's absolute capacity, purging her from any doubt about it once she discovered what was happening to her, and helping her to assimilate the whole experience without shock or dismay. But Zachariah, despite his confidence in Mary's purity and his knowledge of her devotion to her God and her practice of worship, could not suppress his curiosity and asked her about the source of this food. Here there is, for the whole of mankind, a worthy lesson, the learning of which would help immensely in reforming society. If every parent or leader of a group investigated any sudden signs or gradual changes, material or otherwise, in the conduct of those in his charge, whether they were his children or his staff, he would be setting up a barrier against corruption and deviation.

If everyone knew that he would be asked to give an account of any sudden riches which did not accord with his effort, corruption would be checked. Thus Zachariah's concern for Mary, despite his unqualified faith in her fidelity, did not stop him from asking her about the source of her food, to which she replied:

> ". . . It is from Allah: Allah gives without stint to whom He will." (3:37)

This reply came as a surprise to Zachariah, who suddenly became witness to Allah's absolute power and His being above all worldly means. This sudden recognition aroused in his mind an old worrying case, involving the barrenness of his wife and their being without offspring, for, being a prophet, he was fearful that after his death his followers would go astray if they had no successor of his own progeny, to pursue his holy message and carry on from where he left off. He thought of this divine absolute power and its domination over the means and decided to seek its intervention, and prayed:

> "My Lord! Bestow upon me of Your bounty goodly offspring. Lo! You are the Hearer of Prayer."
> (Āl 'Imrān 3:38)

A few moments later, while he was still standing in prayer in the sanctuary, the angels called to him.

> ". . . Allah gives you glad tidings (of a son whose name is John, who comes to confirm a word from Allah, lordly, chaste, a prophet of the righteous." (3:39)

But Zachariah, still influenced by the power of worldly means, or the norms of cause and effect, seemed unsure of the divine prophecy and sought further reassurance:

> "My Lord! How can I have a son when my old age has overtaken me already and my wife is barren?" (3:40)

But Allah reassured him and put his mind at rest and said to him through the angel:

> "So it shall be. Allah does what He will." (3:40)

Here, Allah is drawing Zachariah's attention to two facts regarding His unrestricted will. The first is that it is He who created both causes and effects therefore they do not set limits on His will, and He can dispense with them or impede their laws whenever He desires. The second is that what seems infeasible in human terms is easy and possible in divine terms and that Allah could remove his wife's barrenness and bless her with a child.

Giving in isolation of the means

These words seemed to illuminate Zachariah's mind, and eradicated any doubt left in his and Mary's minds, as to the boundless reaches of this divine will and its ability to work beyond the laws of cause and effect, or the means.

The Sūrah goes on to tell us:

> "And when the angels said: O Mary! Lo! Allah has chosen you and made you pure, and has preferred you above (all) the women of creation. O Mary! Be obedient to your Lord, prostrate thyself and bow with those who bow in worship." (3:42-43)

At this stage, Allah sent the angel to Mary to inform her that He had chosen her and given her preference above all women, so that she might live in constant harmony with His absolute power and capacity, in preparation for the forthcoming miracle of the birth of Jesus. He then purified her by shielding her from all evil throughout her constant practice of worship. Then came the second preference when she, above all women, was chosen to bear a child without the intervention of the usual physical means.

It has always been remarked that in all the faith-related stories and miracles narrated in the Qur'ān, Allah has never called any character by his or her full name, except Mary whom He always refers to as "Mary, daughter of 'Imrān". The reason is that the miracle of the birth of Jesus, or the birth of a child by a female without union with a male, was never to be repeated until the end of time. All the other characters represented moral lessons for the guidance of mankind: they were symbolic of people who live at all times. When Mary's purification was complete and her faith in Allah's unqualified power deeply rooted, the Angels came down to her again to tell her:

> ". . . O Mary! Lo! Allah gives you glad tidings of a word from Him, whose name is the Messiah, Jesus, son of Mary . . ." (Āl 'Imran 3:45)

Yet despite all the preparation that she underwent in readiness for this moment she seemed to be taken aback by the news, and asked:

> "My Lord! How can I have a child when no mortal has touched me?" (Āl 'Imrān 3:47)

Obviously all the faith-enhancing training in readiness for this moment had not fully purged her of the influence of worldly causes. But Allah replied through His Angels:

> ". . . So (it will be). Allah creates what He will. If He decrees a thing, He says unto it only: Be! and it is." (3:47)

Allah did not, however, inform her of how He was to accomplish such a miracle, because He had kept the mystery of creation to Himself and never revealed its secrets to anyone of his creation, even when Abraham asked Him:

> "My Lord! Show me how you give life to the dead . . ." (al-Baqarah 2:260)

He did not tell Abraham how He did it, but He made him go through an experiment which showed him how this divine will worked. He was told to cut a bird in four parts and place each part on the top of a distant hill, and then call the dead bird to fly back to him, which it did.

Similarly, when Mary asked how she would conceive without being touched by a male, Allah did not give her any details, but just told her that He "creates what He will" (3:47).

Why did the Angel come?

The angel that came to Mary appeared to her in human form. Here, some sceptics contend that if Mary had already been informed of her miraculous conception, and if her faith in Allah's absolute power to "say unto a thing 'Be!', and it is" was firmly entrenched in her mind and heart, then obviously, the sending of the Angel was needless.

These people have missed Allah's wisdom and plan in sending the Angel in the shape of a man, for if he had come to her in any other form and delivered his message, and then disappeared without touching her, she would perhaps have doubted that she had never been touched by a man in some way or another. But the fact that the Angel came to her as a man to despatch Allah's message, and his departure without touching her, left no shadow of doubt in her mind about what was happening to her, and convinced her that her conception was a divine miraculous act, independent of human involvement. Allah predicted that the Israelites would cast doubt about this divine miracle, and knew that Mary's encounter with the Angel would give her strength against the slandering gossip that was prone to arise among her own folk. She had to be certain that it was Allah's absolute will that had caused her to conceive.

Yet even when the angel conveyed Allah's message to her she was not entirely free from the grip of the means upon her mind, in spite of all the previous signs that Allah had shown her of His unqualified power, and she said to the angel:

> ". . . How can I have a son when no mortal has touched me, neither have I been unchaste?" (Maryam 19:20)

to which Allah answered through His angel:

> "So (it will be). Your Lord says:
>
> "It is easy for Me. And (it will be) that We may make of him a revelation for mankind and a mercy from Us, and it is a thing ordained." (19:21)

With this last statement 'It is a thing ordained', Allah settled the whole issue once and for all and put Mary's mind at rest. Mary had become fully convinced that her conceiving had been decreed by Allah and that the whole thing should never be brought up again in her mind to be discussed. But she also knew that it would be too difficult for her to convince her people of this divine portent, and decided to disappear from her kin for some time to spare herself their censure and chastisement.

Allah was aware of all the difficulties and agony that Mary had to suffer from the people of Israel whom she knew would never believe her story, no matter how she tried to explain to them how the miracle had happened. To spare her this agonizing experience she was inspired to decline all conversation with man or woman for three days after the birth of the infant, and to let the newly-born baby do all the talking and show the whole of mankind signs of Allah's absolute will at work.

In accurate expression, a few minutes after his birth, Jesus spoke and comforted his mother:

> "Grieve not. Your Lord has placed a rivulet beneath you." (Maryam 19:20)

Thus a few minutes after his birth Jesus performed his first miracle and gave the Israelites stunning signs of Allah's magnificence and power. Before his mother's hand had lifted him from beneath her he asked her not to grieve.

The infant Jesus knew that his mother was apprehensive of the moment when she would meet her people and face their disgraceful accusations and censuring. This apprehension and anxiety were reflected in her wishing death while giving birth to her holy son.

> ". . . Would have I died ere this.
> and had become a thing of naught, forgotten!" (19:23)

Then the holy child, who had just been born, reminded her of her need of food and water to regain her strength and face the events to follow:

> ". . . And shake the trunk of the palm-tree towards you; you will cause ripe dates to fall upon you. So eat and drink and be consoled . . ." (19:25-26)

Then came the greatest portent of all when he told her:

> "And if you meet any mortal, say: Lo! I have vowed a fast unto the Beneficent, and may not speak this day to any mortal." (19:26)

Thus spoke Jesus to his mother, supported by the Spirit and by divine inspiration. He had at this very early age been granted the divine gift of understanding the shortcomings of his people the Israelites, their adamant rejection of Allah's unqualified capacity, and their denial of the Unseen.

Assured of herself and of her God, she took her baby to her own people, who were amazed beyond all bounds and accused her of disgracing the name of her forefathers:

> "O Mary! You have come with an amazing thing.
> O sister of Aaron! Your father was not a wicked man nor was your mother a harlot." (19:27-28)

Now we see that Mary's fears were not wholly unfounded. She was censured by her people who believed only in the means and lived by their laws, and denied all divine power. They did not want to understand, or take the trouble of asking her where the baby came from or whether it belonged to some other woman. But Allah's will and planning were something that the Israelites never acknowledged or assimilated. In this context, the Qur'ān shows us aspects of their scepticism and tendency to slander others, and judges them in terms of their own values and suspicious nature. They had no place, in their code of conduct, for good intention.

But Mary did not try to defend herself; instead, she calmly pointed to the baby in her arms, directing them to seek answers to their questions directly from him. This seemed to puzzle her people, who did not expect such a response and failed to come to grips with the divine absoluteness of power behind the whole phenomenon. They said to her:

"How can we talk to one who is in the cradle, a young boy?" (19:29)

But Allah inspired the infant Prophet to speak, thereby showing them signs of His absolute power at work and what it can do. The days-old baby spoke to them, not as babies talk but in full mature, logical and eloquent expression. He answered them:

> ". . . I am the slave of Allah. He has given me the Scripture and has appointed me a Prophet." (19:30)

With these words, the infant proved to the astounded Jews the divine truth of Mary's story and showed them portents of Allah's absolute power enunciated in the divine purpose underlying his miraculous birth. In saying "I am the slave of Allah" he declared at the very outset that he was but a servant of Allah – thus discarding any notion that he was God or a son of God – and that he was but a Messenger who came to deliver a message from Allah to them. In fact this was Jesus' first miracle, for apart from addressing them in mature logical language, he also informed them of future happenings:

> "He has given me the Scripture and has appointed me a Prophet." (19:30)

Even as a baby, he was full of wisdom and preached to an unbelieving audience about Allah's right way which he himself had been commanded to observe:

> "And (He) has made me blessed wheresoever I be and has enjoined upon me prayers and almsgiving so long as I remain alive." (19:31)

This shows that Jesus was not exempted from the duties imposed on all other believers. He too was commanded by Allah to worship Him as long as he lived.

The verse goes on to tell us that Jesus was told to take care of his mother:

> "And (has made me) dutiful toward her who bore me, and has not made me arrogant, unblest." (19:32)

Here we notice that Jesus only referred to his mother, thereby confirming to the Israelites the miracle of his birth, and that he was an ordinary child, born the normal way.

Here we should pause a while. Mary's coming to her people carrying in her arms her holy baby who was able to defend her in mature and logical terms might in itself have been overwhelming miracle sufficient to convince the Israelites of the truth of her story. But Allah was aware of the stubbornness of the Israelites and their unwillingness to believe in any power other than that of the worldly means, so He bestowed on the newly born infant – in addition to the faculty of proper speech – the power to defend his mother and explain the divine role he was ordained to perform in the service of Allah. Thus Jesus informed them that he had not come to them as an arrogant or unblessed overseer, but rather as a mercy from Allah to turn an ungodly community which had strayed away from Allah's path back to Him, to restore their faith in the powers of the true God and His spiritual Kingdom which they had abandoned and sought security in the means instead of seeking it in their Creator. Then he said to them:

> "Peace on me the day I was born, and the day I die, and the day I shall be raised alive!" (19:33)

The above verse sheds considerable light on the miraculous conception of Mary, the way Jesus was born and the way he died, his subsequent ascension to Heaven and the day he would be resurrected.

In fact, all these issues have never ceased to be debated since they initially arose among both Jews and Christians. Philosophical theories are still being formulated and theologians never stop coming up with new hypotheses about this miraculous birth, disregarding what the Qur'ān has said about them in the truest of detail. Yet all these postulated hypotheses and theories seem to overlook the role of the absoluteness of divine power behind this mysterious birth, as well as the divine portents which Jesus as an infant and as a man was able to demonstrate.

It was this divine power that sent Gabriel to stand by Jesus and give him inspiration every time he was forced into a debate with the disbelievers and the sceptics. Yet the controversy seems to have no end in sight.

But despite all this debate, Jesus' safety from all harm was assured by Allah until He raised him to heaven.

With regards to Jesus' death, the Qur'ān affirms that he was not crucified and that Allah raised him to heaven. In fact the matter of his ascension is not an outstanding phenomenon, for the whole of Jesus' life was but a chain of divine miracles and support from Allah's unrestricted power that defied all the normal laws of cause and effect.

It is illogical for us to believe in his miraculous birth and all his other miracles, and then argue about his being raised to heaven. If we consider his birth, his speaking when he was a few days old and all his other miracles to be true and a reflection of the absolute divine power that supported him, why do we argue about his being raised to heaven, and insist on applying our physical laws to this miracle? If we are convinced that all Jesus' miracles were the product of this divine power, why should we detach the ascension from it? Indeed to affirm this power in one aspect of Jesus' life and deny it in another is self-contradictory.

Furthermore, why should we argue about the raising of Jesus in body or in spirit when the same thing happened to Muḥammad in the miracle of al-Isrā', as already discussed? Those who believe in the absoluteness of the divine will know that nothing can set limits on it and that it is not bound by causes and effects. As the action has been attributed to Allah, then it was He who carried Muḥammad (SAW) to the heavens and raised Jesus to heaven. When the agent is Allah, all physical laws of time and space, as we understand them, become meaningless and inoperative. Any argument that ignores this reality is futile because the executor of these acts is Allah Himself, and not man who is bound by these laws. Nor should Jesus' resurrection become a controversial issue, for the difference between the miracle of al-Isrā' and that of Jesus' resurrection is basically a difference in earth time. Accordingly, Muḥammad (SAW) was carried to the heavens and back to earth in a very short period of time. Jesus' resurrection will take longer. But Allah's actions know no time and are not subject to its physical laws as they apply on earth.

Nevertheless, Allah has predicted in the Qur'ān that the foregoing three issues – Jesus' birth, ascension to the heavens and return to the world – would continue to be debated until the Last Day, and disengaged him from all disputation and conjecture regarding his death and his ascension.

But when talking about Jesus' miracles we should notice that Allah put certain restrictions on his freedom, despite his prophethood and his being supported by Him. This is remarked in Jesus' speech to his people:

> ". . . I have come unto you with a sign from your Lord. Lo! I fashion for you out of clay the likeness of a bird, and I breathe into it and it is a bird, by Allah's leave, I heal him who was born blind, and the leper, and I raise the dead, by Allah's leave; and I announce unto you what ye eat and what you store up in your houses. Lo! herein verily is a portent for you, if you are to be believers." (Āl 'Imrān 3:49)

We notice in the above verse that Allah classified the miracles: some of them were done by His leave, while others were left outside it. And even though Jesus was a Prophet endowed with the divine support to perform miracles, Allah has distinguished between those miracles that he could do within the confines of this support, with no restriction, and those which although divinely supported still required Allah's permission or leave. One of the miracles dependent on Allah's leave was that Jesus was able to give life to the clay bird mentioned in the above verse. Because Allah had kept all secrets about creation to Himself and barred them from all human knowledge, Jesus had to ask Allah's leave and permission in all the miracles involving life and death which he had to perform.